death You!

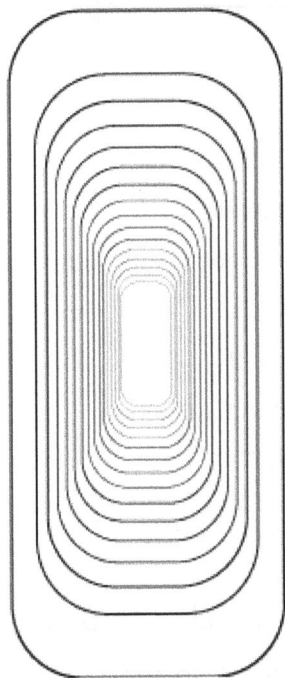

Michael Beloved

death You!

Correspondence   Email

Michael Beloved   axisnexus @gmail.com

7211 41ST Court East

Sarasota FL 34243

USA

ISBN paperback   9781942887553

ISBN epub   9781942887560

LCCN   2023906820

How to use this book:

Make a casual reading initially.

Make a second reading while pausing and considering topics of interest.

Make a third reading while observing the main themes in the discourse.

Finally, make an indepth study of the entire text.

The translation to Sanskrit texts are the author's. For *devanagari* script and word-for-word meanings, please find the full script in his *Bhagavad Gītā Explained, Anu Gītā Explained* and *Uddhava Gītā Explained*.

Table of Contents

Introduction

This content is about death transit which is the shift to the psychic world with no recourse of a physical presence. Generally human beings service a religion by consigning a dead body to a religious ceremony which promotes the idea of life hereafter in the heaven of a deity. However, the same survivors who sponsor the ceremony usually mourn the physical condition of the person's immobile body.

The religious overcoating is more or less, a sham. On this side of existence, the survivors take comfort in the idea that the person shifted to a heavenly world and is better off for it, but these people rarely have mystic perception to verify this idea.

The content of this literature is a broad declaration that what occurs at death of a body is not surprising. In fact, most everything will continue as usual on the physical and astral sides of existence. The world will proceed. The psychic existence will continue. The cosmos will not blink for it.

Chapter 1
The Situation Prior

Death in Fetal State

The beginning of life is termed as birth, which is rated from the time an embryo is deprived of its mother's blood, where it must in a matter of seconds or minutes switch from being, a liquid-surrounded living being, to an air-surrounding one.

It is generally accepted that if the embryo successfully switches to breathing air, its life began at that moment. It is assured of continuing by using air through its nostrils and nutrients through its mouth. Only air and nutrients are required for the life of the body to continue. Anything else like relationship, education, or skill, is unnecessary for mere life to continue.

There are conditions however, and dangerous ones too, prior to this air-breathing birth moment. Such conditions carry with them the threat of death but people may not regard that as a dire event for the entity. Until it emerges from the mother's body, it is not considered to be a functioning human being.

There are exceptions as in the case of a fetus whose parent(s) have social or political importance, where people look forward to the birth of the embryo because they rely on it even before its birth. Even for families which are not famous and which have only local importance, one or more persons who are related, may long for safe transit during the pregnancy and may regret if the pregnancy fails. Some relatives with gripes may long for a miscarriage.

In one way or the other, the threat of death is ever-present. From every angle it assails anyone who has physical life. The beginning of a pregnancy is a marker for the event of a life. Death is present at the onset. As it travels through the father's tubing for entry into the mother's passage, the sperm particle, may be subjected to biological hostility. Its life could end there.

If at that stage there was a psychic potential, a personality, it would be displaced from its sperm body. It may or may not become another viable sperm. Since the sperm is not equipped with memory, we may assume that if it dies during transit through the father's exit or mother's entry, the process is with no objectivity. This is a nature event based on physiological action which is involuntary.

The psychic potential, or personality, will either be assumed as a sperm again immediately or in the near future. It will repeat this behavior until it succeeds to develop further. Once it is not assaulted by death during that transit from the father's body to the mother's, it will become embedded in the body of the mother where it can develop without further biological contribution from the father. The mother's body and that only is the shelter at this stage. This will continue for approximately nine months, in which time, it will become visible as a larger and larger formation in her body. That shows externally as a distended abdomen, a pregnancy.

If the pregnancy fails, people understand that it was affected by death. To protect the host from this dead child, people expect that it will be expelled from the mother's womb as a still born infant which is marked as dead, having a breathless condition which indicates that it is lifeless.

Here again whatever was psychic about it, should be assumed to continue, such that it will again become part of the life-beginning sequence. However, that psychic person began as a sperm particle. Repeatedly it is assumed as a sperm in a male body.

The mental and emotional portion of a lifeform is psychic. The instance of physical life consists of that psychic portion operating a physical body. The process is that if the physical system is unable to respond to the demands of the psychic part, the physical body is regarded as dead.

But that brings into scope the instance of the beginning of the lifeforms on earth, as to when they began and as to their evolutionary changes made to adapt the earth's changing environment. Whether it began yesterday or a million years prior, is not the issue. Something that began yesterday and which mutated rapidly as the environment changed, did so in a certain way, as it responded to the environmental changes. Just the same, something that began a million years ago and which altered as one changing body or which altered as several changing forms over that period, may have changed in the same way even though the rate of alteration varied from a rapid to a gradual process.

Some kind of life began with a psychic entity using physical substance to become a physical body but with that psychic entity remaining as it was but responding differently and adapting to the changes in the environment. Once it began because conditions permitted it to do so, that process continued through reproduction, with the facility for assuming physical life occurring only through bodies, and not directly by becoming part of the environment as an original lifeform.

Death faces each entity which is a physical body. This caused the need for transmigration or shift from a dying body to another living one. Somehow to begin this, there was physical substance and psychic energy. When the physical substance altered and became receptive to the presence of psychic energy and personality, life as we know it began. That evolved further and reproduced as time progressed.

Currently the situation is that new lifeforms are reproduced from old ones. That is obvious, especially in the large, non-microscopic entities. Hence for someone to become a new lifeform, there must be a physical living form from which a new one is reproduced. This suggests that if there is personality as part of the composite of a lifeform, then another personality who has no physical form, takes shelter of one that does. In the natural process, this causes the development of one or more new forms which the tenant(s) becomes, and which develops in the host and then separates from it, to be an independent unit.

The adults who are evidence of survival beyond the sperm or embryo state, may consider the implications. Even now while using an adult body which may or may not be healthy, which may be alive but unwell, one should consider that in the future one may again become an embryo. Of course, if that happens, there will be no memory during the embryonic development. One will lose the memory reference. It will again be an involuntary process which will run its course with no interference from oneself, except perhaps for instincts which one may have, and which nature may accommodate, even though in that state one could not express a coherent desire, nor rational process. Initially, there would be no developed brain for processing information about the environment.

How then could an adult prepare for that possibility? In the first place, it would mean that if one again became a sperm and then embryo, one did not resist the looping process of being psychic with a need for being physical, where the need asserts itself involuntarily. How then could anyone remain as a mento-emotional being, a psyche, and not be helplessly induced into the loop of having a body, being deprived of it, and again becoming a body, repeatedly, with little or no objectivity regarding this process of reincarnation?

It is during the adult stages of a body, that one may examine this natural process, to see if one can gain control or exemption from it. In the adult stage one has a developed brain which is complementary to one's mental faculty, such that one can surmise the situation, gather what is factual, speculate on what is not obvious, and gain insight.

Because the tools for calculating the situation are not available during the embryonic stage, one has no chance to figure this. Even though the psychic entity is intact in full during even the embryonic condition, still, the physical compliment, which is a developed brain, is unavailable. Hence one must use the adult body to know this. Why, one may ask, does one need a physical brain for this? Why could one not do it with only the psychic awareness? The answer is that when the psychic features are combined with the physical embryonic body, some psychic abilities are muted. They are not powered enough at that stage. The reality is that the self needs the faculties of the adult brain for the advanced operation of the psychic intellect.

If the body dies during the embryonic stage, the person will either resume a subtle body which is similar to its last physical form, or it will be re-routed into the father's body and express itself there as a sperm mini-organism. In either case, it will take the natural route which terminates in rebirth, where it will then experience itself as a physical person. The format of consciousness used during the sperm and embryonic stages is that of a sexual urge. In the sperm situation, there is no idea of a physical self, or physical limit, but only as a psychological urge which is alert to move as guided by heat and excitement.

During the embryonic stage the mobile urge is absent. The self uses the format of reception of nutrients and stationary development, with little movement every so often. That is a waiting condition but with patience as if waiting for a signal to act. That motion is to use the senses which will be developed during the embryonic development. All other aspirations, desires and objectives of the self are suspended during that stage. There is no concept of anything other than absorption of nutrients. This evolution from sperm and ovum occurs involuntarily, without figuring and planning.

As iron filings are influenced into an alignment by a magnet, so the energy which is ingested from the mother's body, is formatted by the presence of the self, which at that time has only the urge to develop as its identity format. Everything else about it exist then in a state of stasis but with potency.

Death in Childhood

Termination of life before the end of the teen years, prior to twenty years of age is a surprise event. At the time the entity has little grip on life and little sense of a strong social purpose. It does not have a strong sense of responsibility for others, for its children for instance, or for its parents or grandparents. Usually, it does not have an employment which it feels highly responsible to perform.

Its outlook about death is absent. It does not take the instance of death seriously. Because the body is at its healthiest state, the idea of illness and subsequent demise hardly occurs. It is such that even if there is a severe illness which may result in the cessation of vital functions of the body, still it does not consider the possibility. It looks to life and feels that it will recover from sick conditions.

Ideas from religious indoctrination are hardly considered by youths. They know these views, but they do not place trust in the outcomes which are offered as solutions to the problem of being vulnerable to tragedy. If someone dies in youth, that person will continue existing on the psychic level but in a subtle body which is similar to the physical one it was a deprived of. The self will try to continue its activities by returning to its surroundings, and speaking to its friends and relatives.

This will continue for a time, until this person realizes that it shifted from the physical situation where it participated in the history of earth. At that time, with that understanding, it will become somewhat dismayed. This is due to understanding that it can no longer take advantage of the opportunities offered by history. This person will not however be eager to take another body to be another embryo which will develop into a child form.

Eventually however, when the friends of the same age who have physical bodies, become adults, take employment, and have families with children, then this deceased person who passed on in youth, will become lonely. Having not experienced physical adulthood, having not assumed the additional adult activities and responsibilities of that phase of physical life, this youthful deceased person will become despondent. He/She will wish to be on earth in a more developed body, into an adult state like those youths who were friends, but who shifted with the flow of physical history. This person will then long for the friends to shift to the astral side of life but that will not happen. In fact, the friends who continued in their physical bodies, will be so preoccupied with earthly responsibilities, that their psychic energy will change, making it difficult for the deceased one to locate them.

This deceased person who died in the teen years, will become lonely. He/She will feel the need to be someone's infant but not as an infant, only as a dependent who would have the privilege to participate in history. At that time, there will be attraction to sexual partners, as if that deceased person was to be the child of a couple who are sexually involved.

It may happen soon after, or it may take some time, for this person to be unified with the feelings of would-be parents. Then as fate would have it, this deceased someone will become an urge as a sperm particle, which in the nick of time will, or will not become an embryo. Once this deceased person becomes unified with the feelings of the would-be parent, he/she will lose objectivity, and will be as if it was effaced as a person, and became transformed into being an urge, to move as sperms do when they are ejaculated.

Death in Early Adulthood

Death in early adulthood pertains to those who while being employed have family responsibilities in the form of child/children. Due to investing time in employment, and using some funds for the upkeep of a family, these individuals tap into their subconscious reserves of energies for fulfillment, by invoking a sense of concern for relatives, who must be supported. Some of the dependents may be children. Others may be elderly parents or grandparents. Some may be disabled relatives. There is also the energy for creating, operating, and maintaining an employment, either as a proprietor or employee.

If such a person is deprived of his/her body, there is a feeling of regret, and a sense that a vital opportunity was lost, due to being in a dimension which is out of reach of participation in human history on earth.

When this person is first deprived of the body, there is a feeling of disbelief that it happened. This someone will compare himself/herself with others who still use living bodies on the physical side. The idea will be that life is irregular and unreliable. This will cause an attitude of dismay. That dissatisfaction will reach the surviving relatives and friends. It will impact as a depressing mood.

The concept that someone who dies, abandoned the body, is for the most part untrue. In most cases, one is deprived of the body. One does not shed it. In fact, the action of the psychic energy of a person permanently being disengaged from the body, occurs because the body failed as an operational lifeform, and not because the person committed a mystic action to leave the form.

Most persons who die, feel that they had other things to do which they could no longer complete, because of not being able to operate their dead forms. There is a feeling of being disabled, being without a means of making history. There is a feeling of unfulfillment, as if the scope of life on earth is unreliable.

There is regret and sorrow for such a person, since that someone was unable to complete the support of infants and elderly relatives, and could not share and enjoy festive occasions. This person will hardly think of rebirth, of being someone's baby. The profile required for that will be vacant in the psyche. It is replaced by the feeling that one could host babies, rather than be an infant of somebody.

This person will be drawn into physical situations where adults on the physical side congregate to host others, who are their dependents, friends, and colleagues. When there is sexual intercourse, this person will not be attracted. Because of wanting to host children, the desire to be someone's child is in dormancy in the psyche, as if it does not exist.

Eventually, when this deceased adult realizes that his/her physical ability is ineffective, where that person is ignored by the surviving relatives, acquaintances, and friends, that someone becomes disappointed. He/She sinks into a depressive contemplation, where the conclusion reached is that, *"I am dead. I am no longer of relevance in the world of the living. My social value in the home, community and workplace is nil. What should be done? What is left of me is not physical. It has very little impact on anything. The world ignores me."*

Then this person will feel a soothing energy which will cause a need for compassion from others, especially from others who are physical adults, who could have babies, and who are socially situated to sponson a child. With this new feeling, this someone will feel a repulsion from anyone who is not inclined to having infants. With that there will a drifting force which will carry this person into the association of persons related or unrelated, who are in the mood of having children, and who are involved sexually.

Over time, with this feeling, this person will be attracted to a specific person who either could have children, or who can influence someone to do so. When this attraction is experienced mutually between this person and someone who is an adult, the deceased one will feel that he/she should be closely involved. If that happens, there will be a transfer, where the deceased one will be divested into the psyche of the living adult. This will eventually result in a pregnancy, which if it comes to fruition, will cause that deceased person to develop as an embryo.

In that way the deceased one will loop into the physical world, with no memory of the past life when its body died in the adult stage. This one will operate on instinct using the opportunities it is afforded by fate. Its instinct for physical survival during the adult phase of life will be stronger than it was in the previous life. Even with no memory of what happened previously, it will institute ways of protecting itself from death during the adult years.

Death after Fifty Years

After the flash of youth, which for most human beings passes quickly, there is the advent of the median and senior years which are earmarked by faults in the body. These show externally and are experienced within the form. This causes some reflection about the elderly condition of the parents and grandparents who may or may not be alive. The situation is one of quiet reflection to consider that the body which one has, is no longer in the best condition as it was during the teen and young adult stage.

There is from time to time a consideration about death, as to if it is applicable to oneself, and as to if it was the concern of deceased people, and is the concern of those who are with terminal disease, which show that death is inevitable, at least for people who are unhealthy, and who cannot be cured of a disease.

At fifty years and over, one may think that death is the concern of others, of those who have a terminal disease, those who are handicapped and are immobile, of those whose organs fail one after the other. So long as the body is relatively healthy, someone may avoid considering that death is inevitable, that it is a law of nature which is unavoidable.

It does happen however that some persons pass away at fifty years of age or just after. There may be a rapid deterioration of an organ in the body. Some cells may become transformed whereby they lose their sense of purpose and spoil the area they are located in the body. When someone who is relatively healthy through life dies suddenly, that person is left with no means of social participation. He/She is locked out as it were, left with only a psychic presence, which does not allow full participation in the social history. This deceased person regrets being deprived of the opportunity.

After living for fifty years, that person was somewhat fulfilled in operating a family and in being employed. In some cases, the person may even have served with great recognition in the community. Still, there may be dissatisfaction for being cut off from the world, bared from participation, deprived of a meaningful life. From the hereafter that person would project a dislike for what happened when a debilitating disease killed the body, which was the very means of operating socially.

Recognition was terminated. The eulogy given by living people does not give the fulfillment which was enjoyed before death. A deceased person who passed at fifty years of age or older, will remain near those friends and family in whose company, there was sharing and happiness. Special emphasis will be placed on people who were about the same age. This is due to a curiosity about what other achievements those living persons would attain. There may be envy if any such person becomes prominent in the society, whereby the status of that someone's family is improved.

Those who pass at fifty or soon after, will have little interest in becoming infants again. They would consider the infant and teen years to be unwanted stages because these occur with little or no autonomy, and without the cultivation and use of social skills.

Later however, these persons find themselves to be lonely, as if there are only one or two persons whom they knew on the physical side, and who survived and are still living. Many friends and acquaintances became deceased. Even for these, their achievements became forgotten by most human beings.

This causes loneliness with a longing to be someone's child, to be wanted and cherished, as parents would a long-desired child. At this time, the deceased person who passed at about fifty years of age, will find that the interest in the social affairs of the living is reduced. In its place, an interest in coming under the shelter of two people, parents, will be felt. This person will be attracted to a few people who can beget the body for a child.

If this deceased person is lucky, there will be a pregnancy of which this someone will be the content. It will develop. It will be birthed. It will be an infant but with no comprehensive memory of its past. The birth process which is followed by the growing of the body, is not reliant on the intelligence of the person involved. Nature itself will develop the body, with the self as the occupant spectator.

Death at Seventy Years Plus

The departure from a body at seventy years plus is usually acceptable to one and all, as being the culmination of a life well-lived, with investments in the progeny produced, and the professional accomplishments shown. At the funeral, family members and colleagues speak of the good things the person did during the life.

It is acceptable if the corpse exhibits peacefulness. That is interpreted to mean that life was fair to that someone to allow a favorable end. People imagine a heavenly condition hereafter and speak with glowing terms about it. Besides scriptural guarantees, and their hopes for the person and for themselves, they have little or no evidence for this. Accepting that, which acts as a salve to their emotional injuries, they firmly believe in the wellbeing of the deceased person hereafter. During the funeral, they prepare themselves for turning away from the reality which is that this person who is physically done, was scrapped by time, a cruel power which deprived the deceased of the most desired physical body.

Most persons who must deal with the death of a family member, colleague, or friend, instinctively turn away from considerations about the reality of death. Hence, they do not have to suffer through the sadness and grief which results if someone passes, and there is no way of knowing for sure by sensual evidence, if that person survived as a heavenly being, or became a psychic criminal, who was consigned, or rather, transferred to a hell.

At seventy years of age, no matter how healthy the body is, that person is confronted with the ravages of time. Some of these occurs as

- vital organ malfunction

- permanent nerve and tendon damage

- blood sugar imbalance

- limb deformity and malfunction

- chemical dependency

- irregular cellular growth

- irregular weight

- inability to analyze and remember

- breathing crisis

Many other malfunctions occur. Many are unknown even to the person who uses the body, and who is afflicted with the illness. These are portents of death in that whatever a human being is physically, it does not have the power to completely curb the feature of time which dictates that physical forms must deteriorate.

The attack of infirmity is such that it is a wholesale assault on the principle of individual life. It is relentless. Even though some persons are killed just at fifty years, others die at a younger stage or in the elderly years. One way or the other, after one illness or another, death presents its infallible face.

At seventy, **vital organ malfunction** will occur. For those who are regarded as being healthy at this stage, there will be a point at which one or more organs simply do not function at optimum. Instead, these steadily decrease in efficiency, which in turn affects other functions. If there is medical intervention where an organ is surgically examined and treated or where an organ is replaced, some other organ may fail, resulting in complication. Like an old car whose engine is worn in this part and that part, the body of someone at seventy or older, will reach a stage, where it slows to a terminal stage. Then by one failure or the other, its heart will cease pulsing. Its lungs will cease absorbing. Its blood transport will clog. That will be the end.

At seventy, **permanent nerve and tendon damage** will result. Actions which previously strengthened and enlivened the body may cause extreme pain with inability to heal. Nerves which would normally mend in a matter of hours, days or weeks will remain torn where the cells have no interest in mending splits and fissures. Tendons will become brittle and inflexible, making it difficult to operate the body. This will lead to a bed ridden condition. If the hip joints lose flexibility, the person may be restricted to using a wheelchair, or even to remain in an awkward position, with no hope of resuming mobility. Eventually this will cause so much depression and negativity, that the person may wish for death, or take action to end his or her life. Regardless, death will come when the heart and brain no longer function correctly.

At seventy, **blood sugar imbalance** is likely. This will upset the body's system of digestion and blood circulation. That means that the vital organs will not receive the nutrients which best suit their operations. An anemic condition will result. Medical process will be applied. However, due to the age of the organs and cells, which would normally correct the imbalance, corrections cannot be made. Medical treatment by intravenously applying nutritious fluids into the body may give temporary relied but due to the age of the organs and their deterioration, some parts of the system will be unresponsive. The person will feel a loss of vitality and will gradually yield to the fact that the body cannot revert to a healthy stage. In time, in a short while, the form will be dead.

At seventy, **limb deformity and malfunction**, will be established as the normal state of the body. The person will come to accept this as his/her condition, a stage which has little functionality as compared to how it felt in the teen years and during the early adult experience.

Bone disease will occur. This usually takes years to become established. Some of this could be treated but only early on, at a time when the person had no idea that it developed. This is due to nature's silent but persistent neglect of some functions which it was eager to complete during the embryonic, infant, and teen years.

The same nature which built the body, and which was eager to do so, will itself neglect its maintenance eventually. Because nature so astutely constructed the body, the person who identified himself/herself, as it, has a habit of doing everything besides helping nature in its chore of maintaining the form. This neglect proves to be costly.

The point is that if the body was manufactured to last for one hundred years, if the self who is known as the body was attentive to its care, there would be less illness during that time, so that there is the minimum of its mandatory unhealthy condition.

At seventy, **chemical abuse** of the body by ingesting through the mouth, nostrils, skin, mucus membranes, intravenously, or sexual entry, has dramatic effects on the body. Chemicals may penetrate the brain and cause altered states of consciousness, which may not be properly interpreted by the individual. Besides this, cell structures and muscle may be affected negatively, to form cancerous alterations, which are crippling. In so far as the brain is required for rational behavior, mental functions may be affected. These would result in loss of memory, something that makes many references to be obliterated, where the person loses track of himself/herself, and cannot recognize objects and faces.

Passing from a seventy-year-old body in such a condition may be reflected on the psychic side of life, so that hereafter, the person is discovered to be like an ignorant infant but having a subtle body which resembles that of an aged adult.

At seventy, **irregular cellular growth** accelerates. This happens through the life of the body, in its beginning as an embryo and also during youth. However, the entity hardly notices this until the body reaches an acute stage where for one reason or the other, cells do not complete their functions. In the elderly years this is accelerated where even cells which acted efficiently during many years of the body, fail to keep their working format. These cells either neglect their duties or die in the body and are not replaced.

So many of the bodily functions, its self-maintenance, its decisions regarding what it needs, are conducted by the kundalini lifeForce in the body. It is important to realize that you, as the entity in the body, did not maintain the cells of the form. Some other force did this through the years. The most one could do is to assist the lifeForce when one observed that it needed some service, and could not on its own provide it. During the elderly years, this realization is more of a mental comprehension because the main information at that time, is that irretrievable damage was done. Near the end of the body, one cannot correct a habit or neglect which was to be done many years prior.

At seventy, **irregular weight** may not be curbed. This means that overeating, irregular diet and gland damage which was not curbed years prior, can now be considered but without corrections being made because of a terminal condition of the body. For instance, a person who ate fatty foods excessively, may realize that ceasing that diet would be beneficial. That is the mental. The emotional portion of the psyche may disagree, so that the person is compelled to keep the fatty foods as the diet. Or that person may cease those foods but the cells of the body may not release the fat they hoard.

Obesity may cause problems like artery and vein clogging, heart irregularity and damage to other vital organs. These problems become chronic where they demand attention, and produce stress, forcing the individual to always think of the illness. The psychic portion of the self is fatigued by this. Slowly but surely, the person's will to live is shaken. He/She constantly thinks of death. A continuous depressive state is experienced. Eventually after many days with numerous illnesses, the body reaches a stage where even the best medical assistance proves to be ineffective.

At seventy the **inability to analyze and remember** may be noticeable. The person himself/herself should notice that immediately after an incidence or even after a mental notation about an event, the impression about it vanishes and becomes irretrievable. This is similar to when someone crosses a land border from one country to another hostile territory, where everything that person has, is confiscated by custom officers. The traveler is at a loss of what to do.

The loss of memory which is due to deterioration of brain cells, may be viewed by others, and by the victim himself, as being an introduction to what will happen at the beginning of the next life, where the person will start as a baby, with no integrated information about the previous existence. He/She will be a neutral somebody at the onset, having no comprehensive recall, no reference of time and only the memory, if any, of being forced through the mother's passage, as a beginning.

At seventy, **breathing crisis** may arise. These affect vitality. They bring on an anemic condition which causes weakness and a desire to be reclined. The lungs which began its functions just after the body was birthed from the mother, are stressed.

Lung cells, alveoli, which specialized in absorbing oxygen, and exhaling carbon dioxide, are unable to discern fresh air from polluted gases. With the delivery of fresh air disrupted, the blood stream becomes a poisoned passage. The entire body is ravished with illness, giving the entity no happy feelings. The heart races because it is petitioned through its nerves to increase the pulse rate to compensate for the lack of fresh air in the system.

In this predicament, the person hopes for a way out, for a miracle or medical cure. The outlook is grim. Gone were the happy days of the body. Gone is the vital energy which supported rapid movement and laughter. Everything this person worked to achieve now seems distant and out of reach.

An elderly person, who is deprived of an old body which had terminally diseased lungs, discovers to his/her dismay that the condition of weakness, lack of vital energy, is mirrored on the psychic side. The subtle body mimics many aspects which were experienced in the physical system just before it died. That someone would regret whatever happened which caused the lungs to deteriorate. It may be smoking herbs, excessive alcohol, working or residing in buildings where the air was polluted, or working in mines.

After spending many years breathing anything besides fresh air, the subtle body which survives the death of the physical system, would be afflicted with negative subtle air, and would also be devitalized. After some time, after some years perhaps, the subtle form would, over time, develop a healthy condition, shedding the effects of lung disease.

Even though the departure from a seventy-year-old body is considered to be acceptable, that view is mostly expressed by the surviving family and friends, and not by the deceased individual. This is due to the fact, that there is no definite view about where that person will be once death occurs. The uncertainty about reaching a heavenly place hereafter arises again and again in the mind of that someone.

Many thoughts about the possibility of life hereafter and about reincarnation as well, pop into the mind of that person, but the predominant view is that of being pushed aside, and of becoming irrelevant to history. Each day passes with no improvement in the unhealthy condition of the subtle body.

All social power is confiscated. Some of it is given to others who are incompetent. Some is taken by others who seize it. The person thinks about who is worthy of inheriting property, money, and authority. Efforts may be made to give the expressed wishes and to install preferred individuals but there are doubts which arise as to if the persons selected will be allowed to take the authority or will have the skill to be proficient in the tasks which comes with the responsibility.

As for religion, this person will think of the promises made by religious leaders but due to not experiencing the heavens advocated by those systems, there will be reservations as to the reality of those places. In the end what matters is what is experienced on the psychic side. For most people who die at or immediately after seventy years of age, the mental occupation is with the unhealthy condition of the body. They do not experience the psychic side. They may have beliefs about it and be confident that it exists, but their ideas about the advantages in physical existence will prevail. At death, they continue as they must as a dream body person who is focused on what they knew, and associated with physically before death.

Attaining a heavenly paradise after death is not likely for someone who passes from an invalid or old decrepit body. This is because the subtle body which is itself the heavenly form in a deteriorated condition, must be energized to the heavenly quality before it can transit into and be situated in a heavenly world.

Preoccupation with illness at seventy or later

Survival of a physical body to seventy years of age or older may be regarded as a credit to the person for living a long-fulfilled life. Yet, for many people who reach this age, their lives were unfulfilled, and the effort to appreciate what happened is littered with disappointments and failures. Still, people who are younger may appraise or condemn these persons.

The elderly person must deal with illness, and with the threat of other health issues, which are likely to occur. Day or night, at home or in a hospital, such persons continuously think about the bodily condition. This is involuntarily done with no reprieve. It becomes a meditative state which is negative, because it reinforces depression, and bars the person from accessing a transit to a higher astral realm.

Besides the preoccupation of the mind with the unhealthy condition of the body, there is the constant focus on the social duties which the person is forced to neglect. Imprisoned mentally by thoughts and memories about social participation which cannot be completed, the person is unable to shift to the idea of living permanently on the astral side, voluntarily abandoning whatever it had on the physical level.

Sudden Death

Sudden death occurs with or without prior notice. When prior notice is given, it is awarded with no way to stop it, no way to reverse course and no way to complete obligations after the notice is given. The person is dismayed or may remain calm, acting as if it was expected.

The skip from being a physical someone, to suddenly being a mere psychic being, is a rapid transit which the person notices in astonishment. The person becomes a psychic someone in the nick of time. He/She tries to speak to anyone who is seen but usually this communication is unrecognized by the other person who is embodied, and who does not focus on non-physical reality. This failure to get a response from living people causes dismay. It brings a self-declaration that, *"I am dead."*

In a flash the deceased person who is now only a psychic force like a thought or idea, travels to a family member or dear friend to communicate the diseased condition. Unless the said family member or friend has psychic perception, this fails. In most cases, living people are so physically focused that their psychic perception is suspended. They can neither hear, feel, nor see, the deceased someone.

However, anything which the deceased one thinks of, is played in the mind of those physical survivors, except that they do not recognize this thinking format. It is either ignored or muted by the mind reception mechanism. It is dismissed, or it revolves in a think and response rotation, on and on, but with no comprehension that it is from a family member or friend who was unexpectedly deceased.

The deceased person will notice this confusion in the mind of a survivor but there will be no way to correct it. Then this deceased person will go to someone whom he/she feels can be responsive and who as a result can relate the information to others who are related, and who should be promptly informed.

The deceased person will think of his/her body's disposal, as to how it should be done, as to who should arrange it, as to if there is any possibility that the dead body could be revived. There will be regret that certain functions were not tended prior and certain financial obligations were not met. This person will think like this, *"If I knew this would happen, I would have done this. I would have established that. Why did someone not predict this?"*

Sudden Death for an Infant

When an infant dies suddenly, there is grief and surprise on the physical side. The relatives and their friends are dismayed. They feel unfortunate. They find it surprising that the infant died. Birth is not regarded as an introduction to death. People expect that birth is pronouncement against the possibility of death, a door to life, an introduction to the joys of physical existence.

People regret an infant's death and feel that fate was mistaken. They surmise that fate which should be supportive of an infant's promising future, made a mistake and became a cause for disappointment. "Why," they exclaim, "did this happen? "What did the child do which was incorrect?"

The death of an infant is regretted by family members, who usually have no idea as to why fate acted to deprive them of the child. Even if the infant had a deformed body or was with a terminal disease or defective vital organ, relatives may regard it as an unfortunate loss.

People have little idea of reincarnation. Those who heard of it and who believe it or think that it is a reasonable proposal, do not apply it in a deep sense. The information they have about it, does not help them to overcome grief for loved ones.

For the infant's sake, not much is lost. He/She is left with a psychic body and nothing else. This person will again be processed as someone's child. He/She will again harbor a fear of dying suddenly. He/She has no regret which is due to losing social status as an adult. Instead, there is an effort to retrieve feelings of belonging to a set of parents, and wanting to continue accumulating connections by meeting people of social worth. If the parents of this dead infant are sexually involved, it is likely that the infant will again become fused into the father's feeling and will again become a sperm, which will dart itself to an ovum of the mother, embed itself into her uterine wall and develop an embryo. Most parents, however, will be oblivious to this. They may, however, when this dead infant is birthed again, address it saying. *"You are like your sibling who was our previous child."*

Sudden Death for Young Adult Parent

The death of a young adult parent is a serious occasion of distress both on the physical and psychic sides. On the astral side, the deceased person becomes possessed with sadness. There is a stunned condition of mind. The emotions are grey and cloudy for a time. On the physical side people express astonishment. Some are stunned.

"Why did it happen? Why?" Some opine.

Because the deceased person has no physical access to the child or children who survive, there is a feeling of being severed from reality. Thoughts, of what cannot be completed, flash through the mind with utter distress, and even with anger against the fate, which managed the death and was inconsiderate. It did not consider that the child (children) would be left without the concern and services of the parent.

On the physical side, relatives and friends run opinions and settlements in their minds, as to which person should assume the responsibilities, which were tendered by the deceased person. Some family members and friends meet secretly and give views. Some hold meetings to discuss the issue. Some agree on who should preside and take control. Some others disagree. There are court sessions for legal guardianship where a court official presides over decisions to assign the control of the surviving child (children).

At the funeral, people are distressed. Some speak. Some remain mute. Not a smile is seen. The child (children) does not fully grasp the implications. They feel a loss but at this time the full impact is not realized by them.

On the astral level, the invisible deceased parent goes here and there, speaking to living people mentally but to no avail, because the issue is to be relevant in the physical world, and no one can make that happen. There is distress and more distress. Instead of considering that there should be acceptance of the event, with an understanding that fate is supreme, and its actions are final, usually the deceased parent spends many days grieving, hashing over the sudden deprivation. These feelings bleed into the minds of the surviving relatives and friends, who experience it as a lack of peace of mind, and a compulsion to be at odds with fate.

Sudden Death of a Grandparent

The sudden death of a grandparent is likely to be a silent affair in a family and community. People sense the loss if that person was an active server. However, people do not become as distressed as if this same person was deceased in his/her young adult years. There is a sense that this elderly person lived the life, completed the obligations, cared for others sufficiently, and left suddenly besides.

On the astral side this person moves about slowly, seeing and speaking to those who are dear but who survived. There may be an attempt to instruct and make requests of family members and friends. Because the service energy for that lifetime was expended, this person does not feel as if his/her life was snuffed out inconsiderately. Instead, there is a feeling of release as when a butterfly emerges from a cocoon and flies through the air for the first time.

On the physical side, some relatives and friends may feel happy that this person did not suffer through old age with a decrepit body, or with one which had a failing heart, or some other tragedy. There is a feeling of, *"She/He lived a good life, serving others and rendering kindness in the home and society. This person must be in a heavenly place."*

The deceased one will find himself/herself to be in a psychic body which resembles the one which died in the physical world. It does happen, but rarely, that such a deceased soul experiences itself in a youthful astral body which is profuse with light, shining iridescently and being saturated with bliss feelings. If that happens this person will be out of touch with the survivors who ponder her/his situation and who have no idea what actually happened on the psychic side.

Collective Death Occasion

One may become deceased during a mass killing when that is expected, or when it is not foreseen. One may or may not have time to alert relatives and friends. These are some occasions.

- ethnic or genocidal crisis
- epidemic
- warfare
- crash of public conveyance
- natural disaster

This writer was once in a situation of **ethnic targeting** with inconvenience or death. The situation was such that one racial group which was economically poorer than another, got social control of a capital city. This poorer group looted the business of the wealthier sector. This developed into their committing of violent acts to the wealthier group. There was killing.

I was in the poorer group, but the family I was a member of, did not participate. We witnessed gruesome scenes. We shielded some of the wealthier group by defending them when they were harangued by our ethnic factor.

In such a situation, if one is killed, it usually happens suddenly. One's family members and friends may have no idea about the incidence. Later, one's body may or may not be found. Because of the suddenness of the event, a victim is left to consider it on the astral side when he realizes that he was struct and lost access to physical existence. It is not so much the loss of the body that will afflict one but the loss of the opportunity to complete responsibilities. For infants and youths who are displaced in such situations, there is usually a stunned condition of mind immediately after the incidence. These young ones are baffled and wish dearly to be with their parents, relatives, and friends.

They run here and there in the psychic existence to inquire about being physical. They wonder what happened. Usually, they can make no sense of the events. After some days, they understand that they are parentless and homeless as psychic refugees.

As a child this writer was in a situation of a polio **epidemic**. Then, there was a small pox scare. There was also a measles epidemic. As I recall, the part of the population which was in great anxiety about this, were the parents. Children who are afflicted were miserable but they did not grasp the threat, and did not access any particular value for staying alive. Death was not their concern. Becoming healthy again was but not in the sense of feeling marked for death.

I recall having measles but there were other children who were more afflicted and who cried continuously about it. It itched but could not be scratched without creating lesions. Many children, like myself, simply thought about the playful activities which we normally engaged but which during the infection we could not indulge.

Chicken pox and small pox were scary because of the marks made on the skin, the bodily imbalance, and the strange feelings. But there again, children did not think that they would die from it. Parents were concerned and wanted the medical authorities to cure it.

Kids who pass away during an epidemic are more concerned about resuming their playful habits on the physical side of life and eating the food their parents (guardians) prepare. If an adult passes during an epidemic that person will think of the responsibilities they cannot service from the psychic side. There may be ideas about the wrath of God, the swipe of nature, the carelessness of persons who had the disease but who were not particular to be quarantined.

When someone dies because of **warfare**, it is perplexing because it seems to be non-specific. For instance, during the Vietnam war, I was an electronic repairman for avionic equipment. The gadgets I serviced were used on bombers and fighter jets. If someone was killed as a result by any of the aircraft which I serviced, who was responsible for that?

Someone who was killed by an aircraft which had equipment which I serviced, could not target me as the enemy. The aircraft passed over his head. I was neither the pilot nor weapons operator. How would the victim identify and target me for my part in it.

Thus, when one becomes deceased in warfare, there is disillusionment and mistargeting by the victims. Even the victors cannot be sure about the status of those who were killed. A dead soldier has a difficult time identifying the person who was responsible for his death.

Who is it? The president of the enemy country? The commander of the enemy army? The individual soldier who fired the weapon which killed the body?

Those who survive an assault by the enemy go on living. If they were close to being killed, they may feel blest or lucky, but those who were killed must individually consider the situation. In the back of the mind of a deceased soldier will be the stress for informing family and friends. Some who were politically focused will think about the country instead of the family. These will wonder if their side won the battle.

Some who die in warfare become concerned about their remains, as to if the dead body will be found, as to if it will decay on the battlefield, as to if a wound disfigured it, as to if the enemy will find the corpse and dishonor it, as to if the comrades will retrieve the body and honorably bury it.

After a time, the deceased soldier will travel back and forth between the battlefield and his home. He will do this until he is satisfied that his remains were honorably or dishonorably regarded. As for his relatives, they will think about him as to if he is dead or alive. Some relatives may hear nothing of his demise. Some may be informed promptly. Mostly, survivors will want to procure the body and give it an honorable funeral. Some relatives will consider that war is unjust and arbitrary. Others will feel that the war was worth the sacrifice of someone's life.

Warfare affects people who are not soldiers, even people who are distant from the location of the battles. Many people may lose their bodies in a war. Death which comes as a result of military conflict is not easy to rationalize and justify, either for civilians or for the military personnel. Some who die in battle were forced to wield weapons. These are disappointed if they die. On the psychic side many deceased victims and soldiers, lament, and curse life.

Some people who are unrelated or who are related even, may die when there is a **fatal event of a public conveyance**. Someone who travels with no relatives but with others on a bus, plane, or train, may die in a crash. One victim may have a premonition about the disaster or may have no idea of the possibility.

Passing on that occasion, and finding the self unable to complete the journey on the physical side, would come as a surprise. One victim may even appreciate the event, while another would sorely regret it on the psychic side. In either case, a victim would, with urgency, try to complete the journey by running in the direction of the destination, by shouting to the conductor, driver, or pilot, by trying to help others who are wounded, who wail in pain, where the sounds are heard on the physical and psychic sides.

Officials who were killed in the accident, persons like the driver or pilot, would be uncertain and would wonder if his/her body was killed. In that event, the person would wonder about accountability, if there would be a trial, if the body is wounded only, and will be revived to answer for the mishap. There will be feelings of guilt for an official who feels responsible. One who thinks that he was not at fault may want to slip away from the living and dead passengers.

In a **natural disaster**, some people may die due to the violence of nature. There is the question of who or what caused the scattering wind, the movement of the earth, the accumulation of water, the dust, gas, and heat. Those who are theistic may point a finger at God. Others may attribute it to Nature. In such a situation with no human agency as the cause, people who pass away usually accept the incidence as a destined event which one must accept but which they would rather not think of.

In a natural disaster, deceased persons usually scan their minds to analyze the event. They are particularly curious of some supernatural agency which was involved or if they were targeted by mother earth, or by the wind, rain, or sea.

Death by Suicide

The state of mind and emotions which trigger the impetus for suicide, vary from person to person. And yet, it is based on feeling estranged from some feature of physical life. Most suiciders do not stop to consider what will happen hereafter.

It is an enigma why someone who is aware of reincarnation, would consider suicide. If there is reincarnation where would the suicider arrive after he/she deprives the self of the physical body. How would the suicide benefit that deceased person or someone else.

The tensions felt which bring the possibility of suicide into the mind of someone, are caused by intense and challenging circumstances. For instance, if someone has strong feelings about a political issue, that person may become distraught, to such an extent, that there may be a feeling that if that person died, he/she would be regarded as a martyr, that people would take notice, and agree with the ideas of the suicider. Another example is the case where there is social friction between a suicider and someone who is related, like for instance, a spouse. The suicider may conjecture that if he/she killed himself/herself, the spouse, who is left to content with physical history, will find that circumstances moved in favor of what the suicider desired.

Some person may lose sense of purpose, feeling that life is not worth living. Hence this someone will conclude that the solution is to end the life of the self, so that the self is no more, and it does not have to contend with differences of opinion.

A suicider may be motivated by not having a sense of purpose, or by losing the reason for living, by not being cared for, or by not caring for anyone, not even the self.

Chapter 2
The Event of Death

The event of death is undeclared by anyone. It is unknown. From the side of the living, from the perspective of physical people who witness the death of a body, they, by convention, use a measure to state that death occurred at this or that moment.

The fact is. No one from the physical side can see the moment of death of a body. This is proven in cases where someone dies suddenly, then that person is revived either by medical action or by no obvious activity of anyone on either side of existence. There are cases of persons who were declared dead, then buried, then revived, where after the declaration, the body resumed signs of life.

Modern physicians may commit errors in determining when someone dies. Someone felt that once the last breath or sigh is made, the person is dead, but that was denied in some rare cases, where someone who was believed to have had the last breath, revived.

- Is the moment of death the time when the heart ceased throbbing?

- Is it when the lungs quitting contracting and expanding?

- Is it when there is no sign of bio-electrical activity?

- Is it when a main artery loses fluid?

Survivors Declaration of Death

Usually, the survivors declare death when the vital signs are no longer present. These are heart pulse, breathing action and lack of response to sound and touch. In the modern setting, people verify the conclusion about death when physicians check the body and pronounce its non-functionality.

People expect that medical personnel will do everything possible to revive a body. If the heart still beats, even slowly and imperceptibly, people may hope that the person could be revived. Even if the face shows no sign of life, if the brain appears to be devoid of cell activity, people may hope that the person would recover. If for instance the heart still beats even in a whisper which human senses cannot detect but which shows on an oscilloscope, people express hope.

If someone ceases breathing and if that occurred recently, people may request that air be mechanically impelled into the lungs. This may cause the person to be revived. Even for someone with a body which is one hundred years of age, or someone whose body is damaged beyond repair, people expect that medical personnel can revive the victim.

Eventually however as nature would have it, someone will die, which means that the physical representation of that person, will be nonfunctional. Most people accept this conclusion of a life but there are modern and primitive societies which mummified a dead body with the idea that sometime in the future it would again demonstrate itself as a participating physical person.

One should abandon the idea that one knows when someone died. When the time of death is determined from this side, it is for the most part, approximate. If, however the body was killed in a powerful explosion where no part of it survived and where its destruction was rapid and total, the time of detonation would be the time of death.

In that case, the psychic person who was that body lost every affinity with it because of the wholesale, very radical, disintegration.

The time of death is the moment when the physical system is no longer responsive to the psychic aspects of the person. But this is a rating from the physical side. On the psychic plane, the person may or may not know when death occurred. Nature may not give an alert to the psychic person as to when that psyche was disconnected from the physical system.

We know this, not through speculation, but through the sleep condition, awaking states, unconscious states, and partial observation states. If someone is unconscious both on the physical and psychic planes, there is no idea of time, no idea of self even. Events that occur, either on the physical or astral level, will be unknown to someone who lost track of the objective self, and the invisible and unknowing subjective person.

To tell if there is a gap in time which one did not track, one must have an external reference. For instance, a clock could be used or another event even. If there is no contrasting timing, one cannot tell how long one was absorbed with an incidence or was separated from it.

If someone becomes unconscious just before death of his physical body, and if he was not aware at the moment of death, he cannot know when his physical body died. For that matter it may be moments, minutes, hours or even days before he could admit death. If when that happens, he has no memory for reference, he would be at a loss as to who he is, or he may accept his condition as being a spontaneous person. He may not know if he lived previously even.

On the physical side, people have no way of knowing his awakened or suspended condition. Unless one is a mystic with precise psychic perception, there is no way for one to know how someone whose physical body is dead, realized the moment when he was deprived of its use.

Once when driving a vehicle across the state of Kansas, this writer fell asleep. The vehicle veered to the right where a deep ditch was located. Instead of following the incline downward, it went into the air and flipped. When it reached the highest point in the air above the ditch, I became aware of my physical body which was upside down, as the vehicle was at that moment.

In midair, my body fell towards the roof of the car. At the moment I was aware of seeing the interior of the vehicle and my body which was crumpled in it. In split seconds, the car contacted the earth and the roof crumpled. I opened the driver door and left the vehicle. My physical system was unharmed.

When the vehicle was in the air, I was in the subtle body as my psychic self. Even though I perceived it with psychic vision of the astral form, I was unaware of the condition of the physical body.

More important is that there were some moments when I was unaware of the vehicle and of my physical body. Then I was only aware of my subtle body but with no information about the condition of the physical one. This began some moments before I fell asleep while driving. There was a transit of focal consciousness, where when I drove, I was aware that my focus was suspended bit by bit, but I felt that I could delay this focus arrest. I could not.

I, as the observing feature of self, could not independently maintain consciousness of the physical body. The adjuncts which assist with that, could not continue giving energy for an awakened condition. Hence when the kundalini lifeForce, finally withdrew its support, the observing self could not provide every bit of energy required.

The kundalini withdrew itself as it had to. Then I, the observing self, was left to continue the focus for driving. Since the contribution of the observing self was insufficient to keep the physical system in observational order, that iSelf was shifted into a drowsy state in which assessment of the road, the vehicle and especially, the steer and acceleration, was lost. This happened for moments but for enough to cause the vehicle to veer right at a high speed.

In that incidence, it is obvious that one cannot keep tally under certain conditions of the physical or subtle body. One cannot always resume control of the physical body during an accident which puts it at risk. If, however, one does resume control, one may not know the specific time when the event began. Time proceeds even when an individual's objective rating is suspended.

If this writer had died during that incidence, he may or may not know the time of death of the physical body. When the vehicle veered, I lost track of the car and of the entire event. This means there was a blank consciousness for some moments. When the car veered into the air, I gain perception of the incidence. I saw the inverted air-borne vehicle as a psychic presence. I was located in the air above it. I saw the physical body crumpled, lying in the ceiling. Just then I became or felt as if I was the physical body. I experienced its condition. This was different to peering at it with psychic eyes.

Through this experience, there was some connection between the physical body and the astral one. At no time was the physical one dead. The awareness of it was reduced. Only some of its aspects and condition, was perceived. Otherwise, it was as if it was someone else.

Admittance of Death by a Deceased Person

For living people, the dead person may be regarded in one of two ways,

- as a dead physical body
- as a psychic person who was deprived of physical opportunity.

That would be the view from this side of existence. Those are ideas of the surviving relatives and friends. On the astral side, in the majority of the cases, a psychic person who died, becomes distraught. Even a person who believes in reincarnation, may become unhappy, if his/her physical system cannot be used to participate in history. It is important that during the life of the physical body those who practice spiritual disciplines and who desire to go to a sublime place or condition hereafter, regularly practice the transfer to that location.

This practice is the indication that such a person may transit to a higher realm. The higher states may be experienced in an ordinary or extraordinary way. The basic process is in dream experiences. These are mostly spontaneous where the person did not cause it to happen. In dream states, if before death, one transits to higher dimensions and converses with persons who live there, it is likely that a spontaneous transfer could happen permanently, or temporarily, as soon as one is deprived of the body.

Except for the transfer back to being a physical body, there is no difference between a dream experience when sleeping and when dead. Just as in a dream state some other person will not see the experience but that episode is experienced by the dreamer, so at death, the deceased one's shift to an astral level, will not be witnessed by physical people. But someone who is physical and who has psychic perception may see what happens in the astral existence. There are however only a few humans among thousands who have the perception.

The views of surviving relatives and friends, may affect the deceased one. In addition, that departed person may feel the need to relate to the living people. This emotion may not help the deceased to transit to higher places. Instead, it may cause him/her to remain on a low astral plane or even to descend lower, just to be in a vibratory state which can interfere with the living people.

When a surviving relative or friend or even someone who was hostile, thinks of the deceased person, that thought energy may reach the deceased someone. If the thinking is favorable or unfavorable, the energy will have a proportionate impact. Hostile feelings will have hurtful impact. Happy feelings will be acceptable. As soon as the energy arrives near the deceased one, the mental part of the subtle body will make an effort to respond. This itself is a danger, as it could interfere with the departed one's conveyance to a higher plane.

People usually assume that someone who was pious, will undoubtedly go to a heavenly place hereafter, but the very energy of such thinking could delay or even terminate any transit to a heavenly place. The thought force, though friendly and full of well-wishes, may convert into a stalling energy.

For someone who thinks that the dead body was the total existence of the person, even that opinion may affect the deceased one, as that person may try to correct those ideas by reaching the one who thought that he/she is not existent, to discuss that there is continuation on the psychic side of life, a plane of existence which was used during the life of the body, and which continues hereafter.

The people on the physical side who regard the deceased one as a psychic person, who was deprived of physical opportunity, are usually careless in how they think, and project feelings about the deceased one. Some survivors develop extreme happiness over the death of the person. This happens especially if the person had a terminal illness which was incapacitating or extremely painful. The survivors feel that the deceased one was freed from the accursed condition.

This thinking could interfere with the transit of the deceased person, whereby it would cause the transit to stall, so that the person can hear what projected from the mind of those who render well wishes on the physical side. If the departed one ignored these hopeful thoughts, it is likely that this will be sensed by the people on the physical side. They may feel neglected, which in turn will cause them to project even stronger thoughts, which in turn may brake the transit of the deceased one.

Someone who sends well-wishes which are mild, and which do not have a braking force on the transit of the departed someone, will be appreciated by that dead person, because that energy will have an accelerating effect whereby the departed one will transit even quicker to the higher psychic realm.

Those who regard the dead body as that of a psychic person, who was deprived of physical opportunity, may assess the life of that person, as to his/her purpose life, as to if the life was well-lived and fulfilled, as to where that person may be in the astral existence. These thoughts may reach the deceased one, who may send mental replies, and emit corresponding feelings which will reach the survivor(s).

Since thinking energy impacts the subtle body, one should cease the habit of thinking frequently of those who are departed. Instead, one should only have purposeful communications directed to that somebody. It is not in the interest of a departed person, for a living relative, or friend, to send many thoughts or mental images. If anything, one should think in the positive interest of that departed soul. Even those who have resentments for that person, should cease these, and instead wish the best for that someone.

Once a person lost his/her body, he/she cannot directly participate in history. Hence it makes no sense to be hostile or whimsical towards that individual. Whatever right or wrong, actions or influence, the deceased person expressed, that energy became part of history, and will be resolved by Nature. Hence, there is no point in harboring grudges. There should be a feeling that Nature is competent to dissolve any tension through its use of the time medium.

Usually someone who is deceased, who is deprived of a physical body, does not accept the fact of being permanently deprived of that form. That person feels that he/she must take one action, which is to awaken on the physical side. After years of living as a physical body, where there was sleep and then resumption of physicalness in the form of a physical form, someone has a tendency to live as a physical self only.

There is little acceptance of the psychic self as the essential being. The mental posture is that the physical self sleeps. It may or may not dream while sleeping. It awakens. It acts in the physical world. It again sleeps, usually within a twenty-four-hour period, based on the rising and setting of the sun.

There are three methods used by the deceased person to awaken his/her dead body.

- continue an action
- call for physical help
- awaken as the physical body

At the time of death, a dead person may try to **continue an action** which was partially committed and which he/she felt duty bound to complete. This is frustrating because there will be no physical effect, or there may be a momentary physical action where from the psychic side, there is a miraculous movement of the physical body in its last moments, even when the lifeForce was already disengaged from the body.

There are stories from the time when soldiers used swords, where someone was beheaded on the battlefield and his body remained upright and acted for some moments. This may happen as well when a human kills an animal, where when the animal is fatally injured, its body tries to flee, and does so for one or more steps, until its wounded form collapses.

Someone who partially did a kind act and who suddenly died, may will the self to continue the action, such that the dead body will make an effort to complete that act but it will die anyway. The deceased one will feel as if there was a rapid dephasing of the ability to act, like for instance when someone who acts in a certain way, faints. That person may or may not feel the sudden loss of motion. Because the action power was diminished either gradually or rapidly, the person's objective self may have disconnected from the body, and from its vital energy, before consciousness faded. This could be for a moment or a split second even.

Some who die, may, just as it happens or immediately after, **call for physical help**. Some do so during the last throes of the body. Someone else may call just after the body dies. In which event, the call for help will be on the psychic side, with the departed one knowing or not knowing that it was a psychic sound, which would be disregarded by physical people, who are deaf to psychic events.

Some who call for help, realize that the physical people cannot hear the cry. Some others think that they were heard but that someone ignored the plea. After a time, however, all departed people who reach out to the living people by speaking, come to realize that the living people are deaf to psychic sound.

Some who die during sleep or otherwise, may rest for a while in their subtle bodies. They may attempt to **awaken as the physical form**. This is an involuntary action, used over and over by people who live as physical beings. One carries this method as an instinct in the psyche. One does so, life after life.

I knew a lady who passed on while her physical body was in the elderly years. There was an aneurism in her brain. Her body was kept alive even though her brain died. This was done by mechanically forcing air into her lungs. Eventually her relatives decided that the mechanical means of keeping her body alive, should be removed.

After this she died. I met her on the astral planes. I discussed the futility of trying to awaken her body time after time. Eventually she accepted that her physical participation was terminated. Because she did not want to again be a physical person, she created an astral residence, and lived there for many years.

A deceased person may return to his residence day after day, night after night, with intentions of eating, sleeping, and awakening there. It happens to many departed people. This happens because of the attachment one may feel to being a physical somebody. Unless one works mentally and emotionally to root it out, it is likely that one will behave in this way after death.

Presently the subtle body eats at some place. It is sleeps somewhere. It awakens as something that is interspaced in the physical world. This is an ingrained habit already. It is the likely lifestyle which will be assumed hereafter.

Admittance of Death

Just as some relatives or friends, at first refuse to accept that a loved one is dead, so the deceased person may have difficulty accepting the condition of being dismembered from physical events.

For many persons, this is the worst thing that could happen. Some take this as an insult from fate. Some blame a physician. Some blame a parent. Some curse a government or business official. Some deride God. Some feel that they were cursed. Some reflect that life was not worth the effort.

Even people who had no progeny, who had no cherished someone in their life at any time, even these are attached to life. The impulse to continue living is built into the person.

For most people who die, the acceptance of the event happens with a psychic sigh of: *"I am dead."* That is contradictory because if one can admit, it means that one must exist somewhere somehow. The problem arises with the way we define life. Instead of defining life as the psychic basis for physical existence, we define life as physical presence. That reinforces a denial of value for psychic history.

After death of the physical body, how long will it take for that person to realize, and know for sure, that he/she is no longer a physical reality or as we say, is dead? Some deceased person takes six to twelve months before realizing that the hope to wake up as themselves, as the physical body, is useless. Then, such a self declares, "*I am dead.*"

Some others realize it in moments. For instance, that happens for those who died in a sensational event, like if someone was fatally shot, or if someone died in a plane crash, or if someone was assaulted viciously, or if someone was killed while being kidnapped. The understanding that the physical body is no longer responsive to one's will, depends on the incidence of death.

People who passed on peaceable, especially those who do so in the elderly years, may take some months or longer before self-declaring the physical self as being dead. These folks return to the sleeping area night after night, rest there on an astral bed which feels physical. They rest. They awaken in the morning as usual in the astral body, with it feeling like the physical form which they identified as but which died.

The declaration to oneself that one is dead, does not change the circumstance. Everything continues as usual, with one focusing on whatever was important to one during the physical life. Eventually, however, one will feel attracted to someone who could be a parent to oneself, or one may be attracted to someone who could influence a potential parent. Then one will cease the declaration. One will find that one's attention shifts into wanting to be with parents. One no longer wants to be the physical body one had.

Body Condition / Thinking and Feeling Condition

Death is such that the dying indications witnessed by observers may be at variance with what happens mentally and emotionally to the victim. Once I was present when one person described the last moments of her dearly departed relative. She described the terminally-ill person's condition like this, *"I am pleased to report that my relation passed away peacefully and without stress. By all indications, she went to the heaven of our deity."*

This was a report about a person whose physical body was almost a skeleton when death was near. That was due to the fact that the body ceased to digest food. The person lost appetite and had a cancerous condition in every part.

Many people profess a deity whom they never met. After living for the average lifespan of say sixty plus years and not seeing the deity even once, someone professes that he/she will see the deity. This is based on belief. Besides statements in religious books, and assurances by religious officials, what is the guarantee that any convert will meet a deity at death?

Why not meet the divine being during the lifespan? What is so special about death that the deity will appear then, even though the divine being did not appear for many years during the physical life. Supposed that at the moment someone passes away, there are thousands of other devotees of the deity who also die, what is the deity to do to make himself/herself be seen by each worshipper. Does the deity create parallel versions of himself/herself, thus making it possible to be seen by each member? Otherwise, how is it possible for a multi-apparition to occur?

Will it occur, just a moment before the instant of death?

Will it occur, exactly when death happens?

Will it occur just after, when the person is totally desynchronized from the physical body?

What is the value of the assurance of a religious official that the devotee will definitely see the deity, and will spontaneously go to the realm of that divine person?

At death, the condition of mind of the deceased person may be at variance with the condition of his/her body. In my experience with losing control of a speeding car, if a physical observer saw what happened, his report will not include the complete separation of my subtle body which had no damaging experience and which was in a healthy, non-fearful, state while observing the incidence of the airborne upturned vehicle. The physical body felt different to how the subtle one was experienced.

Someone may be physically distressed or may even be happy on the physical side during the death event. But the subtle form may or may not have a corresponding condition.

For human beings, fear is the word for the general attitude and expectancy about death. Regarding death, we have an innate fear about two features of life.

- pain
- horror

These cause hesitation, panic, and postponement of plans in varying degrees. When there is a threat which indicates death of the body, there may be pain or horror. These are features of impending death, which are mistaken as death itself. Death is neither pain nor horror but due to their affiliation, **pain and horror** are regarded as being allied to and identical with death.

A pain in the physical body which comes from a terminally diseased condition or a fatal wound, is itself not death. And yet, the focus on that pain which may be involuntary and compelling, causes the person to feel that pain to be death. It is however the sensual event which is prior to death.

Once death occurs, the discomfort or disease of the physical body ceases. The departed soul is then transferred to the condition of the subtle body, or it may become unconscious on the psychic side of existence for a time, after which it will awaken and act as it normally does in dreams. For some other person who will die shortly, there may be mental scenes of horror, or emotional experiences which are disconcerting. This person may continue to be involved in those horrible events. But then when the body dies, that someone would detach from whatever it perceived on the physical side.

Its awareness will be psychic, where it may or may not continue to see and/or feel the horrible situation. Its psychic perception of this will be similar to how it experienced similar events in dreams, except that it can no longer retreat to be a physical body and must stay on the astral side.

The natural way to escape from a horrible dream is to awaken on the physical side. Now that this is no longer possible, the person, must deal with the experience head on, or it can transfer into another dimension where the horror has no register.

Death is neither a pain nor a fear. But it so happens that death is affiliated with these, because the physical body usually has a terminal malfunction with pain or fear being experienced. Because of that reference there is confusion regarding the definition of death. One should consider that death is the event of being permanently unable to operate any function of the physical body. Death itself is neither pain nor fear. But these unwanted features are affiliated because they frequently occur just prior to death.

In the event of a sudden fatal accident, there is no time for the person to feel pain or fear. That is due to the rapidity of the disintegration of the body. Then there will be death with neither pain nor fear.

A deceased friend, Sir Paul Castagna, came on the astral side of the day of November 11, 2022. He said that I overlooked something significant about the fear of death. His view is that I did not include the fear of not finishing the mission of one's life. According to him, this fear haunts many human beings, where some years, months or days before death, these persons experience a cold anxiety about dying before completing the mission of life.

He stated that in his situation where his body died of cancer, he could not finish his artistic work and social influence. Once he was told by physicians that he would die, he had many sleepless nights where he analyzed how he could complete the mission.

Moment of Death

The method for determining when a person died, varies from place to place but vital signs which cease, usually determine whether the immobile body is a corpse or not.

Persons on the physical side are liable to misinterpret events. They rarely have psychic perception, which can observe if any psychic content survives, and what condition that psychic self will assume, once it no longer is unified with the bio-electrical impulses in the physical body.

If the heart ceased throbbing, people may conclude that the body is dead; that it died at the moment when the heart became silent. However, on the psychic side of life, the deceased person may have lost control before the time when the heart ceased activity. A body can exhibit signs of life, and the person involved may have no idea that its body still lives. In fact, the separation of the psychic self from its physical body may happen incidentally where the person after some seconds, minutes, hours, days or even years, may be unaware of the condition of the physical body. This happens in trance, seizures, and comas.

An individual does not necessarily feel the moment of death. He/She may have no idea that the body died. If for instance someone is in a dream experience when the physical body dies, that dreamer may not be informed or may not sense the occurrence. If the dream continues where the person does not lose track of the dream environment, that someone may continue in the dream sequence with no understanding about the death of the body and the loss of access to physical history.

Assuming that reincarnation is a fact, persons who are physical now, were physical before. There may be no recall of that. Most persons live as if this is the first life event. There is no coherent reference about a previous history. One lives as if one did not live before. One is engaged currently with the idea that this life is the first one.

If there is a psychic self which survives death, that illusive principle must be present during the living phase of the body. Its operation then would be in concert with the physical life. At death, that psychic aspect has no coordination with physical operations. Since it has no physical facility, it will not have whatever the physical system afforded it previously. These non-available aspects are items like brain-stored memory and patterns of action which were rendered only by the physical body.

Lung Malfunction

Is the death of a body, when the lungs quit contracting and expanding? Can one be certain that death occurred when the breathing apparatus ceased movement? On the physical side can anyone proclaim for sure, that the victim died at the moment when it was determined that his lung functions ceased.

As with any declared cause of the death of a body by persons on this side of existence, who can be sure that a cessation of functions of any vital organ caused death? And even the deceased someone who functions as a psychic being only, may not know the moment when he/she was deprived of control of a part or all of the physical apparatus which was known as the body.

Someone may be unaware of his/her physical body, and that form may appear to be alive to some other person on the physical side. For example, if someone fell from a great height, the psychic body of that person may be displaced from the physical body during the fall or when the body impacted the ground. The body may keep living anyway, where there is involuntary breathing and heartbeat. People on the physical side who observe the body, will realize that even though it is unconscious, it lives.

Efforts may be made to revive it. Suppose during those efforts the body dies, what will be the situation of the person who experiences itself as a psychic presence. It was displaced from the physical body but it experiences itself on the astral side.

To those on the physical side, this person died some moments after falling when the unconscious body lost vitality. To the psychic person, he/she died when during the fall or upon impact, it lost conscious grasp on the physical body because of being displaced from it.

Regardless of what is listed by people on the physical side, it is near impossible for any person to tell the moment of death. The survivors are left to speculate. The instance when there is the last separation of the subtle body from the physical one, can rarely be determined accurately. In fact, it is near impossible for a survivor to know, because the separation from the physical body cannot be determined from the physical side.

Even someone on the astral level, even the psychic self which is shifted from the physical system, may not know the time of death. It is not necessary to know the exact moment. The important information is to know the sequence of events which assail the subtle body. Mostly one should observe what happens at the separation of the subtle body from day to day.

Death is not a special event in that case. Death is a repeat of what happened during the life of the physical body when there was sleeping, dreaming, unconsciousness and the like. Whatever was endured as those events during the life of the body, would be repeated at its death. One should assume that whatever happens will be what happened before, except for the fact that it would be the last instance of the physical events.

Chapter 3
Controlling the Event of Death

For the most part, the event of death, the moment it occurs, may or may not be known to the person who is deprived nor to survivors who are concerned about the body. The event is not controlled by the limited person who was known as it. Nor is it controlled by survivors. Even in the instance where one person kills another, the exact moment for the separation of the astral body of the victim is unknown. This is due to the fact that the event occurs on a psychic plane which is inaccessible to the victim as well as the assailant.

On the physical side an observer is concerned with the vital signs. Questions arise:

- Is he/she aware?
- Is the heart giving a pulse?
- Is the breathing motion continuing?
- Is the face glowing?

On the psychic side, the victim may think.

- Am I alive?
- What happened?
- Can I awaken as my physical self?

Just before death there may be a scaling down of consciousness, where the person feels as if he/she fades from existence. One may feel like a bright light which becomes dimmer and dimmer, until it shines no longer. One may become unconscious or feel as if one is in a directionless place, a nothing land.

Time may be no more. There may be no access to up or down, left or right, in front or behind. Even the idea of death, of termination, may disappear. There may be no idea of the physical body which is recently deceased. The person may continue in that condition for a short or long period. Some residual desires may be activated. Whatever is involuntary in the psychic body will continue to operate with or without input from the observerSelf, who may lack discrimination, and not have a way to gage events.

The idea that death is a radical departure whereby someone will immediately go to a heaven or beatific place, should be questioned as to if such a transfer occurred even once or frequently during the life of the deceased person. If it did, we may be confident that it could again occur. If it did not, it may happen but that possibility would be based not on instances but on belief, and on the tendency to wish the departed, a divine transit.

It should be considered that if transit to a divine place was infrequent, or irregular, or if it did not happen, even once, then what is the likelihood that it would occur at the time of being deprived of physical access to the body? What are the factors which a deceased person operated to cause a divine transfer during the life of the body?

Can the deceased person put those factors into motion at the time of death?

What meditation, or religious procedure, is valid for making this happen?

If during the lifespan, the transit was not due to the action of the deceased, if it occurred on the basis of the action of a deity or by sheer chance, what are the possibilities that this would be triggered again?

If the departure from the body during sleep, did not cause the person to transit to a heavenly place, how is it that the final exit from the body will cause a divine transit. Why would the person not be transferred to the same astral places which he/she experienced during the sleeping period of the physical body?

Exact Moment of Death

In conclusion, it is hardly likely that anyone on the physical side may determine the exact moment when a subtle body of a departed soul was fully disconnected from its physical form. On the subtle side, it is so as well, where a departed soul does not have a clear idea of when it was no longer possible to use the physical body.

A lady, I knew, did not know for over two months that she was fully disengaged from her dead body. She could not perceive it but all the same, she did not experience a disconnection. She repeatedly tried to awaken as her physical self just as she did after each period of sleep.

The disconnection happened, but with her having no experience of it. This lack occurs during sleeping where one sleeps, dreams, and then awakens with no clear understanding of the transition to sleep or dream. The shift from dream or sleep is involuntarily.

If someone noted that during the life of the body, and took the time to study it, one would have a firm view of this but usually someone ignores the psychic events. During the life of the physical body, night after night during the sleeping period, many shifts occur. Some happen when one is in an observational position and can note them, but usually it is ignored.

At death, whatever happens may have occurred before, during a sleeping state, or during an arousal from or induction to sleep, except that death is the last such event in the lifespan of the body. Dream transitions happen repeatedly until the final shift when the physical body becomes disconnected from one's psychic range. Just as during the life of the body, many psychic shifts occur with little or no objective perception, so at death, the final shift may occur with the person having no idea of its operation.

Painful Condition

A painful condition at the time of death may cause the person concerned to focus on the discomfort. This is counterproductive for those who aspire to transit to a heavenly world or pleasant place. It may cause the mind to have a content which is similar to that of a lower realm in which the astral body will be saturated with anguish.

A state of mind is attracted to a similar dimension. A painful death experience may cause the person to transit to a dimension in which painful states are the normal experience. However, someone who for the most part was healthy during the life of the physical body is likely to resume a pleasant state of mind, and may go to a heavenly place hereafter, just after the subtle body is no longer reflecting the condition of the dying physical one.

If, however, the lifestyle contributed to the physical body becoming diseased, that may cause a reaction where the person who tries to release himself/herself from the painful condition, is unable to do so, such that he/she does not experience the death of the physical system, because the subtle body maintains the painful condition, even after the physical body dies. The deceased person may transit to a hellish location in which unpleasant experiences are frequent.

A long illness just before death, one for months or years, in which a painful condition was endured, even one in which a painful condition was abated by pain-killing-drugs, is likely to cause the subtle body to adopt a painful condition and to become somewhat wasted. Even for people who were essentially good, such a condition may cause the subtle body to transit to a hellish location hereafter.

No Feeling of Transfer

When the event of death happens with no feeling of transfer, where the deceased person has no idea, no awareness of any change either in the physical or subtle body, that person is unaware that death occurred. In that condition, this person has no grip on memory or anything from the past and instead feels itself as a glaring consciousness in a fog or in a state of clarity consciousness with no reference to anything from the past.

It is as if time ceased, where it has no prior event nor any outlook for a future. This person's awareness is stunted. It waits in a state of clear, or muddled awareness, for the continuation of existence with no idea that its physical system died.

No Feeling with Sudden Silence

When at the moment of death, someone finds that he/she has no feelings but is aware of a dank silence, that someone experiences itself as awareness in a space which cannot be measured but which is alert, as if waiting for an event.

This state may last for hours, or days, or even years, but it may be instantaneous where it does not proceed through time but vanishes and leaves the person in an astral place where he/she may interact with others, with or without understanding that he/she lost a physical body, and is transferred permanently to the astral world, where one can know oneself only as a psychic being.

There are several existential niches which are saturated with silence, or with hum, or with screeching noise. A deceased person may be transferred into such a place for a short period or for a time. If one finds the self to be there, one may or may not be there with discrimination and memory. In which case, one may be stunned, not knowing what to do because of not having a reference. One would then stay in that state of awareness for as long as it endures.

Blank Out

Someone may blank out just before or at the moment of death. In a hospital, a living physical body may be in a state of unconsciousness at the time death, either for a considerable time before dying or for moments prior. This means that it is likely that one may pass on and be unconscious through the experience.

We should assume that just as an unconscious body usually awakens, so at the time of death, if someone was unconscious both on the physical and astral sides of life, still it is likely that this person would become aware soon after death.

The query is.

What state of consciousness will that person experience itself as, once it becomes conscious of itself after death? Will it remember itself as it was when its physical body functioned efficiently? Will it know who it was or what it did?

shift

One who feels the shift from having a physical body to not having one, where one feels a disconnect from the physical reality, that person knows that it was removed from the feelings of the physical system and is left as a psychic being only. Many questions arise in the mind of that conscious person. These pertain to responsibilities and relationship concerns.

Those anxieties may occur for a moment and then cease. Or they may happen for a time and continue exerting pressure, where the deceased one feels as if he/she lost the opportunities to service numerous responsibilities.

psychic horrors

Some persons experience psychic horrors just before, during, or immediately after the death of the physical body. This may be due to superstitious beliefs, which activate in the mind's imaginative faculty, to bring about ideas which mentally terrify the person, and bring on emotions which are traumatic and scary.

Horrible experiences may happen because the deceased one transited to an astral place where one is subjected to terrible anguish or to being tortured. These experiences arise because of performing vicious acts when one had the physical body, and because of using a faulty lifestyle which was antisocial and vicious.

During these experiences, the person may have no idea that his/her physical body died. There may be a complete loss of one's previous physical history, where one is subjected to terror, and one has no idea of a former existence in any other place. This is like being a newborn infant where whatever happens occurs for the first time.

ecstatic feelings

Death involves the termination of identity with a physical body. This means that the bio-electrical system malfunctions, to make it impossible for the psychic part of the self to connect as, and operate the physical organism. Hence on the physical side it is unlikely that there will be ecstatic feelings.

However, in rare cases, someone could be shifted to a realm of awareness, where there is saturation of ecstatic feelings in the subtle body, to such an extent that the person feels that such ecstasy is physical and psychic simultaneously.

The question is.

Will such a state of consciousness last indefinitely beyond the life of the physical body?

Or will it dissipate slowly or rapidly, where the deceased one finds himself/herself to be shifted into an astral state which lacks the ecstasy.

There are two factors to consider.

- ecstasy within the subtle body because of reconfiguration of energy

- ecstasy outside the subtle body in an astral environment which is always saturated with ecstatic energy

If the ecstatic feelings are expressions within the subtle body, their dissipation will cause a termination, where the individual will find himself/herself to be in another state. This is because of the limitations within the subtle body itself. If the feelings are the nature energy from an astral environment, then so long as the subtle body can remain in that dimension, it will have the ecstasy.

The control of the energy experienced is limited. The individual cannot maintain itself by itself in any environment. It needs support to be in the perpetual condition which it prefers.

heavenly glory

It can happen that at the moment of death there is a slit transit, something so sudden as to be instantaneous, where the person finds himself/herself to be in a saturation of heavenly glory. This may be where there is no other person in the vicinity, and the self is surrounded and penetrated by this glory. Or it may be where there are some persons surrounding in all directions in a heavenly world, a place in which lights abound, with no ushering of trauma, adversity, or displeasure. This may be for a few moments, or for days on end, or forever, in which case there is no resumption of the memory of earthly births, or any other existence ever experienced by the person. The heavenly situation is the all in all and is the only experience known to that translated person.

series of involvements

At the time of death, someone may experience a series of involvements with such rapidity, that in moments, more than one life is experienced, but with no normal rating of time. There would be situations which last for years, one after the other, with one individual or another, such that there are summary experiences with these individuals, either to replay relationship-roles or to complete such feelings and corresponding circumstances.

The deceased person would have no idea about death of the body, but on the physical side, others, the concerned survivors, would be involved preparing the body for disposal, and grieving over their loss.

In some incidences, a departed person would translate to a subtle world and live there from then onwards, with no idea that there was a physical life, a physical body which died, and relationships with others in the physical world. Instead that person will live in the astral dimension, and complete functions there to match whatever association there is in the astral place.

ancestral meet-up

Some deceased persons meet some of their ancestors just after they are deprived of contact with the physical body. Usually, these are favorable assembles but there are instances of a departed person experiencing horrors with one or more ancestors on the psychic side after death. When there are resentments, grudges, and the like, because a living human and his/her ancestor(s) had disagreements, it is likely that unless the ancestors become embryos before the death of the human, there will be obstructive contact when the human dies. At that time, the ancestor(s) will take the opportunity to verbally assault the human who was recently deceased.

Conversely, the deceased person may meet an ancestor favorably, where there are intense or mild enjoyment feelings shared, when they congregated in the astral existence. This happens spontaneously. It ends spontaneously as well.

deity infusion

At the time of passing from a body which is no longer serviceable, someone may become infused by deity energy. He/She may feel a relationship with the deity. A deity may for one reason or the other or just spontaneously without any obvious cause, infuse energy into the subtle body of his/her devotee. This would cause that person to focus intently into a higher plane of existence, somewhere which is the residential domain of the divine person.

Someone may also at the time of death, come under the influence of a negative supernatural person under whose influence, the deceased one experiences intense unwanted traumas. This would happen because the deceased person's psychic energy had an energy which provided a portal for the devil to enter. Such possessions may last for seconds or longer.

Chapter 4
The Life Hereafter

reproductive loop

In a gist, this information could be completed by declaring that the reproduction process is the method of repurposing everything for physical continuation. There are exceptions but these are rare events.

The reproduction loop is aggressively enforced by Nature such that it is hardly likely that any person will not be subjected to it at the time of death, and for that matter, during the life of the physical body.

This applies to every species. Whosoever is here as a physical body, regardless of it being microscopic or gigantic, is in the reproductive loop. As soon as the body dies, the psychic remnant becomes involved in the process of acquiring a new form which is similar to the one used. This is supported by relationship which causes emotional attachment, which is itself the medium of community.

There is fighting in community but that runs parallel to kinship. To resolve the disagreements over resources, some species operate a pecking order, a social disciplinary outlay, in which seniority, and rules of sharing resources, is established. This happens on the physical side when one has a body and on the astral side when one lacks one but feels the forceful pull for becoming one.

What is the general fact about the life hereafter?

It is that as soon as someone dies, the remnant psyche of that person joins the ancestral energy of the family and friends. This causes that person to be positioned in a queue of personalities who form part of a sexual psychic force through which birth opportunities are facilitated.

The time for remaining as a mere psychic force with no physical representation, varies from case to case. It may be a short or long period before an embryo is developed, but it will occur, either in the human species or in some other life form. It will happen in time.

Some individuals remain as a psychic force living in the body of some other person, sharing in that person's activities and being content in that way. Many develop their own forms and become reproductive agents. Eventually, as Nature facilitates, everyone is circulated in the reproductive loop. It depends on how history is formed as per the environmental circumstances.

- *In fact, of that which is born, death is certain; of that which is dead, birth is certain. Therefore, in assessing what is unavoidable, you should not lament. (Bhagavad Gītā 2.27)*

Heaven Hereafter

Many human beings through the centuries since writing was formatted, think that the afterlife consists of a heavenly domain, where a deity presides, and where the faithful will be justly rewarded with heavenly delights. This place may be here on earth or elsewhere in outerspace (the heavens).

This is mostly fantasy but not because it is a fantastic idea. Only due to the fact that for most people this is not experienced from day to day. Even human beings who have a pleasant life with delights, are terrorized when their elderly bodies become sickly with various ailments. They must endure acute illness in the elderly years. In time they too, succumb to death.

The looping force of reproduction is the obsession of nearly every human being. It controls the rich and poor, the beautiful and the ugly, the law-abiding and the criminally-minded. It is prevalent.

Besting the Reproductive System

Instead of staking a claim for heaven hereafter, it is best to secure a favorable format in the reproductive loop. So long as this loop is manifest, it is reliable for producing more infant bodies in any species of life.

It is evident as physical reality. It is not a fantasy or aspiration based on belief. One should understand how to best this reproductive loop, so that one may ride in it with the least inconvenience.

It is likely that if one performs criminal acts, Nature will take note, and issue punitive damages against the self. Hence, one should be socially accommodative, so that Nature may offer opportunities which comprise the least inconvenience. A righteous lifestyle is preferred. Being responsible and reliable is the way to achieve this.

One should carefully note how Nature suggests actions and punishes or positively rewards individuals for compliance. Some returns arrive shortly after the actions are committed, but many occur at some distant time, when it is difficult to trace the consequence to the original circumstance.

There are rules governing conduct in every society. In fact, even the animals have approved and disapproved behavior. Aside from this, anyone who is observant of this creation, and who realizes what happens in the loop of reproduction, may on his/her own, observe, catalog, and form an opinion about how to best the system of Nature's cyclic manifestations.

There are technicalities and exceptions, but overall, this system is standard in the way one acts, and how Nature immediately, or remotely responds. To best the system some basic notations should be made.

- socially approved behaviors usually yield appreciation

- skill which other humans admire, may causes one to become opulent

- kindness to someone positions one, to be a focus of kindness

- healthy eating reduces the risk of illness

These physical activities produce positive psychic energy. This lays a foundation for favorable physical and psychic interchanges in the future, both here and hereafter.

There will always be discomfort, illness, bad luck and whatever is unwanted. The aspiration is for the least misfortune in the life of an individual. What is required in terms of what a limited being can do, is for him/her to acquire the most positive life. The reference for this is Nature, not me, not you, not a human-designed list of approved and disapproved behavior. One must also consider that in the recycling of materials and events, Nature has vast swaths of time to design events. It does not have to present a return for a favorable or unfavorable event shortly within one lifetime. Nature may take decades, centuries or even millennium, for the manifestation of a repercussion. How are we to figure this?

State Immediately after Death

We are familiar with sober awareness, intoxication, hallucination, and the fading awareness before sleep. These conditions of consciousness occur on a daily basis with or without anyone taking actions to produce them. How similar is any of these states to the state of mind experienced immediately after death?

Sober awareness does not rely on the physical brain but it also occurs when there is operation of the brain, or when the brain is alive, but is not actively participating in the psychic events which the person indulges in.

There are states of sober awareness during dreams, even when the subtle body is temporarily displaced from the physical one. Then the psychic self, which is a subtle form, is free from dulling forces. It exhibits clear thinking and lucid awareness.

One who passes from the physical body, and experiences sober awareness, will do so on the astral side of existence and with no cognitive support from the physical brain. Just as during a dream, one may be fully aware or even more aware than when one experienced as a physical body, so after death, one may find the self to be sober and lucid. One may have some idea that one's physical format died. Or one may have no clue of it, and may show absolutely no concern for it.

Intoxication is an adjustment in awareness where the standard view which is output by a bio-physiological body is adjusted. This is done by ingestion of aerosol, or liquid, or solid chemicals, which cause temporary or permanent changes in cell structures such that the normal range of sensual interpretation is altered.

The readings received by the observing principle in the psyche are changed. This causes changes in behavior. It renders inappropriate responses because of the alterations in perception.

As this happens when the physical body is alive, it can happen in the subtle body alone when the physical system is dead. At death the psychic system is no longer anchored to the physical body. Without using the physical reference, it interprets whatever it encounters. This may trigger hallucination which may or may not be interpreted correctly.

Hallucination is a condition of altered perception. It happens when the physical body is alive. It occurs when the subtle body is no longer anchored existentially to a physical system. Hallucination is a switch to one or more dimensions while still having the reference to the physical world. If the observer can reduce the importance of the physical reference, he/she may interpret the new perception appropriately. Otherwise, there will be mishap due to not correctly interpreting the new perception.

Familiarity with other dimensions and their references is the correct way to perceive and interpret hallucination, but it is likely that the view will be lost because of not having accurate reference to the new dimension. This happens while the physical body is alive. It may happen at the time of death or just after. This will cause disarray, confusion, and disorientation. The observer will be traumatized until he/she is re-referenced to the physical plane or to a dimension in the astral which is parallel to the physical level, and which has a similar reality which is steady and timely.

While there is stability of perception when using the physical body, in contrast, the subtle one has instability of perception. This fact is part of the reason why a person becomes attached to physical life. When one views anything in a dimension, if that place does not remain stable to one's sense perception, one is likely to become spooked. One will crave to be physical, where the objects in view remain in their place in a static way for some time.

Everything in the physical world goes through alteration from moment to moment, but most perceptible objects do so in slow motion, so slow that nearly everything appears stationary. This apparent steadiness of the physical world makes the place attractive.

The **fading of awareness before sleep** is a vital study for understanding what will happen at the time of death. One may go through an entire lifetime, and not observe in detail, even one instance of a drowsy condition. This carelessness is to be regretted because some instances of the shift from wakefulness to sleep, which occur during the life of the body, will be repeated at its death. If one was prepared by the study of the shifts before death, it is likely that one will have a grasp on the sequence at death, except that the phase of waking as a physical body will be absent. When at last the physical system is no longer accessible, one will have to continue as a subtle body only.

Does one sleep on the psychic side of life? Will the waking phase just after sleep occur but without identity as the physical body, where one remains in the dream world, awakening there only, with no recourse to physical participation?

After death of the physical system, no amount of effort on either side of the existential divine can cause the physical system to be revived. There is a way out which is to become another embryo. One can however influence physical people by emitting from the mind, ideas which the physical people may absorb and perform. Besides that, there is no way to participate physically. Either one gets another embryo, or one possesses the willpower of others, and makes those persons act on one's behalf.

Those who did not make dream existence a study, and who felt that dreams were merely hallucinations, do themselves a disfavor. After death, what is left to experienced is what was already experienced in dream situations. The more one is familiar with the dream world, as to its operations and shifts, the more one will be capable of negotiating life hereafter.

It is fancy to think that the dream experiences will cease at the time of death, and that one will either be dead forever in every way, or one will be instantly transferred to a heavenly place where angelic beings will entertain one as a special guest. Whatever happened in the dream situations before death, will occur hereafter. Let there be no doubt of this.

No matter what is available after death, the key issue is to be in a position to transit to an agreeable location or to be transported there through some agency other than the self. One should keep the subtle body in the **most sublime condition**, so that it corresponds to the higher subtle zone when it is no longer capable of enlivening the physical form.

Psychological exhaustion at the time of death is undesirable because it will make the subtle body have a vibration which corresponds to a low state on the astral planes. This will make the subtle body gravitate to an unpleasant experience with or without association with other astral beings.

Some humans become exhausted physically when the body fails in the elderly years. This physical condition affects the subtle body causing it to become depleted of psychic vitality. If death happens under that condition, the subtle body will feel incapacitated. The likelihood will be that the person discovers himself/herself to be bed-ridden, unable to stand even, mentally exhausted, saturated with ill-health and emotionally drained.

This person will be in an astral plane, where the atmospheric energy will consist of a depressing influence, which causes torpor, sleep, or total disorientation. By all means everyone who is threatened by death, should maintain the subtle body in a sublime condition. This makes it more likely that one will be in an agreeable and delightful situation hereafter.

Psyche fatigue during the life of the physical body may occur infrequently as a matter of course. If, however it is regular, one should change this by studying the cause of it, and developing a system to cease it. Otherwise, it is likely that the subtle body will have that habit, which in turn will cause the condition to assert itself, after one is bared from using the physical world, and is left with only the astral access.

Even if one is deprived of use of the body during its elderly years, still at that time one should be vibrant, at least in the astral form. There will be a time when the physical system exhibits a terminal condition which is unfavorable. Even then one should maintain the subtle body as best as one could, with the knowledge that the physical system will be destroyed, and one will live only on the psychic side.

A sickly physical body is indicative of a similar situation on the psychic level. One should do anything possible to keep the subtle body in order. The condition of the physical one should not transfer to the psychic side. If it does, one should note it, and do what is necessary to bring the psychic form to the healthiest condition.

Resuming history is an obsession of the subtle body. It does not matter what someone may aspire for or believe, the situation is, that as soon as it realizes, that it is deprived of physical participation, the subtle body involuntarily seeks an embryo.

There is more than one way for Nature to entice one to come back into her loop system of rebirth. It does not have to be sex attraction. It can be for some other fulfilment.

After being departed, sex attraction could cause one to acquire an embryo. But so will be attraction to popularity. Even the desire to eat may cause craving for rebirth. Nature has many attractors which may bring someone to desire physical life. Resuming history is an obsession of the subtle body which seeks to be physical again.

The tendency to be physical is so innate, that even deceased teachers who ridiculed, belittled, and expressed abhorrence for physical existence, become occupied with getting an embryo or with controlling their physical interests from the hereafter.

Under the premise that they have a spiritual mission, they continue the focus on physicalness where they influence their surviving followers to convert others, produce literature of their sayings, build temples, and establish expensive memorials on their behalf.

The **tendency to be physical** is engrained in the psyche, so much so that the realization that the physical existence is traumatic, and worrisome, only suppresses and mutes the tendency. It does not eradicate it. The most one can do to the subtle body is to suspend the influence of this tendency.

Unless one did so before the death of the physical body one will continue to pursue physical interest by exerting psychic pressure on relatives, friends and even to people whom one disliked.

One will indulge in thought hopping, which is natural for the subtle form. It will think, project, wait for replies, then think, project and then wait for replies continuously. A deceased person will inspire physical people to act on his/her desires. Most humans cannot sort an idea in the mind as to if it is their creation or a projection from a deceased or living person.

After being deprived of the physical body, after having no power to awaken as that form, one may still desire to be the body to continue participation in history.

The desires one had when the physical body lived, do not disappear when that body is deceased. Instead, those desire are maintained in duplicate in the subtle body as instincts for actions, and as a need to operate the willpower to cause physical actions.

Some socially powerful people who were politicians, or spiritual leaders, do, when they are deceased, focus even more strongly into the physical world, and become more aggressive about controlling what happens on the physical level. They influence people on the physical side who belief in their ideas. The followers fulfill the desires of these charismatic persons.

Even ordinary people whose influences extend no further than their families, pressure relatives to continue their desires and service the responsibilities which were left behind in the physical world.

Some deceased persons who had strong social interest and who planned physical constructions like homes, offices, or state mansions, may, after being deprived of the physical body, go to a heavenly world. These people remain there only for a short time, for moments in some cases, for hours or days in others.

The strength of their interest in doing physical things being stronger than their desires for heaven, causes them to be pulled to an astral level which is adjacent to the physical world. From that psychic location, they exert influences and continue to motivate physical people to manifest their ideas.

Some are pulled from a heavenly world by the desires of relatives and followers, who lament their physical absence and send call-energies, which serve to attract them to becoming embryos. These persons fit into reproduction energy pockets where they are given the opportunity to be a physical body again. Thus, continuing the instinct for rebirth in Nature's reproduction loop, they are recycled in the physical world, where they fill slots for leadership when opportunities arise.

Some are frustrated in the desire to get a suitable embryo as the son or daughter of a famous or wealthy person. These come out in impoverished, disenfranchised, or dysfunctional families. Nevertheless, they cut their way through life. They seize opportunities to set themselves as famous, wealthy or powerful persons.

It is rare but it does occur, that someone is aware of his/her dying body, then suddenly that person becomes **aware of a heavenly world**. It can happen as well that someone dreamt of being in a heaven, during which time the physical body died, but that person had no idea of the loss.

Soon after however, this person may operate the reflex of awakening physically, but finds that even though the will for this is executed, there is no corresponding action as before. The physical self is not resumed. The person remains in limbo in a psychic dimension, with no understanding of why he/she cannot be aroused as usual.

This results in confusion, frustration, and a sense of urgency. There is a rush to call someone. There is expectation that something will be done, and the person will awaken as the physical body to continue participation in history. This will occur for a time, for a day, or a week, or months even.

Then the conclusion will be that,

"I am dead. My stake in physical history was uprooted. What should I do?"

Noticing that the world continues as if one is irrelevant, there will be regret and consternation. A sense of alarm will be felt. This concerns informing relatives, friends, and others, that one cannot perform duties, and that people who continue in the world, should assume those responsibilities to be sure that they are completed.

The ideas about being in a heavenly place with not arise, or they will surface with little or no relevance, as the focus in the mind will be to complete duties, and to impel others who were under one's influence. This person will continue in the astral world as a psychic being, but with little interest in a heaven, and with sharp focus on becoming a physical body again, but with the status attained before.

By chance, one may meet someone who was related, and who was deceased long before or recently. That person may be happy to see one in one's deceased condition with no physical facility. That someone will begin a conversation to greet one to the astral world. However, one will be stunned at the normalcy of that person, who has no alarm about being barred from physical presence. One will desire to inform that person that it is urgent to return as a physical person, since one has this duty, and that duty, and one has this relationship, and that relationship. But those ideas will only be in one's mind because the other deceased person will have no tendency to be alarmed about not being a physical somebody. One will notice that and will be timid in response to that other deceased self.

It is irregular for any deceased person to get a body immediately after death. Usually there is a waiting period. This is due to complications arising, because the deceased person had untimely death, or because there is a queue of persons who qualify for rebirth from the same potential parents. The others were deceased long before the recently deceased one desired a body.

Persons who die untimely are those who died while using a young body. This may happen because of an accident, or because of the malicious intent of someone who fatally attacked the deceased one. There are many persons who are in the flow of time, and who are in the reproductive loop of Nature. Any of these may acquire a body. Sometimes there is a justle, where one ancestor pushes another out of the queue, or forces someone who qualifies to go to the end of the line of embryo applicants.

There was a case which I witnessed, where some ancestors who were females, were in an orderly lineup for taking rebirth from one of their descendants. Then at that astral place, someone, a male arrived. Instead of being agreeable with the ladies, he stood at the head of the line of applicants. He acted as if he was senior to either of them. As it turned out, this bully got the first embryo. The others were not happy about it but they could do nothing to prevent him.

In this physical world, someone may take advantage of another person. It happens not just here but hereafter. One may assume that once this earthly life is over, one will go to a heavenly place, where God will set things in order, so that no criminal intent is present. Unfortunately, this is not always true.

After being deprived of the physical form, one may somehow immediately merge into the body of one of the would-be parents. This rebirth urgency with no stay in the astral domains is a rare occurrence.

If one gets a body immediately after dying, or if one must wait for weeks, months, or years, one will use the psyche of the parent in whose body one resides, either as a disembodied force, as a sperm particle or as a developing fetus. One will eat when that prospective parent eats. One will act when that person acts. One will astral-project when that person sleeps. These activities may, however, have no coherence.

As a sperm particle in the testes of the father. one lacks objectivity. That departed person will be conscious, but will have no identification as an individual self. Instead, he/she will be as if one were a demanding, desirable, sexually aggressive, force.

Fading away from the Hereafter Condition

After being in the astral existence for a short period or an extended time, a departed entity becomes part of the ancestral energy which forms the loop of attractive reproductive and sexual force. This happens by a mystic attitude of Nature. It is involuntary and automatic. It does not rely on the agreement with the departed person. He/She is like a straw which floats in a river. Sometimes it travels rapidly, sometimes slowly, sometimes it is motionless. In any case it cannot overpower the river but must move as ushered by it.

Eventually, a departed soul feels as if his/her consciousness fades. Its acuteness is suspended but it feels attracted to one, two or more persons who may become its parents or guardians. For the would-be parents, this attraction is felt as sexual invitation.

They interpret this energy as romantic feelings, as desirability, as permissive approval, as a nurturing energy to be expressed and contained. More and more the departed soul feels that he/she relinquishes his/her individuality and becomes part of the reproductive energy of one of the parents, either that of the father or mother.

At this point, the departed soul feels itself to be a powerful urge which is ready to spring into action, to bring the mother and father together for sexual intercourse. Feeling itself to be that power, its only knowledge about itself, is that it is a force for life, which should keep the energies of the parents together.

Before sexual intercourse of the said parents, the entity is transferred to the father's testes, where it feels the impulse to move into the mother's form. With the help of the sexual arousal energy, the entity exhibits a haste impulse, which it functions as, so that as sperm as its body, it propels itself through the mother's passage. It has an attraction power which causes it to sense the ovum.

If the sperm meet a viable ovum, it punctures into it and the formation of an embryo begins. The mind of the entity is completely absorbed in this process, so much so that it has no idea of anything else, not even of what took place a moment ago. The development of the embryo is involuntary. The self involved is subjective to the process and has no observational posture.

They Live On

The run of the clock is time. Human plans work with that. With the rising and setting of the sun, the creatures move to fulfill desires. To be in an advantageous position one has to coordinate with the time factor, such that even if one is vicious, one may be successful, provided that time facilitates.

Both the dead and the living live on, but due to loss of focus through the physical body, the dead have increased psychic perception. The living are handicapped psychically because their physical forms consume much energy from their subtle bodies.

Which is better; to have increased psychic perception, or to be a physical body which can exploit physical objects? It depends on one's assessment for physical experiences. Which is preferred? Enjoyment through a physical body, or enjoyment only through psychic means?

Due to physical focus, those who are deceased are considered to have lost access to the prime pleasures, but they are supposed to be in a heaven, where psychic sensual life is all the rage, and is so satisfying, that the people who live there pity human experience. As a human being rates a monkey, so the angelic people assess the human experience.

Some angelic women cry when they hear of the chores of a human female. Their bodies are bruised just hearing of the services performed by human women. They cannot imagine such a harsh life.

On the physical side the survivors live on. To their view, the situation of the deceased is pathetic. This is because the body which the deceased person was deprived of, is in a pathetic condition which when viewed, evokes sympathy and regret. But on another plane of existence, on the dream plane of life, the deceased, like the survivors, live on. It is just that the surviving physical people insists on physical focus. They, if they consider it even, consider the dream existence to be shifty and uncertain. Hence their regret for the deceased ones.

"Poor fellow/madam. He/She is dead. His good deeds were done. His antisocial behavior was condemned. He lost significance. His opportunity for life is done."

Common Features of the Living and the Dead

The living and the dead have things in common. Among these are.

- thinking construction
- feelings
- mobility
- influence
- sense of self

Those who live, think. Those who are dead, think as well. The difference, if there is one, is that the living has physical obstructions to regulate their thinking. Whatever a man thinks he can freely conjecture but to make his thoughts practical in the physical world, he must think in a way which physical reality accommodates.

In the astral existence, however, there is no physical restrictions and confirmations as we experience on the physical side. A departed self has relatively unrestrained thinking patterns which may infiltrate the mind of any living person. The thinking energy of a deceased person is more amplified than that of a living person. One must remember that both the living, and the dead, live, except that the word, living, is conventionally used to mean physical people as contrasted to dead people who have psychic existence only.

Because the convention is to under-rate psychic existence, we use the word *living* to indicated persons who are represented on the physical side. Others are regarded *as dead* people.

Dead people have a big impact on the living persons because those who are dead experience increased psychic transmission. When a deceased person thinks to someone who lives, the living person is affected by the thinking force.

Without knowing it or without admitting it, a living person is affected by the thinking and feeling of dead people. The evidence of this is as old as humanity. It was known to ancient humans who left stories about ghosts.

A ghost is a deceased person, whose presence is detected by a living someone. That ghost may be unseen to that living self. Some living people see ghosts. This may happen because the psychic eyes of the physical person shifted from physical focus and assumed focus through subtle eyes. There are cases of psychic touch of a dead person to a living one, where the ghost is felt but not seen by the living person.

A living person may hear the speech of a dead person, and not see, nor feel that person. Someone may experience sexual contact with a dead person. That is more than mere feelings. It may have visual and audio perception simultaneously functioning.

For the dead, the common influence for communicating with living people is **thinking construction**. A deceased person will think into the head of a living person. Then, that living person may involuntarily issue a response idea. Then again, the deceased one will think, followed by a mental response from the living person. This may transpire for a time until one or the other ceases the thought conversation.

The feature of this is that the deceased person will sort the thoughts, and know that the replies were given from the mind of the living person, but the living someone may not identify that the thoughts originated from the deceased someone. This happens because living people have a convention where they feel that dead people are inactive. These dead persons are physically dead only. They are psychically alive but physical people understate the astral reality. Still, that does not protect a living person from being influenced by a dead someone.

Feelings are experienced by the living and the dead, but the living experience a smaller range of feelings. This is due to the fact that the living has a physical body which attenuates the psychic range of feelings which the subtle body has.

Physical people, however, are proud of the fact that the physical body channels and utilizes the psychic power of the subtle form. Since dead people have no physical form to experience the attenuated feelings, living people pity the dead. This is because the evidence for life in the physical world is a physical form which is mobile, which is powered by subtle and physical energy.

When a deceased person feels, those feelings are restricted to the subtle body. There are no physical feelings experienced unless the deceased one becomes an embryo or unless the deceased one's subtle body is interspaced into the body of a living person. However, being restricted to the subtle body does not mean having less feelings. In fact, it means having more feelings, having a wider range of sensing. It means having to rely on the body of a living person to detect physical things.

Sometimes, a deceased person will pass through the psychic body of a living person. This may give the living one a shudder. That may produce ecstasy or even abject fear. But the living person who is subjected to that, may have no idea that a dead person crossed through, or interspaced through, the subtle body, the psychic self.

Mobility is experienced by the living and the dead, but the dead have more transits. They move from psychic place to psychic place instantly. In a jiffy, a ghost may transit from one place to another location which is thousands of physical miles away. That is astral projection. While physical people rely on transportation of their bodies and goods by physical means, a deceased person can move psychic stuff merely by willpower.

For the dead, anything means any psychic item, even if such an item has a physical counterpart. However, when the psychic part of something physical is moved, the physical item is not relocated. It remains in its physical position. It is different however for physical people. They can move physical items but they must exert physical power to do so. Hence physical mobility of either a physical body, or some other thing, requires exertion beyond mere thinking commands or willpower.

Physical people do **influence** dead persons, but the influence from dead people to physical ones is more frequent and effective. Stated simply, dead persons prevail over the living. The dead govern the living. This is due to greater psychic powers of the dead ones. Their full psychic power is available as compared to the attenuated, or reduced, psychic expression of the living. Physical people have bodies which consume much energy from their psychic forms.

The living and the dead have a **sense of existence,** except when that existential detector is suspended. In both cases, there is uncertainty. This is due to the involuntary cosmic switching which is beyond the control of a limited self. It is so uncertain that a self cannot absolutely control how long an unconscious state will persist. He/She cannot say for sure if there will be memory, or if there will be only a portion of memory when objective awareness is suspended.

Assuming that the sense of existence is permanent but with a factor of the absolute controlling it, and giving only parttime control to the limited self, when that sense is activated, the self may or may not have portions of memory with it. That means that the bare self is memory-incapable.

It has memory access as it is permitted. It never has access to every sector of memory. It may have no memory. It may have some memory at any given time.

Currently, the evidence for this is present with the self. It has no or some fragmented recall of any existence which was previous to the current life. Its sense of existence must be supplemented with memory, or it is experienced with no memory, as mere beaming awareness, with a short or long range of detection.

When deceased, the person may have memory of his last physical history. Or he may have no recall of it. He could discover himself/herself as mere awareness, with no reference to when he used the body which recently died.

Common Differences between the Living and the Dead

- psychic power increase for the dead someone
- physical access remains for the survivors

There is an automatic **increase in psychic power for the deceased**. This happens as soon as the astral body is no longer interspaced operatively in the physical form. As soon as the physical body is not communicative with the subtle one, the power which surged through the physical system, which supported its nervous system, is conserved, making the subtle body more psychically sensitive.

The living survivors remain with limited psychic ability, such that they do not understand that for the dead person, there is an increase in psychic detection and expression.

Physical access to participate in history, is ruptured for a deceased person, such that direct actions using a physical body is no longer a reality. The survivors continue with physical access.

The dead live as psychic units only. The living live as physical factors with limited psychic reach. Living people underrate the psychic side of existence. They do not appreciate the increase in psychic power for those who died. This causes them to be influenced by the dead without knowing that they are manipulated by the deceased.

Habitats Hereafter

There are many habitats hereafter. These are too numerous to mention except by designating broad categories. The astral world is such that there is an infinite number of dimensions. There are also places which are beyond the astral domains. It is not definitive that a criminal will go to hell hereafter, or that a pious person will definitely see heaven as soon as he/she is deprived of physical access.

One life of an individual for say seventy or eighty years may or may not determine where that person will go immediately after his/her body dies. The complexity of time, the principle of uncertainty, means that the future may not happen as a response to the history of an individual's last life. For that matter the next set of events may have no relationship to the most recent life. Some habitats hereafter are listed.

- adjacent astral realms (includes hazy psychic zones)

- subterranean realms

- paradise

- translation dimensions

- suspension existence spaces

- hell realms

- astral capture zones

- habit holding realms

- immorality hells

- morality heavens

It is likely that most humans will find themselves to be alive hereafter in an astral place which is **adjacent to this physical existence**. Such a place may be a space only or it may have landscape and environment which is similar to this earthly domain. It will not have solid matter as we experience on earth but the state of mental perception may be such that it feels virtually as if it is dense matter.

During the life on earth as a physical body, one will have a few or even many dream experiences which occur in adjacent astral places. These occurrences will be repeated fulltime after one is denied access to be a physical person. When one is dead, where will one awaken? Who will one be?

In the dream experiences, these questions are answered during the life as a physical person. One discovers oneself in a psychic environment which is similar to or different from the physical environment. One should prepare the self to live in such an astral place. That realm is likely to be the habitat hereafter.

During the life of the physical body, when it sleeps, one may on occasion find oneself to be in a zone of energy where one is without definite form, with no limbs or senses, except for knowing that one exists. But one may be aware of no other presence except oneself and only as a self which is conscious, which is aware, and only aware with a limited range of feelings. One may be in such a dimension after death.

Would that be a permanent condition, where one would discover the self to be a sector of awareness and nothing else, and with no other self?

In dreams, one remains in that location for a short period, or for the most, for some hours but not for an indefinite time. If one discovered oneself to be that place soon after one is deprived identity with the physical body, how long would one be as that conscious self with no body?

Persons who use narcotic drugs, and some who are psychotic, may discover themselves to be part of a world which is **subterranean to the earth**'s vibrational frequency. These are reverse places which exist in radioactive time warps where the bodies used comprise radioactive frequencies.

In such places it may be blissful or hellish according to the activity in that locale. A person who is translated to such a place, just after being deprived of the physical body, will have no access to memory of the life on earth, except for recalling events which contributed to that someone's transfer.

For instance, someone who was addicted to a narcotic drug, or psychoactive substance, may remember persons who indulged just as well. If the acquaintances are already deceased, he/she may see those persons in that place. One is not free to do as one pleases in such a place. One comes under the total influence of the narcotic plant or substance which uses energy in one's psyche to satisfy its lifeForce needs.

Someone who is transferred to such a place will try to wonder about how long he/she would remain in that place but as soon as this thinking begins, it will cease, as there are energies in those places, which effectively suppress any thinking which may cause objectivity and resistance to the narcotic influence. After a time however, someone does escape from those places but not by the desire not to be there, only by the exhausting of the energy in the person's psyche, which had the need to use the substance.

Someone could be **transferred to a paradise**. This could happen on the basis of belief in heavenly places, on a pious force based on socially acceptable acts, or on the basis of a deity's action to relocate someone whom the deity favors. This transfer could be permanent or temporary.

After translating to that place, the deceased person may or may not recall the earthly life. He/She may even forget the incidence of death and not know that it happened.

Reaching a heavenly domain just after dying usually includes getting there with loss of memory of the earthly life. There is a risk that such recall could cause the subtle body to degrade to a lower plane, where the heavenly vision or contact would fade. The deceased person will find himself/herself moving away from a realm of light into places of astral fog or darkness.

Most humans who believe in a heaven hereafter, feel that after death, the memory of what happened during the life of the body, will be intact. However even though the memory is stored in Nature, usually, it is not available for perusing. When the subtle body is upgraded to be compatible to a heavenly place, it loses touch with the earthly memories. The self has no way of knowing who it related to while it was on earth. For that matter, the entire earth life may be of no significance. If attempts are made to recall it, those will not be serviced into the mind.

Either at the time of death or some moments or days after, a deceased person could awaken in a psychic dimension to which he/she was **translated**. This is different to being transferred. In a transfer there is some feeling of being shifted or changed, where the deceased one may be surprised to know, that its being made a radical change instantaneously, or in a measured time.

This is contrasted to a translation, where there is no idea of a shift. The change occurs but there is no understanding of how it happened. There is not even a slight sense of the time of the event. Former states are not recalled. There is no instinct to research it. One is like a new born infant with no recall of a previous life, and only with the understanding that one exists, or began to exist, that one is an initial causeless point of existence.

In some translations however, the deceased finds himself/herself with others in an environment which is accepted as the ongoing reality, and which is enjoyed because the body assumed, finds the place to be pleasant or blissful.

At the time of death, a deceased person may be **suspended**. This is when the subtle body enters a trance in which the entity itself becomes unknown to itself. It loses all reference even the idea of itself.

A suspension may occur because of psychological disfigurement of either the dying physical body or the deformed psychic one. A physical body may cause ill-health to the subtle one, but such an injury is temporary for the subtle form, even though it may be fatal to the physical one.

When there is a suspension, the person loses all perception. Even the sense of being, that of existing somewhere somehow, disappears. For all practical purposes, both physical and psychic, the person is no more. There is no register of its features at any place anywhere.

A supernatural being may suspend the being of another person who is under the existential supporting energies of the god. For as long as the god can assert the suppression of the limited self, the person will be cancelled.

At the time of death, someone may be transferred to a place where a **blank state** is ongoing. There is no idea of the self. It is as if there is, was, and will not be a self. The person has no objective nor subjective understanding of itself. It exists but it has no self-awareness. It can be located by someone from a higher dimension but it cannot know its location. Unto itself, it has no assessment of what it is, where it is, or what it would be, if it was released from that blank state.

Persons who are in that blankness, usually emerge from it, but with no understanding that they were suspended by a supernatural person or force. This released soul would awaken somewhere, somehow, but with the feeling that it existed before, even though it has no idea of how it endured a length of time with no comprehension of itself, or of anything else.

The **transfer to hell realms** is possible where some deceased person may go there just prior to death of the physical body, or at the moment when the physical system becomes unresponsive, or after when the deceased person was for a time in an astral realm which is adjacent to physical existence.

The length of stay in such a place varies from moments, to hours, to weeks and even to months or years. It depends on the restraining force which holds the person in that ghastly place. This is related to the criminal acts which were perpetrated by the deceased one during the last past life, or even from lives prior.

Someone may go to a hellish place because of having relationship with someone who is due for that life or is already living in that place. Mere association with a physical or psychic criminal could cause someone, even a saintly person, to see hell hereafter.

In this type of existence there is always thought of escape, except that as soon as such a thought arises, the pains and anguish felt increases considerable. It induces the person to cease considering the escape, and to agree to remain in the situation of being punished. It seems that acceptance of the punishment is preferred when compared to escaping to some other place.

The **astral capture zones** are places which are staked out by one group of departed human beings who were either in a political alliance or a religious affiliation. They capture some of their enemies when those persons become deceased.

The arrested ones are confined, just as in war, one group capture soldiers of their enemy, and imprison such opponents in camps. If a departed soul is captured in this way, it is near impossible for him/her to escape. Such detention may last for months or years. Eventually the capture zone deteriorates. The psychic fences and barricades fade way.

In this world, prisons and detention centers are physical realities for those who break laws and violate social norms. On the astral side hereafter there are similar situations which are hard to avoid if one becomes involved with political, religious, and national conflict.

A deceased person may find himself/herself in a **habit holding realm**. This may happen because of being addicted to a certain food, drug, or behavior. For instance, many humans naturally become sex addicts, having sexual intercourse or masturbation many times per day or week. This may continue on the psychic side of life after death.

These places may be regulated by a supernatural being, or it have no supervising agency. In this physical place, we are aware of persons who have positive or negative habits and whose lifestyle is formatted on the basis of a habit. Some others live in places where a habit is best serviced.

In a habit holding realm hereafter, a deceased someone will be there for a time, for weeks, months or years. Eventually, because of the loss of its sustaining force or motive, the habit wears away. The person experiences being shifted from the confinement.

The desire for taking an embryo will arise. The person will gravitate to a father and mother. In time, it will know itself as someone's infant.

There are **limited immorality hells** which a deceased person may enter after death. These are astral places created by groups of departed people to enforce their religious or social rule which were violated by the followers and by warned potential converts.

This happens because groups of humans either as a clan, nation, or religious assembly, exercise vast power in a society of humans, whereby their authority extends even to the astral world. In such places, their converts who violated proposed moral rules, and others who rejected conversion, are captured and confined hereafter in psychic places.

The controllers of such psychic countries hold courts where the offenders are judged and sentenced according to the statement made in their scriptural text. Such literature may be oral only, or they may be written in books in the physical and astral places where their influence prevails.

Someone who is deceased, and who complied with a religious or social stipulation of a political or social group, may after death be transferred to a **morality heaven**. In such a place, that follower will be rewarded in the way described in the scripture of the sect. It may be that the experience is not exactly what was promised in the doctrine, but it may be so fantastic as compared to the experience of life on earth, that the follower feels no compulsion to criticize it.

This experience of a heaven will run for a time, then the believer will find that he/she is attracted to a physical couple who are to copulate. This energy will operate as an irresistible force, whereby the deceased one will become an embryo. Thus, will end the sojourn in that morality heaven but with no conscious memory of spending time in the paradisical place.

Exceptional Attainment Hereafter

It happens but it is rare that someone becomes an embryo immediately after being deprived of a physical body. Usually there is a queue of ancestors who are due to take bodies one after the other, as pregnancies can happen. Thus, someone who is recently departed is not likely to acquire an embryo, hours, days or even weeks after losing the access to physical history.

However, some persons somehow get an opportunity to become the romantic feelings of two persons who are sexually involved. It is a fact however that there may be forced sexual intercourse with a male forcing himself on a female and strangely with a female overpowering a male, and causing his sexual fluid to enter her uterus. Behind these physical events is the person on the astral side whose influence prevails. Still, that deceased person becomes present as an influence only, and not as a person. The person presentation is suspended. The influence representation manifests as replacement for the person.

Astral Place of Advanced Yogi

For yogis, apart from aspirations for the highest attainment which they are aware of, it is best to endeavor for residence at the place of an advanced ascetic who has an astral domain, where the practice of yoga can continue in earnest. Either one remains in an astral place hereafter, or one again becomes an embryo, or one attains the desired astral or supernatural place as soon as the physical system dies, and one is no longer attentive to a physical body.

Taking an embryo after using a physical form is the least option for a deceased yogi. Such a course is risky. There is no guarantee that one will attain any higher state than the one achieved in the last body. In fact, there is probable cause for becoming lowered and having less practice proficiency.

The concept of making advancement when one takes a human body, is a fantasy. It is believed by many ascetics on the basis of guarantees given by their teachers and literature. Some say that they have seven, or some other account of births, after which they will attain liberation and no longer have to function as physical bodies. How this is guaranteed only heaven knows.

Is it guaranteed by a superhuman teacher who has a physical body? Is it assured by the statement of an advanced yogi who give a promise long ago, even centuries before? Is it a fact that nature will support such a statement by a superior ascetic?

Any such guarantee would have to be serviced by Nature, otherwise it will prove to be invalid. That would be due to pressing circumstances which surround the new body in its infantile, juvenile, adult, and elderly years. A limited self, a yogi even, does not have absolute control, and is not all-pervasive. Hence it is likely that there will be upsets in a new life. These may frustrate the renewed efforts of the yogi.

If on the other hand, the yogi goes to the astral residence of a great guru, he/she will be surrounded by energies which support the completion of the practice. When this is consolidated, one can expect success where the yogi will be elevated to a higher plane and will not suffer a relapse.

Even there however, at the astral place of a great yogi, one may slip and take another body haphazardly. This is because Nature's reproduction energy abounds in some astral dimensions. If a yogi is exposed to it, it is likely that he will be drawn into a loop of reproductive influence. It will be mandatory for him to take rebirth. He will do so with the risks which that entails.

What to do at the astral place of an advanced ascetic, hereafter?

At the astral place of an advanced ascetic there is danger that a student will lose interest in practice. This happens because even if that ascetic avoids others who are not at the guru's place, still someone who is there may carry a tiny bit of reproduction energy, just enough to cause the yogi to be attracted to an embryo.

The attraction may be to a person who is embodied, or disembodied, but its looping energy will pull the yogi into an association, which will cause his subtle body to developed sexual interest, which will be so powerful that he will lose track of yoga practice, and will be drawn into association with those who are to be his/her parents.

To avoid this, a yogi at the astral place of his guru, should keep his attention confined to the interest of the spiritual disciplines which are required for his/her elevation. Visitors from the astral planes and others who have bodies, and who practice in the physical world, should be avoided by that yogi. He/She should know that the danger is ever present and real. If there is attraction it may overpower the yogi. He/She will be controlled by it. The result will be to become an embryo. It may take years or lives to again resume a strong practice.

Advanced yogis establish astral places where one can take refuge but there is no guarantee that such a place will exist for any indefinite period of time. One may hear that such and such a guru has a place, which he will be present at, for a hundred or a thousand years or more. However, such statements are not to be considered as absolute. At any moment, a guru may abandon such a place. Or he may appoint someone to maintain it on his behalf. The guru may disappear. Hence so long as he is resident, one should take it seriously. If he departs, one should find another astral guru and continue the required practice.

Males or females who are at a guru's astral place, should be particular to be sexually neutral. If that is not possible, the student should know that it is likely that he or she will take rebirth. That is due to innate attraction to the reproductive energy of Nature, which presents itself as sexual pleasure.

Sometimes, senior students who managed to quell the reproductive energy, maintain or are responsive to reproduction energy and yet they resist the force for birth. These are cases where the person leaves the residence of the guru for short periods. They enter other astral zones and complete sexual relationships there. Then they return to the place of the guru and persist in the austerities of meditation which they are required to complete.

However, those are exceptions. Others who do this, leave the guru's place, and do not return. In fact, they are drawn into the reproductive loop and appear in the physical world as the child of this or that parent.

Failure to Remain at a Guru's Astral Place

A person who fails to remain at a guru's astral place, will not regret it. This is because the memory of the event will be unavailable to him/her. Instead, there will be an instinctual attraction to yoga practice in the new life. The rebirth situation will be such, that any memory about practice in the last body, will be unavailable in the new body. The ascetic will feel as a new person who just happened to be a child in the physical world, a child for the first time.

The way, the birth situation is rigged, is that Nature causes mandatory obligations to be incurred in the new life. Hence the ascetic begins with an obligation to the parents, and other social units, who assist in child care of the ascetic's immature body. None of this is free. None of this is an expense-less birth right. However, the ascetic may be unaware of the cost. He may take the situation for granted. This is all to his peril.

Sometimes an ascetic is told that because he is a yogi, he does not have to service social obligations from the new or previous lives. However, that is not a fact. Nature will be sure to insist on reimbursement. It does not care who the person is, as to his stature as a divine being, an advanced one, a God, or a dog.

An ascetic is tagged for more than just his obligations which are due to favors rendered to his upbringing. He may be tagged for the obligations of others, like those of his father, mother, grandparents, or teachers. It is in his/her interest to service these efficiently. He should do so in a way which does not generate more liabilities.

Due to irregular political or social events, an ascetic who takes a birth after staying at a guru's place in the astral existence, may be affected by social upheavals, where due to social chaos, he cannot practice, and must be involved in worldly affairs, some which involve warfare or immoral behavior. Such are the risks in rebirth.

At his place in the astral world, Yogeshwarananda discussed his view of the routes usually taken by departed souls. He gave a summary for three ratings.

- normal route
- aspiring siddha yogi route
- achievement siddha yogi route

The **normal route** is traversed by persons who do no yoga. Their experience just prior to death of the physical body, is that of being a physical being with no certainty of being anything else. When the body is no longer responsive, this person feels itself as nothingness. Soon after or sometime after, it feels itself as an astral being, as a dreaming self. Thereafter there is a state of delay. Then after some time, there is the idea of beginning which appears physically as an embryo.

The **aspiring siddha yogi route** is experienced by those who did some yoga practice and who mastered phases of mental retraction and transcendence absorption. These yogis use the physical body to do some practice, but with the understanding that they are psychic beings, who must strive for exemption from inconvenient physical births. When the physical body is no longer functional, they enter a phase of nothingness. Then they awaken in the presence of a siddha yoga teacher. He instructs how they can get a selected opportunity as someone's child, in a destiny which will include more efforts to perfect the yoga disciplines.

The **achievement siddha yoga route** is traversed by perfected yogis, who even before passing from a physical body mastered the yoga process to such an extent that the physical body was no longer of consequence. These persons shifted identity focus to the subtle existence even before death.

After the physical body dies, these persons feel a shift to the astral existence, but they do so in an upgraded subtle body, which transits to the siddhaloka places, where assemblies of advanced yogis reside. This person has no interest in taking rebirth as someone's infant.

The difference between dream and death should be noted. Dream is followed by the usually awakened physical condition. With death one can no longer awakens as, or in, the physical body which one identified as socially.

After death, most departed entities experience food scarcity. This is relieved by possessing the body of a physical person to get psychic food energy.

From my research, I give these locations as objectives for a yogi:

- subterranean *Siddhaloka*
- physical body yoga zone
- *Swargaloka* piety exhaustion heavenly world
- *Siddhaloka* holding zone
- *Maharloka* rebirth resistance zone
- *Janaloka* social resistance zone
- *Tapaloka* total austerity zone
- *Brahmaloka* deity relation zone

These are the details:

After the physical body is no longer accessible, a yogi may go to a **subterranean place** where other ascetics practice yoga. This can be considered as a purgatory. From this place the yogi must take another physical body, but he may do so after being there for a short or long period of time. Then, on the basis of his past social contributions while he used a physical body, he will again be a woman's child. The situation of that subterranean place is such that the yogi is not a regular ghost. He continues to do practice. He associates with likeminded ascetics. The guarantee for him is that when he gets a new embryo, and can connect with a teacher in the physical world, he will resume the practice.

The **physical body yoga zone** is this physical existence which we currently endure. It is a valuable opportunity. From this vantage a yogi may achieve salvation so that he develops in the subtle body, a resistance to taking physical forms.

The *Swargaloka* **piety-exhaustion heavenly world** may be achieved by a yogi. It is not a recommended objective. A yogi may be required to go there if he had certain enjoying desires when he previously used a physical body and did positive social acts. This place is a danger because the subtle body as it is experienced there, does not permit one to have discrimination. This means that while one is there, one will not have the understanding or motivation about liberation. These will be in the psyche as they were before while one was on earth, but these would be suspended for the duration.

After using one's pious credits in the Swargaloka heavenly place, one will find oneself to be in the subterranean world with other people who are urged to come back into the physical world to participate in its history. From there, one will eventually find oneself to be transformed as an embryo.

The next higher location is the *Siddhaloka* **holding zone**. This place is desired. From here one may go higher without having to use a physical body to do austerities. At this place one can continue practice while in association with advanced yogis. The key factor about this place, is that a yogi can attain this location only if he developed resistance to physical rebirth. This is simple enough but it is a tall order, because it means that the yogi is resistant to gender differentiation, and the energy flows which are overpowering, when one is in the presence of someone to whom one is sexually attracted. This includes the attraction to affection which itself is a currency of sexual love.

In the Siddhaloka holding zone, a yogi may complete the austerities, which would cause the subtle body to be formatted with higher energy, and higher perception. There, a yogi can self-focus more efficiently. He does not have to deal with digestion, social involvement, and event interruptions. A yogi can develop more efficiency of control of the psyche while at this place.

The next level is the *Maharloka* **rebirth resistance zone**. If a yogi reaches this place, it means that his subtle body has no attraction to taking rebirth. He no longer has to be alert about the possibility of taking an embryo. At this place there are no thoughts, ideas, or motivations for physical history. The subtle body is such that it always looks away from earthly existence as a matter of course.

The next location is the *Janaloka* **social resistance zone**. This place is where the yogi is separated from others. This is where the concept of having a social family, or being part of a social family on earth, no longer occurs in the mind. The pull to be part of a social clan either as the head of the family or as co-head, or as a dependent in it, is not experienced at this place. Persons who reside at this place greet each other cordially, just as strangers who meet at a club, but who are not related, and who though cordial, have no desire to bond with each other as family members.

The next zone is *Tapaloka* **total austerity zone**. This place is the final place for purifying bad motivations and very subtle corruptions in the psyche. These subtle energies are hidden but they undermine a yogi's quest for liberation. Here one meets great yogins who assist in making the final advancement.

The last and highest of the zones which one may reach with the subtle body is the *Brahmaloka* **deity relationship zone**. This is the environment where the *Brahma,* the creatorGod, resides. At that place one comes to terms with the planetary creator. From this place, one may go even higher but not with the subtle body. That form does not manifest beyond this place.

Subtle Aspects which may cause Reincarnation

- touch sensation as softness, smoothness, or silkiness

- perceptual sensation as round, oval, or curvaceous objects

- taste satisfaction in nourishing and sweet foods

- sight perception of color

Touch sensation as softness, smoothness, or silkiness is hostile to the liberation of any yogi. In the astral existence a yogi may underrate the power of the touch sensation to cause a loop energy which may compel him/her to be attracted to future parents. The result of that event will be birth as a baby, with no control over the early stages of that life, and only with minimal effort being made in the adult years of that body, where there will be enticements to use the sense of touch for pleasure fulfillments. A yogi is not needed. Nevertheless, he/she will get the feelings of being essential to social events. Taking the touch sensations seriously, the yogi will wholeheartedly indulge. This is compared to an antelope which with satisfaction, quenches its thirst in a pond which is inhabited by alligators. The touch sensation funds socialization which is a hub for rebirth.

Perceptual sensation as round, oval, or curvaceous objects are billboards for reproduction. These signs hail the astral travelers, encouraging them to rest their weary feet and enjoy a much-desired meal, at the restaurant of sensations. In the astral existence, there is a feature which is alluring. It is when an event seems physical even though it is astral. This causes a reawakening of the desire for physical participation.

The need to be physical becomes so powerful that the yogi forgets his spiritual aspiration, He consents to be part of a psychophysical event which results in his/her assumption of an embryo. Thus, the loop of reproduction proves to be compelling.

Taste satisfaction in nourishing and sweet foods is carried in the subtle body during the life of the physical one and hereafter. It is so compelling that it is difficult to detach from it. This need is supported by two factors, namely, the nutrition need, and the flavor appetite. If either or both of these express strong urges in a disembodied person, he/she may be drawn into an eating event of physical people. The result of this is to enter the reproduction loop to become a child of those people. Thus, rebirth will spontaneously occur.

Sight perception of color is another basis for taking an embryo. The departed person may have no insight about the attraction to rebirth through sensual exposure. But that ignorance does not inhibit the urge for being physical. A self may be conveyed into the body of a perspective parent after seeing the voluptuous body of that person on the astral side of physical life. This attraction may abruptly end that departed soul's awareness of the psychic existence, causing that person to become feelings for sexual indulgence, in the body of the physical person. This urge if fruitful will result in an embryo, with the disembodied person only feeling as if it is the reproductive fluids of the two parents.

Hereafter with Little Change

For most people, death will be the same as before. Even people who rely on religious doctrine to control the situation hereafter, they too may discover to their dismay, that death is a continuation of what happened in the subtle existence while the physical body lived. The subtle body will, more than likely, repeat its lifestyle, not adapting to the religious expectation of the deceased person.

The familiarity one had with physical persons, places, and things will be there in the subtle form after there is no responsive physical body for the person concerned. This means that the deceased soul will pursue a thinking relationship with persons who were important during the life of the physical body. These include relatives, friends, business associates, enemies, and even outright criminal elements. The subtle body will continue its behavior unabated.

A radical change is hardly likely. It can happen that a law abiding and socially acceptable person, may suddenly and unexpected find himself/herself in a heavenly world hereafter. That could be with faint memories of the life the person lived on this earth. Or it may be with no memory of that situation. It is a question of how long would that person remain in that heavenly realm.

A criminal and socially unacceptable person may find himself/herself to be in a hellish situation where he/she is pursued by others, just as if he/she was an animal which was violent to humans, and was to be killed. Some criminals find themselves under supervision, by people who restrain the subtle body, and inflict grievous harm to it.

Some criminals may have no memory of their hostile acts. They will say, *"Why am I here? Who are you? What is my offense? How can I flee this suffering."*

Hope for a Heavenly Situation Hereafter

Someone who is deceased may, on the basis of religious belief, long for a heavenly situation just after the physical body is no longer accessible, and the person fails repeatedly to awaken with the privileges, which were due to his/her physical body. Some of these features were intangible, as for instance, respect which is given to elderly persons.

When an elderly individual finds that he/she can no longer be present physically to collect those tokens of appreciation, the deceased one may lament that death occurred. With no one offering honor, there may be a gap in the psyche of the deceased person. Prior to death, that offering though subtle, was felt in the emotions as a positive contribution to the elderly one.

Feeling despondent, that deceased elderly someone will think about his/her religious beliefs. He/She may feel that the likelihood of getting a reward of heaven may yet occur, if only there was patience, where the deity of the faith would have time to act, to bring this disappointment to an end. That idea will give some relief. The mind will again rehash about losing the important social position as a family member, and as someone who was knowledgeable, and was consulted.

A haze will appear in the mind of this person. With it, will be the recurring idea that the deity should facilitate transportation to the heavenly place.

Realism after Death

A deceased person's realistic hope is to expect the same psychic prohibitions which he/she endured during the recent life. Even though there must be more dimensions and conditions of existence than one could experience during physical life, still, to be practical in the world hereafter, one should be of the opinion that there certainly will be perception and communication, just as there was when the last physical body lived. These references were acquired in dreams. For those who were supersensitive, some psychic events were acquired even while fully conscious as the last physical body. There should be an open attitude, and a readiness to experience new domains, but one should not exert expectations which are not supported by previous experiences, and which are beliefs, which one did not confirm as factual reality.

Rapid Thought Switching

Some deceased person may find that due to anxiety over loss of social benefits on the physical side of life, he/she lives in a state of rapid thought switching. This will terrorize the mind of anyone on the physical side to whom such thoughts are projected or intended. The negativity of this is that the deceased person, and those on the physical side who are targeted by the arrow-like thinking projections, will suffer from mental anxiety in thinking of the death event.

Persons on the physical side will mentally review what happened as the cause of death, and also of the services which the deceased person performed, which are neglected. The emotional exchanges which were positive will be recalled but the happiness of that will convert into sorrow and numbness.

Wandering Search soon After Death

There is a danger after being deceased, where one may become a wandering somebody. Such a person is called a ghost by those who experience the psychic presence of the deceased someone. With a loss of purpose, feeling untethered, like a boat with no anchor, this person may go from place to place in the astral world, but to places which are mirrored like the physical reality, which the person is now deprived of.

Being lonely, feeling disappointed, being deprived of the pleasures which physical presence affords, this deceased soul will wander in the astral domains, shifting from place to place, which corresponds to the physical reality which was known before. He/She will harass living relatives and friends. Such a being is not dead. He/She is alive but with no physicalness, no direct access to be part of history.

What a Deceased Person should avoid Seeing

A deceased person who does not want to again become a physical person, should by all means gather his/her wits, and remember the hassles which accompany physical life. It has physical enjoyments but it has trauma as well. Having considered that a physical body facilitates stress and torments, comparing its disadvantages to its rewarding experiences, he/she should, based on decisions made during the life of the dead physical body, be convinced that anything which may cause one to loop back into physical existence, becoming an embryo, should be avoided.

One should know that regardless of one's aspirations, regardless of the strength of willpower, if one connects with Nature's reproductive loop energy, one will become an embryo. One's determination is no match for Nature's allurement. One should not be arrogant, feeling that no matter what, one will not take a body. It is a matter of not linking to a reproductive loop. Once one connects to a loop in the form of a set of physical parents or to their energy, one will become an embryo. One will again experience oneself as someone's infant.

On the hereafter side, one should avoid seeing, thinking of, or remembering the following.

- humans coupled sexually

- animals copulating

- someone to whom one is sexually attracted

- infants nursing or playing

In the astral existence hereafter, one will be more sensitive to psychic acts, much more than one was during the physical life. The increased psychic perception will make one, to be acutely aware of mental and emotional movements of people, who are physically based. Such sensitivity could be to one's detriment. It could be to one's advantage as well.

Those who practiced yogic meditation and other systems of mind and mental image control during the life of the physical body, may monitor the increased psychic perception carefully. In a way that makes it unlikely that one will take a haphazard rebirth. Others however, having no control over the increased psychic abilities, will be harassed by what is heard, seen, or detected.

As soon as one gets even a notion of a couple being sexually engaged, one should leave that place, and get beyond the range of the participants. This is because the link perception to those physical persons, is part of an already formatted rebirth, for anyone who is on the hereafter side. If one is attracted, and is drawn into the experience, there is every likelihood that one will become an infant of the persons involve.

Life as a Living Physical Body

In so far as life is only a living physical machine (body), it begins as the threat of death, when one is confronted with the fact, that the value of life is nil. This is because one cannot guarantee that one can be a physical body forever. The reality is that this life as a physical body will be terminated, and rapidly too, within one hundred and fifty years for the most.

The idea is floated that science may give a method for prolonging physical life, even to extend it indefinitely. That is not the reality at the moment. There is no physical evidence that it was the reality before. The conversation began about people living for thousands of years. There are scriptures and legends that attest to that. But even so, death happened because no one who is alive now, can prove that his body survived for more than one hundred and fifty years.

The threat of death looms over everyone. That itself is the promise of live, overturned. Death is the end of life for the physical body, a time when the biological rhythms stall for the last time

Interim Education and Preparation

Life as the psychic body of a self, does not begin as a baby. That psychic self is ongoing for as long as there is psychic energy to support its existence. Education about death should be acquired while the physical body lives, and hereafter while the being is shifted into being only a psychic entity. Preparation for living as a subtle body, as contrasted to being a physical person, should be made. That is the priority for life. It is better to focus on life as being the subtle body, leaving aside the stress for life as a physical system.

The threat of death is present even when one is in the womb of the mother. It presents itself at every opportunity by reminding one that the physical body can be harmed. It is ever present as sleeping sessions when one loses track of the self as a physical reality.

Social Necessity

To some extent, it is necessary to be social involved. One begins this life being serviced by others. In some cases, one experiences the last conscious phase of this body, while being catered by others. One is obligated. This life is hemmed with obligations. These liabilities cause compulsive focus on the physical plane. A countereffort should be made to study the spiritual shift, where the life of the physical body is no longer the priority. The psychic system is the enduring one. Even though it craves physical register, it is still the essential life, the base for physical interaction.

With haste, one should repay the ancestors, and seniors to whom one is obligated, for acquiring the physical body. But one should do so without losing focus on the essentiality of the psychic body. One should simultaneously service social obligations, and focus on a spiritual shift, so that the life desired is the psychic one.

Religious Destinations Hereafter

Most religions offer the convert, some suffering release and happiness hereafter. Some doctrines offer neither, except the abolishment of personality which is the target of trauma. Either one becomes perpetually happy, or one is de-existed where no unhappiness is possible, because one cannot be targeted by unpleasant states, if one does not exist.

These promises are questionable. If there are sublime spiritual states for assumption after death, those places, or existential conditions, should be available while the physical body lives.

For those doctrines which offer erasure of personality, the question arises as to what or who caused the personality to be in existence in the first place. If one did not produce the self that one is, how can one guarantee that one will eliminate that very self, which was caused by another agent or principle.

I had an experience at an astral place which was supervised by a devotee of a religious sect. There was a symbolic ceremony which focused on the dietary shift of human beings, from being meat eaters to being vegetarians. There was a ritual in which two sheep were killed, but their blood was diluted with water, to indicate that if one eats meat, one may in the process of time, develop a less violent dietary process, so that the strong taste of blood is no longer acceptable. Thus, one dilutes it.

After this ceremony with primitive animal sacrifice, there was a shift to another astral place, one that was sublime in comparison. In that place, cows were free to roam and were milked by humans. There were students who were supervised by multi-racial teachers.

We were to go to the cow pastures, but there was a chasm to cross. The senior instructed that I should mount his shoulders, which I did. He stepped into the chasm and floated over. There was a large cow which drank water from a clear pond.

The senior devotee said that I had four books which he would review. I told him that I have forty books, which were present in a room, which was assigned to me. He looked at the shelves but did not see the books. In that dimension one can see only what one is inclined to viewing.

This is a place where some devotees of the sect go hereafter, as a substitute for the spiritual realm of the deity, which they could not achieve. These places exist on the basis of the senior people in the religious society. The leader of such a place may have a physical body or he may be deceased. By making this psychic facility, he caters to the needs of any followers who become deceased, and who remain loyal to the sect, even though its guarantee for transit to a spiritual heaven did not happen.

Chapter 5
Bhagavad Gītā Extract

These selected verses from *Bhagavad Gītā* pertain to the situation hereafter. Because Krishna declared himself as the Supreme Being, I present some verses which were part of the dialogue between Arjuna and Krishna. These statements relate to existence and death.

There was never a time when I did not exist, nor you nor these rulers of the people. Nor will we cease to exist from now onwards. (Bhagavad Gītā 2.12)

This is a declaration of the perpetuity of the coreSelves. This does not mean that the selves are always aware of their individual existences. It signifies that no matter what, each self has perpetual value. Despite limitations, each self is qualified as continuation.

The circumstance of this statement by Krishna was a battlefield on which Arjun was a prominent warrior. Krishna was Arjun's chariot driver. Moments before the battle was to begin, Arjuna become emotionally distraught. To encourage him to be a determined warrior, Krishna reminded Arjuna that the warriors on either side were continuous selves.

Arjuna's emotional response to the scene of the battle was based on his visual perception and its outcome projection, which was that each self was a physical body, which may be imperiled in a horrific battle.

Krishna deprived Arjuna of this view by citing a known belief of the time, which was that even though the self functions as a physical body, that person has a perpetual background.

The problem with this statement is that it has no physical support. If true, this is a statement of psychic declaration. Hence, to prove this using only physical perception would be impossible. Krishna presented this premise at the beginning of the discourse with Arjuna. For us, we may accept it for the time being. Perhaps Krishna will provide some way for confirmation of this existential perpetuity of the non-physical identity which for the time being, we consider to be a physical body.

As the embodied soul endures childhood, youth and old age, so another body is acquired in sequence. The wise person is not confused on this topic. (Bhagavad Gītā 2.13)

This establishes an abstract principle which serves as the subtle substrata for the childhood, youth, and elderly conditions of a physical body. It continues to exist while there are physical developments and when those operations are no longer visible. At the time of Krishna and Arjuna, this was a belief of many human beings, but their confidence in it was based on verbal evidence presented by philosophers of the time.

Temporary things demonstrate changes which in time bring about partial or total deterioration. There may be alterations or deductions from any object. The idea is that all changes which occur, happen on an abstract basis, which is difficult to define. There must be a reference but if that is transcendental, physical perception cannot access it.

Of the non-substantial things, there is no enduring existence. Of the substantial things, there is no lack of existence. These two truths were perceived with certainty by the mystic seers of reality. (Bhagavad Gītā 2.16)

Proportionately, whatever will survive the death of the body is the endurance. Even if the psychic side will not persist as is forever, it is the more enduring factor when compared to the physical body. Hence, one should begin the spiritual inquiry by acknowledging the self as the psychic reality which will be the remnant of the person after death. That is not an absolute conclusion but it is where the investigation begins. It is based on the reality of the physical world which is contrasted by the reality of the dream existences.

For the physical body there is no enduring existence. The evidence for this is the aging of the physical form, and the deaths or deterioration of the physical bodies of senior relatives like the great grandparents. The firm indisputable conclusion is that the physical body and its physical identity or social tag, will disappear. Even if surviving relatives maintain a memorial to remind the world of a deceased person, still eventually those relatives will be removed from the face of history. Eventually there will be no trace, nor anyone who maintains the memorial.

The first reference for endurance is the psychic aspect of the self which persisted in dream experiences. It does not matter if ultimately this tag is discovered to be partially unreal. The value is that one must begin where one is located as a physical body. One should calculate the values from there. Someone, a physical body, is here on earth as part of history. That is accepted even for those who insist that there is no value in a physical body. Even they are tagged as a body, and must commit acts for its survival.

The body will die. That we know. Hence, the investigation is about what will survive. Other than physical materials, the body has emotional and mental operations. These are the psychic aspects which may survive. We know this because of having dreams, supernatural perceptions, and psychic communications. What format will the remnant psychic aspects take when there is no longer a physical body?

Know that indestructible factor by which all this world is pervaded. No one can accomplish the destruction of that everlasting principle. (Bhagavad Gītā 2.17)

For us, the assumption is that there is an indestructible factor by which the world is pervaded. This declaration of Krishna cannot be verified by the physical senses of a human being. Even convincing statements by scientists which explain a subtle underbasis of matter, cannot be verified merely by the senses of the body. Scientists use technological instruments to delve into the atomic structures of the elements. The products of technology give us confidence that the discoveries and declarations of the scientists are valid. A human being cannot figure an everlasting principle which cannot be destroyed.

In fact, of that which is born, death is certain; of that which is dead, birth is certain. Therefore in assessing what is unavoidable, you should not lament. (Bhagavad Gītā 2.27)

In the physical dimension which we are so familiar with, and in its corresponding astral places which we experience in dreams, the formations live and die, and then recycle into new formats.

Whatever is formed physically, and which has cellular construction, will die. It has a psychic remnant which survives but which is not detected by physical means. That subtle body lives as it did, even before the birth of the dead physical body.

However, the remnant self is present when the physical body lives as well as when that physical someone dies. The essentials remain alive when the physical system is no longer responsive to it. One should be confident, that part of the human person is psychic substance, which transcends physical existence. Its existence is not risked by the abrupt or gradual termination of the physical system.

The living beings are undetected in the beginning of a manifestation, visible in the interim stages, and are again undetected at the end of a manifestation. What is the complaint? (Bhagavad Gītā 2.28)

The initial mystic event which is the precursor of the birth of a baby is unknown to the physical parents of that child. It is an event. It is known but the circumstance and information occur in a psychic domain which is inaccessible to most parents. Hence, we assume that the beginning of a pregnancy is incomprehensible.

People know that if a woman's menstruation does not occur, that may indicate a pregnancy. In fact, anytime seminal fluid makes contact with a woman uterine passage, there is likelihood of a pregnancy. But those are physical indications. The psychic events prior to that are unseen.

Once the pregnancy develops, and a child is born, that is visible to physical people. But again, when that child grows into an adult, its elderly years are highlighted by death. This is routine. Who can object to it?

In the body, in all cases, this embodied soul is always non-killable, O descendant of Bharata. Therefore you should not mourn for any of these beings. (Bhagavad Gītā 2.30)

The psychic content of the physical person is not killable by physical means. First, we must establish that there are things which are part of the physical self, but which are non-physical. These aspects of self escape physical damage. There is displacement from a physical body. The raw identity part of the physical person is psychic. The prominent dispersal of that raw energy is known as the physical self.

The value of the physical body is overstated. This is why we frequently mourn for physical people who are dead. It is because we underrate and even ignore the psychic aspects of self.

Arjuna said: What about the undisciplined person who has faith? Having deviated from yoga practice, having not attained yoga proficiency, what course does he take, O Krishna? (Bhagavad Gītā 6.37)

This is an inquiry about the prospects for a person who developed faith in the idea that there is a psyche which would survive the death of the physical body. Will that person have an advantage when he/she can no longer relate physically?

If someone did yoga practice and did not fully gain confidence in the psychic self, through experience of that self as separate from the physical system, will that someone be in the same doubtful condition, as any other person, who did not pursue spiritual investigation before death?

The definition of yoga is not given in this query of Arjuna but its basic objective, is indicated. It is that if one is proficient in yoga during the life of the physical body, one will experience the remnant psychological energy and will begin, if not complete, the transfer of self focus into that energy before the time of being deprived of the physical body. That is the least attainment for a yogi.

If at the end of one's life, one recalls Me in particular, as one gives up the body, one is elevated to My condition of existence. There is no doubt about this. (Bhagavad Gītā 8.5)

This declaration of Krishna was used by many people as an assurance, a guarantee, that if at the end of the body, one can remember Krishna, specifically, one would be translated instantly to a sublime spiritual condition in association with him.

The problem with this statement is that it has this stipulation.

- recall Krishna in particular

Does this mean a full recall based on knowing Krishna personally? Does this mean a momentary memory about Krishna? How can anyone guarantee for himself/herself that he/she will recall Krishna at the end of life? Who knows what condition he will be in at death? What control does anyone have so that the mental condition will satisfy this stipulation?

If there is no quality to the recall, then every person who remembers Krishna at the time of death, should by this guarantee, become instantly elevated to Krishna's condition of existence. But if it depends on a particular quality of the recall, further clarity would be required to define who can successfully use this statement.

Moreover, whatever texture of existence is recalled when a person abandons his body in the end, to that same type of life, he is projected, O son of Kuntī, always being transformed into that status of life. (Bhagavad Gītā 8.6)

The key to this equation is the Sanskrit word *bhâvam*. I translated it as texture of existence. This is an accurate rendering because it is not what a person conveniently or under pressure, remembers, but rather his/her basic psychological condition. It is the state which is the underlying attitude and outlook of the person.

Someone who dies, will find that his psychic condition is the basic state which he experienced previously in dreams and thinking. He will resort to a psychic condition which is exactly the same as what he switched to during the sleeping condition of the physical body.

One may or may not remember Krishna at the time of knowing that one was deprived of physicality, but regardless the basic state of mind which one experienced during the life of the physical system, will again prevail except that it will be without usage of the body.

With a mind that does not venture outwards, which is disciplined by yoga practice, a person goes to the divine Supreme Person, while deeply meditating, O son of Pṛthā. (Bhagavad Gītā 8.8)

This pertains to a yogi who is proficient in meditation practice and who, during the life of the physical body, practices deep psychological penetration of his/her psyche. Because of achievements in meditation during the life of the physical body, he goes to the divine Supreme Person, when that body is no longer available as his physical form.

That yogi mastered mind control to such an extent, that the outward going tendency of the mind, which is its natural posture, ceased. That is replaced by the reverse situation where the mind folds inward as its involuntary condition.

He who meditates on the Person Who knows everything, the most ancient of people, the Supreme Supervisor, the most minute factor, the one with unimaginable form, with a radiant body, free of grossness, (Bhagavad Gītā 8.9)

The guarantee about those who recall Krishna in particular and who would attain Krishna's condition of existence, just after being unable to be his/her physical body, is better defined in these verses. Here the particulars are given, which would disqualify most of the devotees of Krishna. This is because the majority are not proficient in meditation.

This specific Krishna is the Person who knows everything. He is the one who is the most ancient of people, not because he stated this, and one has confidence in his words, but due to one's realization in meditation. One must be revealed about Krishna as the Supreme Supervisor, the most minute factor, the one with unimaginable form, who is himself a radiant body which is free of grossness

...and that meditator who even at the time of death, with an unwavering mind, being connected devotedly, with psychological power developed through yoga practice, and having caused the energizing breath to enter between the eyebrows with precision, goes to the divine Supreme Person. (Bhagavad Gītā 8.10)

These are more details about what should be done by a yogi if he/she would attain a dimension of transcendence in relation to the divine Supreme Person, just after losing identity with the physical body.

These actions of the yogi are psychological events not mere beliefs nor demonstrations of faith. Somewhere else, Lord Krishna or some other person may promise or advocate that any devotee, particularly those who are not expert at meditation, may attain the world of Krishna, but here this pertains only to the great yogis who qualify as described.

The technique of causing the energizing breath of the subtle body, to enter the brow chakra with precision, is practiced in *samyama* meditation, which is the progressive mental control for internal discipline. It requires mastership of *pratyahar* sensual energy withdrawal from the features of physical existence, even from physical devotional practice, at least during the time allotted for the meditation practice.

One turns away from every aspect of physical existence, and folds over the focus, into psychic sorting and application, so as to open higher perception between the eyebrows, or through the intellect orb which is in the head of the subtle body.

After a time, the intellect itself is silenced. The yogi may use the sense of identity which surrounds the coreSelf. These are perception orbs which manifest to the yogi within the psyche. Just as an embryo has limited perception means, not even visual access, but just as in time, it develops eyes and other sensual access, so the yogi begins this practice with no psychic senses, nothing besides attention or alert awareness. Then, in time after hours of meditation daily, he develops supernatural perception.

A devoted connection with Krishna is required. If the yogi does not have that, or if he is devoted to another deity, he may reach some other transcendental place or person, and would be liberated according to the status of that destination or deity.

I will briefly explain the process to you, which the knowers of the Veda describe as imperishable, which the ascetics who are free from cravings enter and who desiring to be transferred there, they follow a life of celibacy. (Bhagavad Gītā 8.11)

The focus on existence is a dual consideration of *to be* or *not to be,* with those who want to be, having one or the other interest, to be physical as we are currently or to be psychic, with no physicality.

Those who want *to de-exist* hereafter, are not concerned even with the possibility of being recycled as an infant in some species of life.

In the time of Krishna, some people, had the aim of being translated to an existence in which the self only experienced what was pleasant.

Some hints are given in this verse as to what some ascetics did to secure transit or translation to *aksharam*, the place where everything in imperishable. One must be.

- free from craving
- be celibate

Those are two of the requirements. The listing is completed in the following verses.

The state of being free from craving means that the senses must be disinterested in physical existence. This happens after a yogi traced the sensual quest backwards into the psyche, to discover how his interest was diversified, into a quest for objects through five sensual orifices; hearing, touching, seeing, tasting, and smelling. Initially this yogi becomes obsessed with disciplining and depriving the five senses. Later when these are tagged, he discovers that it is the interest of the self, which is the cause.

This interest is the direct handler for the self, its one arm for grasping physical or psychic objects. When that interest is retracted and used to focus on the self, a concern about reality arises. This causes an investigation into extra-dimensional situations to find what is compatible to the self. Instead of a denial of, *I am not this, I am not that*, there is assertion into what else there is.

Controlling all openings of the body, and restricting the mind in the core of consciousness, situating the energizing energy of the soul in the brain, remaining fixed in yoga concentration, (Bhagavad Gītā 8.12)

These are more of the stipulations for achieving transit to the place where everything is imperishable.

- controlling all openings of the body
- restricting the mind in the core of consciousness
- situating the energizing energy of the soul in the brain

- remaining fixed in yoga concentration

These are psychological disciplines which must be mastered in mystic yoga practice. One must be a devotee of Krishna and be a proficient yogi as well.

Controlling all openings of the body is both a physical and mystic method. It is acclaimed in the Patanjali yoga thesis as *pratyahar* sensual energy withdrawal. There are nine openings with the skin as an additional one which covers the entire body and which is embedded with hairs. The obvious openings are two eyes, two nostrils, two ears, one mouth, a genital, and one anus. Information about the external environment is garnished by some openings. That is reported to the intellect which catalogs the information, and routes it through a process for conclusions.

A yogi must carefully control the nine openings and the skin, so that he/she does not become reliant on the intellect's conclusions. This skill is preparatory for advanced meditation.

Restricting the mind in the core of consciousness is a meditation practice. Modern devotional authorities disregard this requirement. They cite the golden avatar, Sri Chaitanya, to state that one should focus on the Krishna deity who is external to the body and individual mind. In fact, once when I attempted to restrict the mind in the core of consciousness, a Swami of a devotional sect threatened to expel me from a Krishna temple. He stated that the seniormost person in the sect outlawed such meditation activity.

The mind is by nature a sense object grabbing psychic mechanism. It is against internalization for self-research. It is a struggle for a yogi to meet the requirements listed in this verse.

Situating the energizing energy of the soul in the brain is a kundalini yoga practice. It is part psychic and part physical, with breath infusion and contractions combined with inner focusing and directing of the lifeForce energy.

The lifeForce is centralized at the base of the spinal column both in the physical and subtle bodies. This must be adjusted by the yogi. Over time doing breath infusion, striking at the base, the kundalini shifts upward and eventually it becomes established in the head of the subtle body. It loses interest in the lower areas. Its focus into the head of the subtle body helps the yogi to reduce focus on physical pleasure sensations.

The value of this is that at the time of death, the lifeForce will not have a compelling interest in sexual indulgence. That will free the person from the compulsion to become an embryo.

Remaining fixed in yoga concentration is a lifelong aspiration. On and on, day to day, a yogi must strive for this. Step by step, day by day, he/she should decrease the interest in physical history. He/She should shift to psychic events as the priority.

The idea that physical actions in worship and adoration of Krishna is sufficient, is questioned by Krishna's statement in this verse. If someone focuses on physical aspects of Krishna worship and states that these are spiritual/psychological movements, does that convert those physical acts into being inner yoga concentration? Each devotee should reasonably consider this.

...uttering Om, the one-syllable sound which represents the spiritual reality, meditating on Me, the yogi who passes on, renouncing the body, attains the highest objective. (Bhagavad Gītā 8.13)

These complete the list of the psychological disciplines which must be mastered in mystic yoga practice.

- uttering Om, the one-syllable sound which represents the spiritual reality

- meditating on Krishna

- yogi who passes on, renouncing the body

It was required, at least in the time of Krishna that a yogi, if he wishes to translate to the divine environment, should be versed in **uttering Om, the one-syllable sound which represents the spiritual reality**. Nowadays some devotional authorities leave Om aside. They present the value of chanting holy names, usually the Hare Krishna *Mahamantra*. Claiming that the *Bhagavad Gita's* instruction was for an era prior, they advocate a different mantra.

Yogis, however, who accept Krishna as He presented himself in *Bhagavad Gita*, should heed his stipulations. This will guarantee for them that they could hold Krishna to the methods given to Arjuna.

The act of **meditating on Krishna** should be practiced during the life of the yogi. But at the time of being permanently disconnected from the body, the yogi should intensify that already cultivated focus. Yogis who did not practice during the life of the body, and who attempt to do this when the physical body is near death, will not get the result of the practice. Still those incompetent ascetics should make the effort, but they should not think that the full benefit of the practice will be theirs.

Meditation on Krishna includes preliminary self-realization, which is discovery of the aspects of the individual psyche. First, one must realize one's psychological parts. When that is fully catalogued and controlled, one may approach the Supreme Being, Krishna.

Those who neglect the practice of self-realization, may rationalize the lack of that method, but it is difficult to see how they could approach the transcendence of Krishna. For the most, their achievement will be to acquire an embryo so that they could again focus on the physical aspects of Krishna, those properties of his which surface in physical history.

The **yogi who passes on, renouncing the body**, and who satisfies the other requirements listed by Krishna, will be translated to an imperishable domain, where Krishna is the resident deity.

He whose mind does not go to another focus at any time, who thinks of Me constantly, for that yogi who is constantly disciplined in yoga, I am easy to reach, O son of Pṛthā. (Bhagavad Gītā 8.14)

Recall of Krishna at the time of death, will be of the correct reach, if the yogi does so with some supportive mystic actions. Whimsical recall, haphazard connection, will not suffice. During the life, the yogi's mind should have no other constant focus besides Krishna. That may happen only if the yogi was versed in meditative focus on Krishna.

Thinking of Krishna constantly should be a disciplined conduct even before the death event. But this is not shallow thoughts or whimsical chanting. It is thinking of Krishna as his life is described in the *Srimad Bhagavatam,* and reaching him according to what visions of Krishna the yogi experienced during life.

Approaching me in this way, those great souls who went to supreme perfection are not subjected to rebirth in this shifty, miserable location. (Bhagavad Gītā 8.15)

The guarantees given by Krishna in *Bhagavad Gītā* are to be taken seriously. Those which were issued by devotional teachers, or by persons who are rated as incarnations of Krishna, are as good as those who issued those other decrees. One should not confuse modern assertions with the direct certification of Krishna.

It is interesting that devotees of Krishna ridicule these stipulations, and admonish that if one follows these, one will not attain Krishna, because it is too difficult to practice this in the current era.

Up to Brahmā's world, the populations are subjected to repeated births and deaths, O Arjuna. But in approaching Me, rebirth is not experienced, O son of Kuntī. (Bhagavad Gītā 8.16)

The cosmology described by Krishna includes a highest heaven beyond which is another world, the imperishable place which has only imperishable objects. Up to *Brahma's* world means from subterranean places which run parallel to but which are more enduring than this earthly place, this place itself, the physical realm, and psychic heavens which are above it.

The heavenly places, which are superior in duration to this physical place, have relatively long duration, but life there does not extend forever, and the fear of losing register there is present in varying degrees. The most secure heaven is Brahma's world but that place though the ultimate in those heavenly places, also comes to an end, although it is again enacted after a blank time span.

Krishna stated that in approaching him, rebirth in these places is not experienced. This is due to the upgrade of the body of the yogi, where, due to association with Krishna, the yogi's psyche goes through a transformation which keeps him linked to Krishna, with a psyche which is similar to Krishna.

Those who know the day of Brahmā, which has a limit of one thousand time cycles, and the night of Brahmā, which ends in a thousand time cycles, are the people who know day and night. (Bhagavad Gītā 8.17)

The situation we are in is timed to operate, and be disabled, at regular intervals, except that for some, the duration is miniscule, and for others it is near infinite.

The person factor is current. The environment is evident. Some persons have a lifespan that is unimaginable, while others like an insect or unicellular organism may last for weeks or moments.

In this physical creation and in the obvious psychic aspects of it, there is ignition, shine and burn out. This is repeated again and again as materials are created, used, and recycled. The conclusion is that for perpetuity, one should find another environment, a place in which the radiance is constant with no extinguishment. That is why one should do investigative yoga.

It would be great if one could cease involvement here, turnabout and discover if there is an imperishable all-radiant place. However, since this environment is so shifty, one should strive with the knowledge that it may take many lives to complete the study, and reach the conclusion about reality.

When the day of Creator Brahmā begins, all this visible world is produced from the invisible world. When his night comes, the manifested energies are reverted back into the invisible world. (Bhagavad Gītā 8.18)

Whatever is sensually perceptible in this world, which was apprehended in the past, now or in the future, arrived here as an expression of the invisible world. But again, it will de-exist by reverting into its origin. As this world retrogresses, it becomes more abstract, assuming forms which we fail to detect, and which to us are as nothingness.

The in and out, up and down, versions of reality, which we encounter during the life of a physical body, is part of the kaleidoscope of reality. It shows itself in part and remains unmanifest in part. It runs as events. It flames out as unsensational blank energy.

O son of Pṛthā, this multitude of beings which is repeatedly manifested, is naturally shifted out of visibility at the arrival of each of Brahmā's nights. It again comes into existence at the onset of Brahmā's day. (Bhagavad Gītā 8.19)

This is the streaming video, produced by the reality, rendered from itself as a limited version of what it is, which is on the other side of the existential divide. Whatever was here prior, whatever is here now, and whatever will be in the future, is part of the turn of this reality display, which assumes temporary designation repeatedly.

There is also the rendering of personality with permanent coreSelves, who wear various social faces which are masks for relationship needs. Over and over, again and again, a corePerson discovers itself to be existing in this, but feeling itself as a produced self, in a theatre based on the onset, development, and death of a physical body.

But higher than this, there is another invisible existence, which is higher than the primeval unmanifested states of this dissolvable creation. When all these creatures are disintegrated, that is not affected. (Bhagavad Gītā 8.20)

Krishna informed of another invisible existence, a higher place. That is the spiritual realm where there is no indulgence in temporary reality. The primeval unmanifest states of this dissolvable creation are in psychic realms. Some of these can be detected by a yogi, but the majority are realized only as subtle energy, in which shapes and forms cannot be cognized.

This itemizes two invisible worlds. One is the reverse source of this existence. The other is beyond this visible situation and its origin. Both are invisible but one is higher than the other, and is not related, and does not produce this visible scene.

The continuous disintegration of lifeforms, and the collective total disaster of those forms, does not change the primeval unmanifested source condition. It certainly does not affect the other invisible existence which is higher than this, and higher than the source for this.

That invisible world is unalterable, so it is declared. The authorities say that it is the supreme objective. Attaining that, they do not return here. That place is My supreme residence. (Bhagavad Gītā 8.21)

The manifestation and removal of formation stages happen on this side of existence. The situation beyond that is the place of no return, a location which Krishna admitted as his supreme residence.

Krishna's province is the ultimate environment. It is the supreme objective of the yogis. That place is a match for the yearning energy for fulfilment and completion of desires. It is a place where all sensations respond for perfect happiness of the individual who resides there.

In this world satisfaction happens part of the time with disappointment and frustration using up the rest of the time. In that other place, Krishna's domain, the only desires which arise are those which are fulfilled instantly.

That Supreme Person, O son of Pṛthā, is attainable through a devotional relationship and not by any other means. Within His influence, all beings exist. By Him, all the universe is energized. (Bhagavad Gītā 8.22)

There must be a cultivated and active devotional relationship between Krishna and the yogi. Stated precisely, that person must be a devotee of Krishna. However, this does not mean that the devotee should not be proficient in yoga and should only be chanting the name of Krishna, and doing ritual worship of the Blessed Lord.

No other means but devotion will cause the devotee to translate to Krishna's perpetual spiritual place after death, and even during the life, during dreams, visions, and apparitions. But the devotee must be qualified in other skills, habits and mystic methods as elaborated by Krishna in this discussion with Arjuna.

As in Arjuna's life, devotion to Krishna included service actions, which fulfill the instructions for social activities as suggested by the Lord. If one lives being occupied in a way which satisfies these requirements, there is every likelihood, that one will transit to Krishna's paradise after the final desynchronization from the physical body.

O bullish man of the Bharata family, I will tell you of the departure for the yogis who do or do not return. (Bhagavad Gītā 8.23)

In the time of Krishna, an important topic for ascetics was the ideal plan for transmigrating to a desirable location hereafter. Yogis got descriptions of various psychic realms, along with methods of flight to such places. If a yogi was proficient in these transits during the life of the physical body, it was assumed that he/she attained a desirable realm hereafter, or that he/she took an embryo with the intention to succeed during the next life.

Those who returned went elsewhere, either permanently or for a short or long period, after which they assumed identity as an infant of parents. Those who did not return, eradicated in their psyches, the need to be a participant in physical history. They were not attached to any attainment which requires the use of a physical body.

The summer season, the bright atmosphere, the daytime, the bright moonlight, the six months when the sun appears to move north; if at that time, they depart the body, those people who know the spiritual dimension, go to the spiritual location. (Bhagavad Gītā 8.24)

This does not cover mere passing on during the summer season, the bright atmosphere, the daytime, the bright moonlight, or the six months when the sun appears to move north. It is more than this. Some are of the opinion that if they could arrange death during the summer season, they would migrate to the dimension stipulated in this verse. However, that is incorrect.

Why? Because one is required to know the spiritual dimension (*brahmavidah*). This means that during the life of the physical body, one must practice reaching that place, and know how to access it through elevated consciousness, where one actually transits there in meditation, or otherwise. Even someone who is a devotee of Krishna, even a well-known publicly acclaimed devotee, would not qualify under this verse, unless he/she was versed in reaching the spiritual location, during the life of the physical body.

Merely imagining that place on the basis of descriptions in religious text, does not quality one. Reading about and becoming versed in preaching about that place, as one understood it in texts, does not qualify one to go to that place. One must actually transit there during the life of the physical body, in meditative states, and even at times when one is awake as the physical body, and has apparitions or visions into that spiritual place.

The smoky, misty or hazy season, as well as in the night-time, the dark-moon time, the six months when the sun appears to move south; if the yogi departs at that time, he attains moonlight, after which he is born again. (Bhagavad Gītā 8.25)

For the yogi who happens to be deprived of his body at the unfavorable time which is described in this verse, it is likely that he will again take another body. This brings to our attention that the physical and psychic environment may be an impediment, whereby our aspirations will fail, due to lack of assistance from the heavenly bodies, the planets, and stars, even the earth.

The influence of the smoky, misty, or hazy season, as well as the night-time, the dark moon time, the six months when the sun appears to move south, will frustrate the plan of the yogi to reach a transcendental place hereafter. The environment has an effect. It is not that the yogi is all-powerful, and can force Nature to be supportive.

The light and the dark times are two paths which are considered to be perpetually available for the universe. It is considered so by the authorities. By one, a person goes away not to return; by the other he comes back again. (Bhagavad Gītā 8.26)

This statement is a terrible one because if one accepts it, one can understand that one is limited, and is in need of positive influences.

The pivot of these attainments or the lack of any, is based on one single aspiration, which is to avoid taking another physical body. Persons who find the physical life to be acceptable are not addressed in these verses. This is for seasoned yogis who are desperate not to return as someone's baby.

A yogi must take advantage of the light times. He needs assistance from the environment. If Nature is set against his aspirations, he must again take another physical body.

Knowing these two paths, O son of Pṛthā, the yogi is not confused at all. Therefore at all times, be disciplined in yoga practice, O Arjuna. (Bhagavad Gītā 8.27)

There must be clarity about the environmental influence and its imposed limitations. A yogi is not the Supreme Lord. He is not the Absolute. He does not control the subtle climate and all surrounding psychic energy. He is affected by the environment. To be realistic he should study how he is influenced by what surrounds him on every side, in any of the environments he switches to, or is shifted into by other powers.

The best position with the most leverage is attained by practicing yoga and making the best out of the various situations one may be exposed to. A yogi should estimate his chances to go to a higher dimension. The proficiency he attains while using the physical body will hardly increase hereafter. Thus, he can have some idea of where he will go, once he can no longer use the physical body.

The yogi, having known all this, goes beyond the good results which are derived from study of the Veda, beyond religious ceremonies and disciplines, beyond austerities and beyond offering scripturally-recommended gifts in charity. He goes to the Supreme Primal State. (Bhagavad Gītā 8.28)

A detailed study of the psychic environment which supports the existence of this physical world, as well as some insight into whatever is beyond that, is vital for a yogi. No guess work! No hope based on speculation! No mere faith in a deity or scripture! No confidence because the religious teacher said something with emphasis!

Only mystic penetration, where a yogi directly perceives higher realities, and knows the passage to those places, will guarantee the routing to an imperishable location after death.

This must be achieved in meditation before being deprived of the use of the physical body.

The subsidiary aspects have value but if they are not reinforced by direct mystic penetration, their usage will not give access to the transcendental places.

The **good results which are derived from study of the Veda** are manifested in this dimension now and in the astral existence hereafter. However, while enjoying the benefits in the astral world, there is in the background, the lingering need for physical existence. This is due to the fact that a transit to a heavenly place on the basis of Vedic study carries with it the threat of rebirth, of being projected into a reproductive situation. As soon as the results are exhausted, the person will find himself/herself being attracted to perspective parents. This will terminate as becoming an embryo, but with the instinct to again study the Veda, and again get the result of a vacation in an astral heaven hereafter.

Ultimately, **religious ceremonies and related disciplines** cause anyone who is complaint, to be distracted from the objective. They focus on accumulation of money, or some other value which is wealth. Those who want money are induced either by tradition, or intuition, to confirm to what is stipulated in a religious doctrine. Apart from ritual or mere attendance, there are disciplines which must be completed as required by the sect. Once these are done the person feels that he/she appeased the deities and environment, and will be successful by getting value in the physical world.

A yogi leaves this aside because he sees that wealth is power, which converts into responsibility, which in turn converts into accountability, which when enforced brings on shame and hard labor. It does not matter if the present body has aristocratic status. There is no guarantee that in the future one will not assume an undesirable body. To avoid this, a yogi bleaches the desire for aristocratic status from the psyche.

Austerities for physical conquest is a way of getting leverage in the physical world. A yogi must leave such efforts aside. By all means, austerities must be performed but only for organizing, and elevating the psyche. The idea for this is that the coreSelf should be in a dominant position over its adjuncts. It has a sense of identity, an intellect, memory, and sensual energy. These should be brought to order, so that their interest supports the education of the coreSelf, and gives it control over the psyche, where those adjuncts do not conspire to undermine the effort of the core to supervise its self (psychological aspects).

When someone **offers scripturally-recommended gifts in charity,** there is a feeling of happiness. There is approval from members of the sect. There is inner assurance that one did what was correct, and will be rewarded amply. Even though it is honorable, a yogi leaves that aside.

When as instructed by a parent, a child gives money to a beggar, the child gets a merit for complying with the parents' request. The child did not earn the money and will not get the pious credit from giving the coins. It is the parent who will get that reward.

Nature is the force which funds everything. What a human does which is a compliance with an encouraged act, is not accredited to the human agent. This is why a yogi eases himself/herself away from charitable focus. It must be realized also that the development of wealth, for the sake of offering charity to others, is a perverted practice which ultimately causes conceit in the self.

O son of Kuntī, all beings retrogress into My own material nature at the end of Brahmā's day. I produce them again at the beginning of Brahmā's next day. (Bhagavad Gītā 9.7)

Cosmic death happens when a star explodes or crashes in on itself. Everything which evolved from whatever there is, will in time retrogress. But it will again emerge as the systems operate in compression and expansion cycles.

We can perceive this on the physical plane. Krishna explained it from the personSelf perspective, saying that at the beginning of *Brahma's* day, whatever was folded in, again emerged, and expanded as development.

The knowers of the three Vedas, the soma drinkers, and those who are reformed of bad tendencies, worship Me with sacrificial procedures. They desire to be transferred to heaven. Attaining the merit-based world of Surendra, the king of the angelic people, they enjoy celestial delights in the astral region. (Bhagavad Gītā 9.20)

Most religious people are hopeful for transfer to the heaven of their preferred deity. While living they want to be successful by means of conveniences and wealth. This is for the comfort of the physical body. The person is a psychic phenomenon but its feels that its self is mostly physical, and that physical conveniences are fulfilling.

People who have theistic inclinations, try to adhere to moral stipulations, as defined by their religious teachers and textual instructions. This contributes to law and order in their societies. Some worship Krishna. Some worship another deity or a devil even.

If the procedures and supernatural authority are valid, the devotees of the particular religion may be transferred to that deity's paradise. Attaining that merit-based world, seeing the deity in full glory, the follower enjoys celestial delights in the astral heaven.

Having enjoyed the multi-dimensional, angelic paradise world, exhausting their pious merits, they enter the world of short-life duration. Thus adhering to the tri-part Vedic injunctions for righteous life style, those who aspire for pleasures and luxuries get the opportunity to go to heaven and come back to the earth again. (Bhagavad Gītā 9.21)

Supposing that after death, someone shifts to the multi-dimensional angelic paradise world of the preferred deity. How long would that person remain there in a sublime beatific state of consciousness? Since the cause of the transit there, was religious focus on earth in the recent physical body, then when the performance energy which supported that transit was exhausted, that person would resume life in the physical world as an embryo, being again relegated to physicalness in this world of short-life duration.

Thus, by complying with the moral stipulations of a religion on earth, a practitioner got heaven hereafter in some psychic realm, then got birth as someone's child, whereby that good person would again stick to morally approved behavior, and would strive for pleasures and luxuries, and then again would return to heaven, for as long as the investment in morality would support a sojourn in the heavenly place.

Those who satisfy the supernatural rulers, go to those authorities. Those who satisfy the pious ancestors, associate with such departed spirits. Those who try to satisfy the ghosts, go to those beings. Those who try to satisfy Me, surely approach Me. (Bhagavad Gītā 9.25)

Krishna presents himself as the Supreme Personality of Godhead. He is also a Personality of Godhead in the individual sense. He is God. He is also a god, all at once. Whosoever is accepted by anyone as the Supreme Person, is also free to be a limited agent under certain conditions. Being God does not mean that the said divinity may not relate or demonstrate in a limited format.

Those devotees of some deity, if they follow the stipulations of that person, may go to the realm of that divinity after death of the physical body. It is possible. In fact, one may do that and not be aware of the fact that there are multi-divinities. Unless more is revealed to one, one is left only with a limited view of Godhead. One is likely to feel that only the deity one prefers is an authority.

Those who get the approval for righteous conduct from a deity, are likely to be translated to the realm of that supernatural person. All the same, those who go so far as to accepted their pious ancestors as psychic authorities, will go to their departed relatives after death.

Those who satisfy the ghosts may go to such psychic people as soon as their bodies die. And Krishna alerts that those who worship him, may go to him after death. The transit in the afterlife depends on the actions and directive energy during the life of the physical body.

Arjuna said: What is material nature? What is the person? What is the living space? Who is the experiencer of the living space? I wish to know this. What is a conclusion? And what is experienced, O Keshava, pretty-haired One? (Bhagavad Gītā 13.1)

For those who inquire about death, as to the impact of it and about the alternatives beyond it, these questions of Arjuna have significance. Someone comes into this world from somewhere or from nowhere, depending on one's opinion. That baby is confronted with physical objects which are part of the reality here. The physical person and everything which is external to its form are part of Nature.

One should, if one has the interest, investigate the origins. What is Nature? What is the person which is a physical object in combination with mental and emotional energies? What is the living space, wherein mental and emotional formations occur? What is the objective contrasting egoSelf? What is an opinion? What is experienced as detected events?

The Blessed Lord said: This, the earthly body, O son of Kuntī, is called the living space. Those who are knowledgeable of this, declare the person who understands this to be the experiencer of the living space. (Bhagavad Gītā 13.2)

The analysis of what may occur at the time of becoming conscious, after being deprived of the ability to arouse as the physical body, begins with an understanding about the psychic side of the body. If there is no psychic side, then the fact is a simple one; death of the body is the end of all aspects of the personSelf.

Krishna presents the view that the physical person which we consider to be the body, is actually not the person. It is a living space which is a container for the aspects, which in summary, are addressed as the body.

If one experiences the format of oneself as Krishna reported, one is regarded as an experiencer of the body. The experiencer or coreSelf is one aspect in the living space. The addition of adjuncts to that core is termed as the psyche, the psychological combination which by convention is regarded as a person.

Know also, that I am the experiencer of all living spaces, O man of the Bharata family. Information of the living space and the experiencer of it, is considered by Me to be knowledge. (Bhagavad Gītā 13.3)

For the study of the afterlife, as to if there is one, as to if one should prepare for it, that education is necessary. Apart from a psyche which is a psychological container, which houses a coreSelf and adjuncts, there is a superObserver, who resides in a super dimension from which he has access to all limited psyches. That person is the Supreme Being. He is Krishna. Spiritual vocabulary about the selves and superSelf is rated by Krishna as knowledge.

As for this living space, as for what is, as for what kind of environment it is, as for the changes it endures, as to what causes it to change, as for he who is involved, as for his potential, hear from Me of that in brief. (Bhagavad Gītā 13.4)

An in-dept understanding of the living space and its contents is necessary, if one is to penetrate the hereafter before one is deprived of the physical body. After birth, one came to know oneself as the physical body. And yet, one desires to know what this body will develop as, and when it will be terminated. If something will be left as a remnant of the self, and if that something will be an emotional and mental formation, then one should become familiar with it, while one functions as the physical form and is identified as it.

What is this physical self? What kind of environment is it? What are its developments? What pressures are it under? What is the observational factor in it? Would it be possible for the observer to second guess what will happen at death, when the cohesiveness of the physical person is fragmented?

This was distinctly recited many times with the various Vedic hymns and with the Brahma Sūtras, conclusively with sound logic, by the great yogi sages. (Bhagavad Gītā 13.5)

The information about the coreSelf and its current environment which is a psychological chamber or psyche, was divulged by some yogis before the time of Krishna. They presented their conclusions in the *Brahma Sutras* and *Upanishads*. Some accept that literature as the final information. And yet, Krishna, the person who presented himself as the Supreme Being, found it necessary to review those conclusions and present a new thesis which contained some of what the previous researchers declared.

The major categories of the elements, the personal initiative, the intellect, the unmanifested energy, the ten and one senses, the five attractive objects, (Bhagavad Gītā 13.6)

...desire, hatred, pleasure, pain, the whole body, consciousness and conviction; this is described with brevity, as the living space with its changes. (Bhagavad Gītā 13.7)

Besides the coreSelf, the stalwart observing factor, there are other features which comprise the psyche.

- major categories of the elements
- personal initiative
- intellect
- unmanifested energy
- ten and one senses

- five attractive objects

- desire

- hatred

- pleasure

- pain

- whole body

- consciousness

- conviction

The **major elements** are exterior and interior. From the materialistic viewpoint, it is exterior as the earthly and atmospheric environment. From a yogic viewpoint its interior presence is the challenge. This is researched in advanced meditation. One must assess the influence of Nature as to if one can control it.

The **personal initiative** is a gift of existence. Each coreSelf has this ability to know itself. However, this feature is not available at all times. We find that we are aware and then there is a gap through which we are unaware. This must be investigated in meditation. Using schematics given by Krishna and by advanced yogis, one should plunge into the psyche to know the truth about this.

The **intellect** is an invaluable award as it allows for comparison between one perception and another. It rates events and objects. It is also misleading because if it has incorrect information, it draws faulty conclusion. It is however, indispensable. This mean that the yogi should calibrate it during usage.

The **unmanifested energy** is ever present. No one can see it with physical eyes. Recently scientists show sufficient energy where no one can deny that it exists. In meditation, it may be seen or perceived in some way. How does it figure in hereafter?

The **ten and one senses** and the **five attractive objects** assail every creature. There is an ongoing effort to control the senses and to limited or expand the availability of the five attractive objects. Yogis must figure how to reduce their influence.

During the life of the body, if one spends most of the time satisfying the senses and procuring the attractive objects, one will have no time to rate the sensual influences.

Desire and **hatred** are phases of yearnings, with desire being the major force. Hatred is a reaction when an event does not match a yearning or a potential feeling. A yogi must research this to understand how the psyche is motivated with eagerness or hesitation.

Pleasure and **pain** are sensual interpretations. These may be accurate or inaccurate. A yogi should check to understand how it is configured by Nature. A resistance to this should be developed in the psyche.

The **whole body** experience is spontaneously felt from time to time. It reinforces the idea that the self is a physical body. A yogi must meditate to understand that the body is a composite.

Even though **consciousness** is assumed, its level varies and its presence is inconstant. This is a large study in meditation practice, as to why consciousness varies and even disappears on occasion.

Conviction is an attribute which arises when the personal initiative and the intellect are linked. It is required when there are decisions and strong opinions. A yogi should disentangle the personal initiative from the intellect. Then he can curb the sensual energy so that it does not mislead the core, nor cause it to endorse activities which inconvenience it.

Lack of pride, freedom from deceit, non-violence, patience, straightforwardness, attendance to a teacher, purity, stability and self-restraint, (Bhagavad Gītā 13.8)

..indifference towards the attractive objects, absence of motivated initiative, the perception of the danger of birth, death, old age, disease, and suffering, (Bhagavad Gītā 13.9)

...social and emotional detachment towards child, wife, a home and whatever is related to social life, being always even-minded towards what is desired and what is not wanted, (Bhagavad Gītā 13.10)

...unswerving devotion to Me, with no other discipline but yoga practice, resorting to a secluded place, having a dislike for crowds of human beings, (Bhagavad Gītā 13.11)

...constantly considering information about the Supreme Spirit, perceiving the value of the science of reality; this is declared as knowledge. Whatever is contrary to this, is ignorance. (Bhagavad Gītā 13.12)

The topics and features for education are:

- lack of pride

- freedom from deceit

- non-violence

- patience

- straightforwardness

- attendance to a teacher

- purity

- stability

- self-restraint

- indifference towards the attractive objects

- absence of motivated initiative

- perception of the danger of birth, death, old age, disease, and suffering

- social and emotional detachment towards child, wife, a home and whatever is related to social life

- being always even-minded towards what is desired and what is not wanted

- unswerving devotion to Me, with no other discipline but yoga practice

- resorting to a secluded place

- having a dislike for crowds of human beings

- constantly considering information about the Supreme Spirit

- perceiving the value of the science of reality

Whatever information or education one acquires which is contrary to this, signifies an indulgence in ignorance, and an involvement or focus on subjects which will diminish enlightenment.

I will explain that which is to be experienced, knowing which one gets in touch with eternal life. The beginningless Supreme Reality is said to be neither substantial nor insubstantial. (Bhagavad Gītā 13.13)

The eternal life is apart from this physical existence and from its psychic supports. However, the supports are the first level of investigation. When a yogi has insight into the supports, he may extend his interest into what is higher. He should be progressive in meditation, so that he makes contact with the beginningless Supreme Reality, which is such that some say it is substantial, and others rate it as being insubstantial, because they cannot objectify it.

Everywhere is Its hands and feet, everywhere Its eyes, head and face, everywhere is Its hearing ability in this world; It stands, ranging over all. (Bhagavad Gītā 13.14)

The beginningless Supreme Reality is the most sensitive detection factor in this creation. Subsequently nothing happens without its minute observation. The calculation we should make is that it monitors every personal and impersonal occurrence. Nothing escapes its vigilance.

It has the appearance of having all sensual moods, and It is freed from sensuousness. Though unattached, It maintains everything. Though free from the influence of material nature, It is the experiencer of that influence nevertheless. (Bhagavad Gītā 13.15)

It is simultaneously attached and detached. It is the adjuster but it cannot be modified. It is related to everything and yet, no other reality is positioned to censor it.

It is outside and inside the moving and non-moving beings. Because of Its subtlety, this beginningless Supreme Reality is not comprehended. This Reality is situated far away and it is in the location as well. (Bhagavad Gītā 13.16)

It is less than a whisper's distance from anything, and yet it is out of reach of everything. The investigation into its existence is never completed.

It is undivided among the beings, but It appears as if It is divided in each. It is the sustainer of the beings and this should be known. It is the absorber and producer. (Bhagavad Gītā 13.17)

It is confidential with the individual selves, but some are unaware that it has a relationship with each. It is the background for confidence but a self may not accredit its supportive lift.

This is declared as the light of the luminaries, but It is beyond gross or subtle darkness. It is the information, the education and the goal of education. It is situated in the psychological core of all beings. (Bhagavad Gītā 13.18)

In the dimension of selves, it is the core of cores. And yet, it may not impose its presence on anyone.

Thus the psychological environment as well as the standard knowledge and what is to be known, was described in brief. Experiencing this, My devotee draws near to My state of being. (Bhagavad Gītā 13.19)

If a yogi investigates the Supreme Being sufficiently, that ascetic will translate to Krishna's state of being. In that transcendental condition the yogi will slip away from all negativity which is related to death of the physical body.

Decay does not affect such a yogi. The zones which produce negative states of mind become distant and are not perceptible to him.

Know that both material nature and the spiritual personality are beginningless, and know that the changes of the living space and the moods of material nature are produced from material nature. (Bhagavad Gītā 13.20)

The spiritual personality, the coreSelf, is partially expressed through a physical body. When a self is freed from having to share its energy with material nature, it can experience its person radiance.

Then the changes of the living space and the moods of nature become a distant event which were relevant when the self was inducted in the enterprises of Nature.

Material nature is said to be the cause in terms of created work, sensual potency and agency. The spiritual personality is said to be the cause in terms of experiencing pleasure and pain. (Bhagavad Gītā 13.21)

In the study about death, there must be clarification about the physical person, regarding its dissolution as a functional living body. What, if anything, will remain from the physical system when it perishes?

If the person is only a physical system with bio-electrical parts, then the inquiry into death ends with the cellular destruction of the body. Otherwise, to catalogue it, a non-physical inquiry begins.

The self is plagued with pleasure and pain. Those are sensations felt by the personality. Krishna tags the spiritual personality part of the psyche as the cause of those feelings.

However, since the self may feel that it is the cause in terms of created work, sensual potency, and agency, then to make sense of Krishna's denial of this, the self must detach itself from the sensations, and observe them from a neutral position. This must be done repeatedly during meditation and even during states when one is extrovertedly focused. Most of the practice must be completed before death of the physical body.

The spirit, being situated in material nature, experiences the modes which were produced by that nature. Attachment to the modes is the cause of the spirit's emergence from realistic and unrealistic situations. (Bhagavad Gītā 13.22)

The psychic aspects of the physical person should be sorted. Once this is achieved, the spirit or coreSelf should be segregated. If one is unable to do this, one should study the theory of the self from *Bhagavad Gītā* and supportive literature.

After understanding the theory of this information, one should learn meditation to eradicate the ignorance in the psyche. Chapter two of *Bhagavad Gītā* has details about sorting the intellect from the coreSelf. That is *buddhi* yoga, the meditative and physical practice of isolating the analysis equipment from the observing self. When *buddhi* yoga is achieved, *atma* yoga or the focus on the uninfluenced coreSelf should be practiced.

The core is less than the physical person, because it is the corePerson with assistance from psychic adjuncts, which when linked to a physical body, is summarized as the full physical person. When that physical format is no longer sensitive to the core and its adjuncts, that remnant something is termed as a subtle body. Then it experiences subtle material nature only. However due to an innate attachment to Nature, this self is attached to the various fluctuation of Nature. This is why it experiences and is conveyed through realistic and unrealistic situations, which traumatize it.

If one does not understand this theoretically, and if one does not practice to perceive these operations of Nature, one will be drawn into a haphazard rebirth, involuntarily becoming again an embryo of some species of life. One will have no choice in the matter. One will only comply with the process.

The observer, the permitter, the supporter, the experiencer, the Supreme Lord and the Supreme Soul as He is called, He is the highest spirit in the body. (Bhagavad Gītā 13.23)

There are basically two observers, permitters, supporters, and experiencers, in a psyche. One is the Supreme Soul, the highest personSelf in the body. The other is the limited self. This one is documented and checkmated repeated. This one is influenced by its sense of identity, its intellect, its memories, and its sensual feelings. This limited one is insensitive to the superior person, who is the Supreme Soul.

The limited self, is as much a person, as the Supreme Soul, except that the limited one is irresistibly attracted to the displays of Nature, whereby for the most part, he/she is inattentive to the opinions of the Supreme One. This causes regret on the part of the limited one who consents to actions, which cause anguish and short-term happiness.

He who knows the spiritual person and material nature, along with the variations of material nature, is not born again, regardless of his present condition. (Bhagavad Gītā 13.24)

A certain degree of objectivity is required to gain exemption from rebirth. As it is, each physical person is tagged with specific associations and conditions of existence, which put him/her under a course of evolution, and under subjugation of pressures, which cause him/her to be born again. This is done under the auspices of material nature with little input from the Supreme Being.

To twist oneself from this, one must increase the submission to the God, and reduce one's attraction to Nature. Since this requires massive mental and emotional detachment, it is abnormal for most entities. But if somehow, by the grace of God, someone can single out the spiritual person, and sort what of the self is material nature, recognizing the variations of Nature which are misleading, that person is likely to resist the compelling cycle of involuntary death, then birth, then death, then birth, over and over.

Some perceive the spirit by the spirit through meditative perception of the spirit. Others do so with Sāṁkhya philosophical conclusions and others by yogic disciplined action. (Bhagavad Gītā 13.25)

The untangling actions are mystic movements made to sort what is spirit, and what runs parallel to it, but which is not of the same enduring quality. It happens in meditation (*dhyānena*) that one perceives the radiant coreSelf in contrast to the analytical faulty which drums thoughts, ideas, images, and memories.

There are other methods. For instance, a person may study the *Sāṁkhya* philosophical conclusions, which Krishna taught Uddhava. Some persons by imbibing that information, do contemplations which actuate the supernatural senses.

Others merely by yogic disciplined action, functioning with detachment while acting socially, feel the subtle body as distinct from the physical one, even though one is interspaced in the other. This causes a pin-pointing in consciousness where the person can realize that consciousness outshines physical life.

But some, though they are ignorant, hear from others. They worship and by their confidence in what is heard, they also transcend death. (Bhagavad Gītā 13.26)

There are cases of devotees of Krishna who did not practice yoga and did not become proficient at transcendental meditation, and still these persons developed a resistance to haphazard rebirth. Such people did during the earthly life hear about Krishna and/or read about him. Somehow they accepted the authority of Krishna.

Merely by confidence in Krishna's statements and in subsidiary information given by great yogis and devotees,

some persons who lacked mystic perception, experienced a
psychic transformation and transcended death.

**As for anything that is produced in this existence, be it a
stationary or moving object, know, O strong man of the
Bharatas, that it is produced from a synthesis of the experiencer
and the living space. (Bhagavad Gītā 13.27)**

Whatever happens in this environment, regardless of if it
is alive or dead, stationary, or mobile, all of it, is a synthesis of
the experiencer and the living space. In any direction, up or
down, in or out, one will find those two factors. However, it is
multi-dimensional, such that one's sense perception may not
grasp it. When one perceives nothing, that does not mean the
absence of everything. It should be concluded that one has
insufficient sense perception.

**The Supreme Lord is similarly situated in all beings
without perishing when they disintegrate. He who perceives
that, really sees. (Bhagavad Gītā 13.28)**

Verification for the existence of God is hard to attain.
Basically, one has two ways of perception. The obvious
method is to use the senses of either the physical or subtle
body. That gives perception of what exist side by side in the
physical world and in the astral existence. But there is another
perception which is perception in the psyche. This means in
the physical body or in the subtle form. This internal vision is
developed by yoga practice.

The first step is to perceive the coreSelf in the psyche.
Seeing God in the self means seeing God in the psychic
compartment of the subtle body. This is because the self itself
resides in that psyche with its adjuncts. When someone says
that he/she meditates in the self, the meaning is that the
meditation is based on inner focus within the psychic container
which houses the self and its adjuncts.

However, Krishna gives more information, stating that the
Supreme Lord also exists in the psyche. The discovery of this
Supreme Person is difficult. In the first effort, the discovery of

the coreSelf is a rare achievement. That core is so subtle, that even to itself it is hard for it to perceive itself. And the Supreme Lord is more abstract even. That makes it extremely rare for one to perceive the God in the psyche.

As for seeing God in his environment, one must first go to that place. One must also have spiritual senses while residing in God's domain. If one transits there somehow but does not have the spiritual sense perception, one will not see the divine being.

Even here in this world, if a mammal is born blind, it cannot see the environment which it discovers itself in. One may be in an environment and not perceive the objects which are present. One may transit to a transcendental plane and not perceive a single object there. These are the difficulties.

Seeing the same Lord being situated everywhere, he does not degrade the soul by his own soul. Subsequently, he goes to the supreme destination. (Bhagavad Gītā 13.29)

When an advanced yogi, or a blessed spiritual-perception devotee, has direct perception about the Supreme Lord being in the psyche of every limited entity, that devotee experiences a checking force which does not allow self degradation. Over time, he/she transits to the supreme destination. This happens during the life of the physical body and when that body becomes unresponsive and is declared, dead.

The variety in this world is present even in the uniqueness of the limited entities, but it is a single God who inhabits the various entities, even though the deity is in a dimension which is remote, and which transcends even the radiance of the limited selves.

It is compulsory, that if one does not have the vision of the presence of the Supreme Lord in every psyche, one will be distracted by other influences, which will result in actions which cause the degradation of the self.

He who sees, that in all cases, the actions are performed by material nature, and who regards himself as a non-doer, truly sees. (Bhagavad Gītā 13.30)

Before death, it is imperative that the self understands that it has a limited position as part of the development of its physical body and the environment. This realization is part of the preparation for death. If one knows this, one will know that death is inevitable. The remnant features which survive death, are the issue.

As a concept, the form of the self poses as a physical body but that is the self with a mask covering. It is not the self in fact. For the most, the self may be the subtle body, the event wanderer who acts psychically in dream experiences. But even that is not the self, as the subtle body may be discovered to be a container, in which is housed psychic energy, a focusing observer, an analytical faculty, memory, and sensual apparatus. What then is the segregated self? It is the focusing observer.

The question is. How can this bare self be isolated? The sorting process is done in advanced meditation. Then it is realized that the focusing observer is a combine of a sense of identity and a coreSelf. Both the sense of identity and the core, are transparent. Each is neutral. However, there is notation which is that each has inclination for dependence. Each is subjected to influences.

The person who sees that in all cases, the personal or impersonal actions are performed by material nature, and who regards himself as an energy-providing factor, truly understands this situation. This does not mean that this person is free to be inactive only. This person has the insight but he/she does not have the absolute authority to desist from all actions.

When a person sees that all the various states of being are based on a single foundation, and only from that everything emanates, then he reaches the spiritual plane. (Bhagavad Gītā 13.31)

One must do more than see intellectually that the various states of being are based on a single foundation. The perception must induce the individual to act while respecting the whole existence, and the individual who is the ultimate entity. A limited self must realize itself as an unnecessary accessory, which is useful to this totality. That transfers the person to the spiritual plane.

Since this imperishable Supreme Lord is beginningless and devoid of the influence of material nature, even though He is situated in the material body, O son of Kuntī, He does not act or become contaminated. (Bhagavad Gītā 13.32)

There is a difference between the Supreme Lord and the limited entity. The highlight of that is the Lord's neutrality in reference to the influence of material nature. For the limited self, material nature is challenging. It swipes the limited beings and affects their attitudes and responses. Some of the limited selves escapes from total dominance but many are held by it repeatedly.

Even though the Supreme Lord is situated in the psyche, he transcends its influences, but the limited selves are affected. They are required to react to its physical and psychic operations. By itself, Nature cannot fling itself into manifestation. It relies on the power of God and the limited selves. However, the limited ones cannot fully govern their liaison with it.

As by subtlety, the all-pervading space is not polluted, so the soul, though situated all over the body, is not affected actually. (Bhagavad Gītā 13.33)

From one perspective the limited self, the soul, is not affected, but when it is involved either voluntarily or involuntarily it feels fluctuations as if those were its energy. Hence it is affected but it is also not affected.

Nature in any physical or psychic aspect, cannot bring about the dilution of the limited self. The core's radiance is constant. The problem is in its sharing of its energy with the

Nature. It feels this sharing but at no stage does its power become exhausted. The core cannot be used to a finish, where it is reduced to nothing. When its involvement with Nature causes it to be somewhat expended, the association between itself and nature is automatically suspended.

As the sun alone illuminates the whole world, O man of the Bharata family, so the user of the living space gives feeling to the entire psyche. (Bhagavad Gītā 13.34)

Material nature is a power which challenges the coreSelf, the spiritual person. However, as the user of the psyche, the core gives feelings to the entire psyche. In the physical body, in the subtle form, the self energizes the potency of nature. This is how the individual experiences through its psyche.

Those who by intuitive perception know the difference between the living space and the experiencer, as well as the liberation of the living being from material nature, go to the Supreme. (Bhagavad Gītā 13.35)

The death situation, the transit of the self from its physical body, varies from person to person. Due to millions of dimensions, there is no telling where someone will transfer to or be transferred to, soon after being deprived of the use of a physical body.

In the astral existence hereafter, a bigger issue is stability. Who knows for how long a departed person will be in any astral place? In comparison, those in the physical existence can rely on gradual decay of the materials. Rarely is there rapid deterioration.

Before the physical system dies, the partitions in the psychic world should be known. One should develop the intuition to know the difference between the psyche, and the coreSelf, which is the main resident of it. This psyche will transit out of the physical body which was patterned like it.

The Blessed Lord said: I will explain more, giving the highest information of all knowledges, the very best. Having experienced that, all the yogi philosophers went away from here to the Supreme Perfection. (Bhagavad Gītā 14.1)

To achieve the Supreme Perfection, one is required to understand the material nature, and the spiritual personalities. This must be understood intellectually at first but that must be developed into direct mystic perception.

Resorting to this experience, being transformed into a nature that is similar to My own, they are not born even at the time of the universal creation, nor are they disturbed at the time of dissolution. (14.2)

The Supreme Perfection includes direct experience of the relationship between Nature and the individual selves, as well as the dimensions which are available to the selves, and the situation and remoteness of the Supreme Person.

One who becomes focused on the origins, experiences a transition to a nature which is similar to Krishna's. That permits exemption from being born at the time of the universal creation and being suspended at its dissolution. It is because such a person is not sapped by a relationship with Nature. His/Her radiance is not consumed inefficiently by the Nature's proximity.

The extensive mundane reality is My womb. I impregnate the essence into it. The origin of all beings comes from that reality, O man of the Bharata family. (Bhagavad Gītā 14.3)

Even though the immediate crisis is the upcoming death of the physical body. That by itself is not a shocking event. The ongoing trouble is the involuntary use of the self's psychic powers by the mundane energy.

To understand how the self is linked to Nature, to figure if the self can either restrict, or terminate the use of its powers by nature, *that is investigation*.

Krishna informed that the extensive mundane reality is His womb. He claims that he impregnates the cosmic lifeForce into it. That combination produces all beings in the material world. That is our involvement. The solution is that even though the limited self is involved here, it did not select to do so.

It discovered itself to be in this situation when its existence entered an objective awareness phase. The realization is that since it did not cause itself to be aware here, it is likely that it cannot by itself free itself from Nature's association. It should sponsor a relationship with the Supreme Person and get from him a method of release from this situation.

Forms are produced in all types of wombs, O son of Kuntī, I am the seed-giving father. The extensive mundane reality is the great womb. (Bhagavad Gītā 14.4)

The material existence in its visible and invisible formats, is a cosmic womb, within which diverse forms are produced in all types of hatching chambers. Krishna presents himself as the cosmic impregnator.

The subtle part of this, the psychic parallel, is worthy of investigation. If the physical creatures had enduring forms, their focus into the physical world would be warranted. Since the physical selves do not endure, it is paramount that the remnant psychic aspects be recognized.

Clarity, impulsion and retardation are the influences produced of material nature. They captivate the imperishable embodied soul in the body, O strong-armed hero. (Bhagavad Gītā 14.5)

This is the explanation given by Krishna, regarding why the limited selves are in this creation and are dominated by its events. There are overriding influences which spread as physical or psychic perceptions. The selves cannot resist nor be objective to every display which they encounter.

The spreading influence of Nature will continue hereafter. At that time, there will be no relief from it. It will be pressing from all sides. Thus, it makes sense to tally the self's resistance while it is a physical system which awaits the ending of that body.

Regarding these influences, the clarifying one is relatively free from perceptive impurities. It is illuminating and free from disease, but by granting an attachment to happiness and to expertise, it captivates a person, O sinless one. (Bhagavad Gītā 14.6)

It is not freedom outright. When there is any, it is a choice of influences. There is no place where one or a combination of the three mood operations do not surface. A yogi must study each feature. He/She should learn how to recognize each, and sort the combinations which prevail in any event.

The clarifying influence is relatively free from perceptive impurities but that one, like the others, bullies the coreSelf just as well. However, if there is a choice, the yogi should agree so that the clarifying influence prevails. It the least of the obstructions. It yields the least unwanted trauma.

A self relies on this clarifying influence to cause accurate insight but it should be kept in mind, that there will be an attachment to happiness and to expertise, such that it is likely that one will do anything and everything to have happiness be the ongoing mood in the psyche. A yogi should resist becoming addicted to this clarifying energy.

Know that the impulsive influence is characterized by passion. It is produced from earnest desire and attachment. O son of Kuntī , this mode captivates the embodied soul by an attachment to activity. (Bhagavad Gītā 14.7)

The second influence is the impulsive one. This is characterized by passion. Under its influence, the self acts irrationally as if under a compulsion. Earnest desire and attachment are its urgency. That motivates the self to consent for acts which were not properly vetted.

But know that the depressing mode is produced of insensibility which is the confusion of all embodied beings. This captivates by inattentiveness, laziness and sleep, O man of the Bharata family. (Bhagavad Gītā 14.8)

The depressing influence of Nature benefits someone by inducing and enforcing sleep, which allows the lifeForce to refurbish the physical and subtle bodies. By producing inattentiveness and lazy states, it may influence a being negatively. It causes insensibility which results in intellectual confusion, wrong decision, and incorrect action.

The clarifying influence causes attachment to happiness. The impulsive one causes a need for action, O Bharata family man. But the depressing mode obscures experience and causes attachment to negligence. (Bhagavad Gītā 14.9)

A yogi should study the negative aspects of each of the three influences. One should avoid their overcast conditions so that one can be selective to get the best of each. The clarifying influence results in happiness but if someone becomes prone to that, he will make decisions and commit actions just for the enjoyment. This will result in wrong actions which will yield unpleasant feelings.

The median influence, the impulsive mode, causes a need for action, even when that should not be committed. The depressive mode dulls discrimination and presents procrastination as the solution.

One should self-critique inner behavior, monitor social interactions and adjust how one interacts with the environment within and without the psyche. The main focus should be to set the coreSelf and its adjuncts in order.

When predominating over impulsiveness and depression, clarity emerges, O Bharata family man. Depression rises, predominating over impulsiveness and clarity. Similarly, impulsion takes control over depression and clarity. (Bhagavad Gītā 14.10)

The three influences surround a person on all sides, both in the physical environment and in the subtle world. The moods are prevalent inside the psyche and outside of it. Understanding this and knowing their pervasive energies as facts, a yogi should be vigilant.

It is important to know when one is under the spell of a particular mode. The preference should be to be under the clarifying influence. When a lower mode is useful and must be accepted, one should carefully monitor it. For instance, when the physical body is tired, it is best to surrender it to the lowest of the influences, the depressive influence. But one should do so only for a limited time. One may also give the body over to the depressive mode while the astral body shifts to the clarifying influence. Then when the physical system was rested, the astral form may again become alert in it, assuming the clarifying mode in both the astral and physical situations of self.

When clear perception, true knowledge, is felt in all openings of the body, then it should be concluded that the clarifying mode is predominant. (Bhagavad Gītā 14.11)

A detailed understanding of the features of the psyche would be beneficial for preparing the self to make the transition from being a physical being to being a psychic one. No one should assume that he/she will get the best outcome hereafter. Just as in dreams, one may experience pleasant or unpleasant conditions, it is likely that the states one is shifted to at death, may be to one's liking, or it may be unpalatable.

To gain an advantage, one should do meditation to learn how to insist that the psyche has clear perception. The senses should be alert and should report truthfully about the environment. The lifestyle should be adjusted to facilitate the clarifying influence. Whatever one does during the life of the physical body which causes an increase in the influence of clarity, will be serviceable when that body dies, and the psychic form no longer has a physical parallel to relate to and control.

Greed, overexertion, rash undertakings, restlessness and craving, these are produced when impulsiveness is predominant, O strong man of the Bharatas. (Bhagavad Gītā 14.12)

Lifestyle adjustments must be made. The yogi must struggle with behavior which is counterproductive to the aims of yoga. He/She should rigidly check and recheck, gage and calibrate relationships, and even hidden actions, and wishes, which run contrary to the recommendations of yoga.

Until the yogi can find a way to either eliminate, or neutralize them, some unwanted features should be suppressed for the time being. The unwanted genetic urges in the physical body and the corrosive tendencies in the subtle one, which a yogi discovers but cannot eliminate, should be neutralize. This means that they should be disabled. These will continue existing in the psyche but with no action being committed on their behalf.

Greed, overexertion, rash undertakings, restlessness, and craving, are the expressive forces of the impulsive influence. The yogi can quiet these, where their operative powers become suspended, and do not dominate the psyche. In meditation, a yogi should strive to silence these urges.

Lack of clarity, lack of energy, inattentiveness and confusion emerge when depression is predominant, O dear son of the Kurus. (Bhagavad Gītā 14.13)

Each of the three influences have positive functions. Each have negative applications. Even the superior influence has a happy mood expression which is addictive and ruinous.

A yogi should study the positive applications as well as the negative uses. The activation of an influence may be involuntary, like for instance when drowsiness or sleep takes control of consciousness. To make this positive, a yogi should voluntarily surrender the physical body to slumber.

When there is confusion which is due to mental exhaustion, the yogi should position the body so that it can recuperate. When there is lack of clarity, a yogi should not push on with mental activity. The admittance is that with the observing self as an assistant, nature runs the operation of the body. If the self cooperates with the clarifying influence and facilitates the impulsive and retardative energies when they assist the clarifying mood, that yogi will get the best service from Nature.

When the embodied soul goes through the death experience while under the dominance of the clarifying mode, he is transferred to the pure worlds of those who know the Supreme. (Bhagavad Gītā 14.14)

The pure worlds of those who know the Supreme, is a range of transcendental territories where advanced selves abide. To reach that place after not being synchronized with the physical body, a yogi must practice during life, to conduct himself/herself under the dominance of the clarifying feature. If he consistently lives like this, he has no other special effort to make during the physical life. His conduct will be as dictated into his mind by the influence of the highest mode of Nature.

If one did not apply the self consistently to the highest mode during the life of the body, one cannot suddenly confirm to it at the time of death.

Having gone through the death experience in the impulsive mode, the soul is born among the work-prone people; likewise when dying in the depressive mode, the soul takes birth from the wombs of the ignorant species. (Bhagavad Gītā 14.15)

The state of mind at the time of death has a heavy bearing, on where someone will be present, after being psychically disconnected from the physical body. The general attitude towards people and circumstances during the life of the physical body, prevails at the time of death, such that those who are generally in the impulsive mode, will gravitate towards materialistic people, who will copulate to produce an embryo.

Those whose moods are usually expressive of the depressive mode, are attracted to people, and creatures who are motivated by that energy. They come out again as progeny of humans or animals, who are driven by the depressive energies.

Those who are anchored in clarity, go upward. Those who are impulsive are situated in the middle. Those who are habituated to the lowest influence of the material energy, the retarded people, go downward. (Bhagavad Gītā 14.18)

The passage from this physical focus to the psychic one at death, begins during the life of the body. It begins when the entity's psyche becomes emotionally interlocked with that of the parents. Whatever condition the entity assumes at any time, can be the basis for its next presence. The changing altering condition is what matters, not the belief structure nor lofty aspirations. As the bright ideas of a poverty-stricken man has no impact on his poor condition, so the hopes for divinity or heaven after death, does not affect the stark reality of a dead religious man.

People who are anchored in clarity, provided they do not digress to physical focus, are guaranteed to go upward. But if they are mostly anchored in the influence of clarity but habitually or by duty, swim down to lower levels, they are likely to take birth under one or the other two modes. This is the answer to question as to why a saintly man is sometimes discovered to commit actions which are questionable.

Those who are impulsive by nature, and who have leanings towards clarity, should execute self-discipline, so as to wean themselves from the advantages of impulsion, and train their adjuncts to become attached to the clarifying influence. But as for those who are saturated by the lowest influence, those retarded people will go downward. They are pulled to lower habits which reinforces their stagnation.

When the observer perceives no performer besides the influences of material nature and knows what is higher than those influences, he reaches My level of existence. (Bhagavad Gītā 14.19)

The arrival at Krishna's level of existence is an existential, rather than locational one. It can be both but at the minimum it is existential, where the yogi devotee may be using a physical body, and participating in physical history, and still be in contact with the realm of Krishna, and with the perceptual privileges, which anyone has who contacts those dimensions.

The yogi devotee may be totally translated to Krishna's realm, where that ascetic is unaware of this earthly situation, and is only present elsewhere, in dimensions which have no exhibition, nor motivation from Nature, as we experienced it on this plane of existence.

During the life of the physical body, one should make it one's habit to regularly shift from physical focus. One must also come to know that Nature is the prime mover here, and that all other actors, the limited entities, render expression of glaring power, which is used by Nature in its operations, but with an entity being tagged with responsibilities, according to how its radiance is consumed by Nature.

When the embodied soul transcends these three influences of material nature which are formulated in the body, he is released from birth, death, old age, and distress, and attains immortality. (Bhagavad Gītā 14.20)

Even if someone is not a Krishna devotee, even if that person never heard of Krishna, and has no idea of Krishna's existence, or even has no view about a Supreme Person, that someone if somehow, he/she transcends the three influences of Nature which comprised the psychological content of his body, he/she is released from birth, death, old age, and distress.

No matter who he is, or what his beliefs are, the immortality of an entity is a principled fact. He only has to repossess himself by tapping into origins. A limited entity does not have to believe in Krishna to become immortal. He/She is perpetual regardless. The spiritual status of a self, is a reality no matter what, no matter if that entity is unaware of its perpetuity.

The key factor is focus. If the perpetual entity focusses on what is temporary, he/she will experience the running shifts of that, and will draw conclusions in reference to that. As the reference for itself, a self will rely on its focus, which means that it will feel perpetual if it is in contact with what is enduring. Otherwise, it will sag accordingly.

The Blessed Lord said: The yogi sages say that there is an imperishable Ashvattha tree which has a root going upwards and a trunk downwards, the leaves of which are the Vedic hymns. He who knows this is a knower of the Vedas. (Bhagavad Gītā 15.1)

Nature is a converse configuration. It is something that is perpetual but only as its origin. Its expressions are in alteration at all times. Because of a need for position, we are of the view that we can make this Nature stand its ground. However, there is no hope for that. This Nature will perpetually change and yet, its origin is stable even though we do not perceive how that is so.

Branches spread from it, upwards and downwards. It is nourished by the mundane influences and the attractive objects are its sprouts. The roots are spread below, promoting action in the world of human beings. (Bhagavad Gītā 15.2)

Now, at this time, the selves should figure the design of Nature. One should spend the greater part of this life, cracking the code of this existence of which we are a part. For the time being, we have some objective awareness which should be used to discover the ins and outs of this cosmic and local situation.

The fantastic scenes which bewilder us, the extensive operation of this cosmic engine, the chaos which we are constantly being threatened by, the overpowering psychic and even physical formation influences, should be investigated. Can we discover a reference, which we can use to navigate this ocean of terrible wonders?

This Nature, this tree-like structure is a living organism. That is its mystery. As bacteria float through arteries, so we travel on a planet which floats through outerspace. This bewildering reality which is ever-altering is a puzzle to be solved.

Its form is not perceived in this dimension, nor its end, nor beginning nor foundation. With the strong ax of non-attachment, cut down this Ashvattha tree with its well-developed roots. (Bhagavad Gītā 15.3)

The attempt to comprehend this cosmic situation is both a physical endeavor and a psychic one. Unfortunately, a limited entity is equipped with limited senses, and cannot on its own grasp the total situation. Even when compared to some other species, the human sensual range is challenged, as for instance, in the case of vision, which many birds have greater range. In every sense, there is a creature which has a greater sensing capability.

On the psychic front, we are limited. We cannot see dead people. We cannot see the atomic activity. Even if one performs mystic practice and restricts physical sensual interaction, still, one would acquire only partial insight.

The form of the psychic Nature is not perceived in this dimension. Neither its end, nor beginning, nor foundation is visible to our sensual perception. Arjuna was instructed that to curtail, and perhaps remove its influence, he should with the strong ax of non-attachment, cut down his reliance on Nature which has well developed roots, which feeds on everyone who is attached to it.

Such a discipline should be done during the life of the physical body. The resulting detachment would render the yogi with a subtle body, which has psychic perception during the lifetime, and increased intuition hereafter.

The detachment from Nature is a curtailment of the reliance on it. But then, the yogi should redirect his endeavor energy to find that place which is to be researched. He should aggressively pursue that place, the location which frees a self from the need to return to this world after death.

While the gravity of this world which pulls the selves to it, is its stability, the adhesive which attracts a self to the divine situation, is its compatibility to the quality of consciousness of the segregated coreSelf, an existence with no misleading adjuncts.

It is natural for such a yogi, to have the attitude that he takes shelter with that Primal Person, the Supreme Lord, from Whom the creation emerged in primeval time.

Those who are devoid of pride and confusion, who have conquered the faults of attachment, who constantly stay with the Supreme Spirit, whose cravings have ceased, who are freed from the dualities known as pleasure and pain, these undeluded souls go to that imperishable place. (Bhagavad Gītā 15.5)

A yogi must strive for this within the lifespan of the physical body. If he/she fails to achieve that, the endeavor may continue on an astral level hereafter. Or if he/she is unable to maintain subtle existence, and takes another physical body, the instinct for the quest will prompt efforts for this in the new life.

Eventually a time will come when the yogi always resumes the quest when he/she has a physical body. Then in time, a final effort will succeed so that he/she is not attracted to physical history. With the pressure to be physical gone, that person, being devoid of pride and confusion, who conquered the faults of attachment, and who constantly stays with the Supreme Spirit, with cravings ceased, being freed from the dualities of pleasure and pain, will go to that imperishable place, having lost the need for physical history.

The sun does not illuminate that place, nor the moon, nor the fire. Having gone to that location, they never return. That is My supreme residence. (Bhagavad Gītā 15.6)

Krishna described his supreme residence as being self-illuminated with all materials there having inner and outer illumination, there being no need for a sun, moon nor fire. For humans the need for light for seeing and heating, is a craving. On earth, it is provided by Nature through some luminaries and combustive materials. Without that this universe would be a cold and dark place. But the spiritual world is different. It is where reliance on heavenly bodies and flammable materials is absent.

My partner is in this world of individualized conditioned beings. He is an eternal individual soul but he draws to himself the mundane senses of which the mind is the sixth detection device. (Bhagavad Gītā 15.7)

There are personality and materials. This existence comprises both, but with the personalities being interspaced or completely segregated from the materials. There are cores to the personalities but this depends on the combination formats of the psyche of the individual.

In this world, the majority of persons are conditioned individual selves, such that the core of the person is masked by many materials, thus blinding the core. There is a magnetic attraction between the conditioned individuals and the materials. This causes the core to be other than its bare self, to be a combination being with adjuncts which adhere to it.

Even though a limited self is eternal (*sanātanaḥ*) he/she attracts the mundane senses of which the mind is the sixth detection device. Accordingly, one is prejudiced due to reliance for interpretation on adjuncts.

There is a concern about this however. The God regards the individualized conditioned being as his partner. God has a responsibility to arouse them from the drowsy state which prevents them from gaining full insight.

Regardless of whichever body that master acquires, or whichever one he departs from, he goes taking these senses along, just as the wind goes with the perfumes from their source. (Bhagavad Gītā 15.8)

In so far as one considers the self to be identical with its physical body, that someone loses some of itself when the physical system dies. Even though our perception of a self is based on its physical acts, it psychic register persists after death.

Regardless of how it was born, or how it came into being, someone's death means that he/she took his/her psychic sensuality. These drift with him/her through the psychic existence, just as the wind goes with the perfumes from their sources. Death is physical absence only. Death does not abolish psychic presence.

There is a coreSelf which is impeccable, and which is imperishable. There is also a coreSelf with clean adjuncts. This person will persist with changes until the end of time. It does not mean however that the coreSelf is perpetually objective to itself or to anything else. The objectivity may be suspended by natural and supernatural motions.

From the perspective of being a physical body, the personSelf is transcendental to that physical system. It is the core with tarnished adjuncts. Because the adjustments vary from time to time, this personSelf fluctuates but with the original spiritual self enduring.

Regardless of the species, at death of the physical system or at the onset of the life of it, the remnant self transits to another dimension or location. It takes the psychic senses with it, just as the wind goes with the perfumes from their sources. It has no choice in the matter because it is fused to its adjuncts.

While governing the sense of hearing, the vision, the sense of touch, the sense of taste, the sense of smell and the mind, My partner becomes addicted to the attractive objects. (Bhagavad Gītā 15.9)

Even though the self is addicted to the attractive objects, it feels justified in doing so. This is because it became aware of itself in this event which is the earth's history.

The objectivity of the self is further deceased by its involvement with the sense of hearing, the vision, the sense of touch, the sense of taste, the sense of smell and the mind. Most of these utilities are involuntary. No choice is made by the self, for it is influenced supernaturally. It takes special austerity to gain some detachment from the decisions projected by the senses in the psyche.

The dismissal of a self from this physical event, means that its subtle senses, and their required supports, must be disconnected from its physical body. The physical application of its psychic presence ceases, but in the subtle world everything else remains as is.

The idiots do not perceive how the spirit departs or remains or exploits under the influence of material nature. But those who have the vision of reality do perceive this. (Bhagavad Gītā 15.10)

Many human beings lack the insight to know or even speculate about the perpetuity of a self. They have no idea about the departure of a spirit, regarding if it becomes irrelevant to this situation, and applicable to any other.

The endeavoring yogis see the spirit as being situated in itself; but even with exertion, the imperfected souls, the thoughtless ones, do not perceive it. (Bhagavad Gītā 15.11)

Some people have intuition about the coreSelf. Others are oblivious to it and consider only physical reality as of substance. This makes it obvious that each person is endowed with varying degrees of insight.

Most of the persons who believe in a perpetual self, have no perceptive evidence about it. This is because it is difficult to sort the self from its adjuncts, which assist it in detecting whatever exists besides the self.

And I entered the central psyche of all beings. From Me comes memory, knowledge and reasoning. By all the Vedas, I am to be known. I am the author of Vedānta and the knower of the Vedas. (Bhagavad Gītā 15.15)

Due to a lack of control over memory, knowledge, and reasoning, a limited self is not guaranteed objective perpetuity but it should assume that it is eternal but with limited objectivity.

The Supreme Being subsidizes the deficiency in the limited person by providing some memory, knowledge, and reasoning. The shuffle of these psychological aspects is governed by the God in consideration of the needs of the limited persons.

These two types of spirits are in this world, namely the affected ones and the unaffected ones. All mundane creatures are affected. The stable soul is said to be unaffected. (Bhagavad Gītā 15.16)

The degree of affectation is the measure of influence over a coreSelf which exists in association with Nature. The environmental influence is both physical and psychic, with its psychic spread being the prevailing force, as it is applied while the self behaves as a physical body, and while that self does not have the means to do so.

Broadly speaking there are two categories of spirits with each type having many sub-divisions. It is listed by how it can ignore, resist or be non-impervious to the urges of Nature.

Those who without restraining themselves can ignore Nature, are rated in the highest category, that of being unaffected. This is not based on a plan to resist but on the quality of the spirit itself.

But the highest spirit is in another category. He is called the Supreme Spirit, Who having entered the three worlds as the eternal Lord, supports it. (Bhagavad Gītā 15.17)

This is a similarity between the personSelf of the limited spirit and that of the Supreme Being, in that apart from being individuals perpetually, they inhabit a psyche. Despite this, the limited spirit is prone to being influence by the adjuncts it uses. But the Supreme Spirit is transcendental to the cosmic being which it is.

The eternal Lord supports the cosmic manifestation, and to an extent the limited spirit contributes to the support of his/her psyche. While the limited spirit must take help from God and Nature, the Supreme Lord fully supports and is a necessary contributor to the cosmic situation.

As an act of existence itself, the eternal Lord makes Nature perceptible, and then inhabits, and supports it. The limited selves are assailed by this cosmic manifestation. In fact, we are bewildered by it.

Since I am beyond the affected spirits and I am even higher than the unaffected ones, I am known in the world and in the Vedas as the Supreme Person. (Bhagavad Gītā 15.18)

This is the pronouncement of Krishna, as the Supreme Person. What can be said about it? Who can deny this? Who can prove this?

There is sufficient evidence in our experience for inferior, superior, novel, or ordinary, people and things. Whatever is the source of this creation, can be understood as being diverse with complete and incomplete, fragmental and total, competent and incompetent, features.

I constantly hurl the despising cruel, vicious, lowest of humans into the cycles of rebirth in the wombs of wicked people. (Bhagavad Gītā 16.19)

Apart from the innate attraction we have to particular features of this existence, there are impositions of Nature and the mystic actions cast from the mind of God. These may be in a person's favor.

A person's disruptive behavior or his positive acts, attract unfavorable or favorable reactions. Some of these reflexively reach the actor. Some come as a result of the blessings or curses from other limited entities, and from superior ones.

Rebirth is a natural process, a recurring procedure. It has spaces in it, where a supernatural being may intercede to promote desirable opportunities, or to cause further degradation, by assigning someone to a dysfunctional human birth environment, or an animal womb

Thus, O son of Kuntī, entering the wombs of the wicked people, the blockheads, after not associating with Me in birth after birth, traverse the lowest route of transmigration. (Bhagavad Gītā 16.20)

There is an evolutionary pressure in material nature. This has a subtle body application, but it is illustrated in the physical world, through the appearance of various species of life.

Even without divine influence, someone would strive to gain a higher footing, as he transmigrates in or through various species of life. Nature applies a pressure such that an entity feels that he/she should accomplish improved situation and dominance.

There is an uplifting pressure which is applied by the presence of the Supreme Lord. From the bottom, there is a pushing force. From the top there is a pulling force. These complement each other. These are applied by Nature and the Supreme Lord respectively.

At some point, a limited entity realizes the presence of these two influences. He/She utilizes this. Those who respond only to the Nature energy, who ignore, or simply fail to detect the influence of the Supreme Person, take to a non-productive degrading lifestyle. From the astral side, when no physical body is used, deviant people enter the wombs of wicked persons.

Due to not associating with Krishna, in birth after birth, someone who is insensitive to his influence, takes many bodies in the lowest species, or in the lowest of human families.

Craving, anger and greed are the three avenues of hell which degrade the soul. Therefore one should abandon this threefold influence. (Bhagavad Gītā 16.21)

During the life of the body, someone should act in a way which is likely to yield positive circumstances hereafter, and in the future physical life, if there is to be one. The senses should be monitored so that addiction to pleasure is not developed. If anyone becomes addicted, he/she will commit violence to procure whatever features support the unwanted habits. This will project the entry to a hellish life here and hereafter.

Being released from these three avenues of depression, O son of Kuntī, a person serves his best interest and then goes to the highest destination. (Bhagavad Gītā 16.22)

Courses of behavior will be developed. That is the way of Nature. We observe it even with the animals. A yogi should study how particular urges encourage their corresponding habits, and how certain lifestyles sink a person to a hellish condition in this physical world, with the likelihood that it will continue on the psychic planes hereafter.

Whosoever discards the scriptural injunctions, and follows the impulsive inclinations, does not get perfection or happiness or the supreme destination. (Bhagavad Gītā 16.23)

The individual should behave for his/her self-interest, not just in the short term by fulfillment of urges for pleasure, but also in the long term. One should learn that a short-term fulfilment, which is immediate and pleasant, may result in long term anguish and dissatisfaction.

The Blessed Lord said: According to innate tendency, there are three types of confidences of the embodied souls. These are clarifying, motivating and depressing. Hear about this. (Bhagavad Gītā 17.2)

The three influences are ever-present. They cannot be abolished. They are a perpetual part of the Nature energy. It is a matter of which of the influences will prevail on an individual.

Each person's attraction to these energies varies, where generally in one individual, a certain percentage of the clarifying, motivating and depressing energies prevail.

A yogi should self-observe to know how he is influenced to make preferences. He/She should curtail unwanted moods and urges, and accommodate more of the desired features. There is a psychic portion of these influences. That part will go with the person to the psychic side of existence when his/her body dies. Hence it is in someone's interest to act in a saintly manner during the life of the physical system.

Confidence becomes manifest according to the essential nature of the person, O man of the Bharata family. A human being follows his trend of confidence. Whatever type of faith he has, that he expresses only. (Bhagavad Gītā 17.3)

Even though someone repeats his/her behavior, it is still possible for someone to change persistent habits. But that requires effort at self-restriction and self-application. There must be a certain amount of exertion before a persistent habit would be altered. Even if it is changed, it may not remain so for a long time, as the psyche regularly resumes its bad behavior.

As Krishna stated, a human being follows his trend of confidence. Whatever faith in whatever principle or action he commits, that he repeatedly expresses. This is the curse of behavior. Every yogi should realize this, and not understate the difficulty in establishing the required lifestyle.

The clear-minded people worship the supernatural rulers. The impulsive ones worship the passionate sorcerors and the cannibalistic humans. The others, the retarded people, petition the departed spirits and the hordes of ghosts. (Bhagavad Gītā 17.4)

It is not important to categorize oneself as being clear-minded, passionate, or retarded. The relevance is to realize what behaviors one exhibits which are in particular categories. Honesty in self-analysis is the cure. That will empower the individual to make changes. These adjustments must be applied with determination, where the yogi is committed to working with himself/herself for an extended period to bring about the necessary changes.

Association is important. If one is in relationship with saintly persons, it is likely that one will gain support to act in a pious way. Conversely, even a pious person may be degraded if he/she associated with a criminal-minded personality.

In the psychic world, as it is on earth, there are godly and devilish individuals. Thus, we find that clear-minded people worship the supernatural rulers. The impulsive ones worship the passionate sorcerers and the cannibalistic humans. The others, the retarded people, petition the departed spirits and the hordes of ghosts.

Once someone pins his behavior and can properly categorize it, he/she can take steps for self-upliftment, where step by step, there is gradual but certain elevation. It is a matter of side-stepping lower influences and substituting higher behaviors.

The Lord of all beings is situated in the central psyche, O Arjuna, causing all beings to transmigrate by His mystic power, just as if they were fixed to a spinning machine. (Bhagavad Gītā 18.61)

There are two personProjectile influences. The supervisory one is noted in this verse as the Lord of all beings who is situated in the central psyche of every living unit. His presence as the centralized personal force, causes the limited selves to transmigrate just as they were hurled about but kept harnessed to a spinning machine.

The elemental personProjectile is the limited personSelf which is influenced by other such selves and by Nature at large. This self, a relative being, is attracted to Nature's psychic and physical sense objects. Instead of absorbing the influence of the Supreme Lord, they feel compelled to access other urges. However, one can only do that in so far as the Supreme Lord does not hold one's attention.

With your whole being, go only to Him for shelter, O descendant of Bharata. You will attain the supreme security and the eternal place by His grace. (Bhagavad Gītā 18.62)

Now and hereafter, a yogi should sincerely and fully accept the influence of the Supreme Lord. He/She should abide by the requests of the Lord as they are itemized in the *Bhagavad Gita*.

Chapter 6
Anu Gītā Discourse

Anu Gītā is the conclusion of the *Bhagavad Gita*. It is vital for all readers of the *Bhagavad Gita*. It completes the study of the self and its opportunities as explained by Krishna. An ascetic spoke the *Anu Gita*, but he did that at the request of Krishna, who wanted to convince the *Yadu* family group about the seriousness of preparing to transmigrate from physical existence.

After the battle of *Kurukshetra*, with their enemies dead or effectively suppressed, Arjuna and his brothers relaxed. On one occasion when Krishna visited with them, Arjuna requested a repeat of the *Bhagavad Gītā* information and revelation. Krishna refused to indulge Arjuna. Instead, Krishna repeated the incidence of the ascetic *siddha* who instructed the *Yadu* clan. *Anu Gītā* specifically targets the destinations hereafter, and the methods of achieving those places, by lifestyle adjustments.

Janamejaya said: O brahmin, while sitting at leisure in the state assembly-hall, after eliminating their opponents, what discussions transpired between Keshava Krishna and Arjuna? (Anu Gītā 1.1)

This discussion occurred after the Battle of *Kurukshetra*. Its prelude was the *Bhagavad Gītā* which was delivered openly on the battlefield. Both conversations provide technical information on birth, death, and commencement of existence in some place, here or hereafter.

The *Bhagavad Gītā* was delivered in a tense atmosphere when millions of soldiers confronted each other. Their weapons signified death.

However, after the opponents of Arjuna were silenced by death, Arjuna and his brothers, the victors, established the kingdom and began to enjoy the sovereignty. It was at this time, that Arjuna realized that the revelation of the Universal Form and the information given by Krishna which concerned the supernatural existence, was not in the forefront of his mind.

He was vacant of it. This caused Arjuna to request a repeat of the information and revelation. *Janamejaya*, a great grandson of Arjuna was curious to know what Krishna and Arjuna said to each other in the leisurely atmosphere of peace time. He inquired from *Vaiśampāyana* about the verbal exchange between his great grandfather and Krishna.

The questionnaire of Arjuna about the Battle of *Kurukshetra,* concerned the implications and liabilities of political violence. The answers from Krishna focused on these ideas.

Every soldier on the battlefield was a perpetual being, who used a physical body, which would be killed either on the battlefield or elsewhere.

Fate is supervised by a supreme being, who was revealed as the central figure in the Universal Form, which Krishna displayed to Arjuna.

A person's lifestyle results in a certain fate hereafter, where he/she may again become a physical being, or may go to some psychic or spiritual locale.

Krishna is the Supreme Lord. It is in a limited self's interest to comply with Krishna ideas.

Vaiśampāyana said: Having autonomously secured his kingdom, the son of Pṛthā, in the company of Krishna, enjoyed with delight that luxurious assembly-hall. (Anu Gītā 1.2)

This is sad because of the portrait of Arjuna painted by Vaiśampāyana. This is to be regretted by all devotees, and by yogi-devotees as well. This was a sarcastic remark about Arjuna's behavior after the war. It does however portray accurately, Arjuna's general attitude of self-importance, but it was something to respect. It was not an empty boast, nor a statement of arrogance. Arjuna was in fact, one of the greatest warriors who ever lived.

Someone may deduce that Arjuna was the greatest. Then his attitude would be justified as being mere fact. Yes, but as great of a warrior as he was, he was not the king of the country which he was engaged to defend. He was a brother of the King. That sovereign was *Yudhishthira*.

There is an idea however that Arjuna was special, and that his authority superseded that of the king. This is because Arjun has a special charioteer, who was Krishna, the self-declared, and generally accepted, Person of God. Some feel that since Krishna was cheeky with Arjuna, the importance of Yudhishthira as king was rightfully diminished.

That view however falls flat because *Yudhishthira* was an agent of Krishna. It was *Yudhishthira's* connection with Krishna which permitted that *Yudhishthira* was king. At the time of enjoying the kingdom after the battle, Arjuna felt that he won the battle. In fact, he did not. If anything, it was Krishna's disciplinary energy which saturated the victors, causing them to be victorious.

Review the statement again:

- *Vaiśaṁpāyana said: Having autonomously secured his kingdom, the son of Pṛthā, in the company of Krishna, enjoyed with delight that luxurious assembly-hall.*

Suppose it was announced like this:

- *Vaiśaṁpāyana said: Having with his four brothers, especially the king Yudhishthira, autonomously secured the kingdom, the son of Pṛthā, Arjuna, in the company of Krishna, and his brothers, enjoyed with delight that luxurious assembly-hall.*

As soon as Arjuna's mood included his brothers, especially King Yudhishthira, the mood changes, the behavior is adjusted, the inflated pride is reduced.

What was the ego crime committed? It was that Arjuna gave little or no importance to the empowerment of Krishna to Yudhishthira, or to anyone else for that matter.

A devotee must wonder if Lord Krishna noticed that Arjuna underrated Krishna's empowerment of Yudhishthira. Arjuna was of such a mood, that caused him to overrate his importance to Krishna. This is not healthy for a devotee of Krishna.

Once, O King, it so happened, that while enjoying together, those two companions went with their folk to an area of that place which was like being in the celestial world. (Anu Gītā 1.3)

It may be observed from the literature, that Krishna encouraged Arjuna to be proud of their friendship. However, it was up to Arjuna to realize the negative effects of their familiarity, where in more than one instance, Arjuna allowed that relationship to cause him to disrespected relationships, which Krishna had with other devotees. One must protect oneself from arrogance.

When a devotee becomes arrogant, the God may, or may not render a corrective treatment. Then it was up to the devotee to recover himself by sobering the mind, by recognizing the glory of other devotees. We repeatedly see that when a devotee is specially empowered by Krishna, that great personality may become affected negatively, where he insults, berates, and even manhandles other devotees, even when it is not his duty to do so.

This makes extra chores for Krishna, and for the other devotees, who notice the prideful attitude of the offending person. If a devotee does not self-observe his inflation, he will not act to correct himself. In other words, humility will not come to the rescue. That means that he will be ruined. Either

Krishna or another devotee would correct the offender, or that person is left to self-discover his defect, and to correct himself accordingly.

Even people who are rated as pure devotees or as teachers of devotees, or as incarnations of Krishna, may on occasion act offensively, based on misestimation of their value to Krishna. And of course, if not corrected promptly, anyone who does this is ruined.

The situation was such that Krishna and Arjuna were enjoying life on earth in a way which was comparable to that of life in the *Swarga* angelic realms. That is the astral domain of the Indra demigod. Compared to life on earth, that environment is heaven. It is not Krishna's residence which is described in *Bhagavad Gita*. Nevertheless, it is legendary for the enjoyment had by its denizens.

One can read between the lines. One may get the gist of what *Vaiśampāyana* conveyed, where Arjuna enjoyed himself to the fullest, while Krishna was detachedly involved. The way that Krishna does this is explained in *Bhagavad Gita*. Krishna encouraged Arjuna to be detached even while acting in the physical world, but Arjuna could not apply this advice in every circumstance.

Then being accompanied by Krishna, Arjuna, that son of Pandu, while viewing that delightful place, spoke these words: (Anu Gītā 1.4)

The presence of Krishna is such a wonderful event, that even the thought of it, brings happiness to a devotee. It causes wonderment!

Only in Krishna's presence will the devotee maintain a detached condition, and still commit to worldly events, even heavenly life on earth. But if a devotee switches or is switched to unrestricted enjoyment while being with Krishna in the physical world, then even then, that person will make incorrect inner movements, which Krishna will be aware of, and which may cause the Lord to retreat from the devotee. This is for the devotee's protection, and to service the responsibility of the Supreme Being for the puny self, which is a limited psyche.

It just happened to cross Arjuna's mind that something he self-observed should be presented to Krishna as a request for a favor.

The happiness and psychological release he enjoyed, after acting as the principal warrior on the battlefield, faded. With that a hazy memory of Krishna prebattle discourse, and the delivery of the Universal Form, came into focus. However, the recall was blurred. Despite its importance, Arjuna could not bring the information and supernatural experience into focus. Feeling forlorn, he decided to request a repeat. He wanted Krishna to recap the details, and re-infuse the apparition of the Universal Form. This time, he mentally pledged, that he would surely retain the experience.

O superman, person who is the son of Devakī, just before the battle, I perceived your infinite control and your supernatural majestic form. (Anu Gītā 1.5)

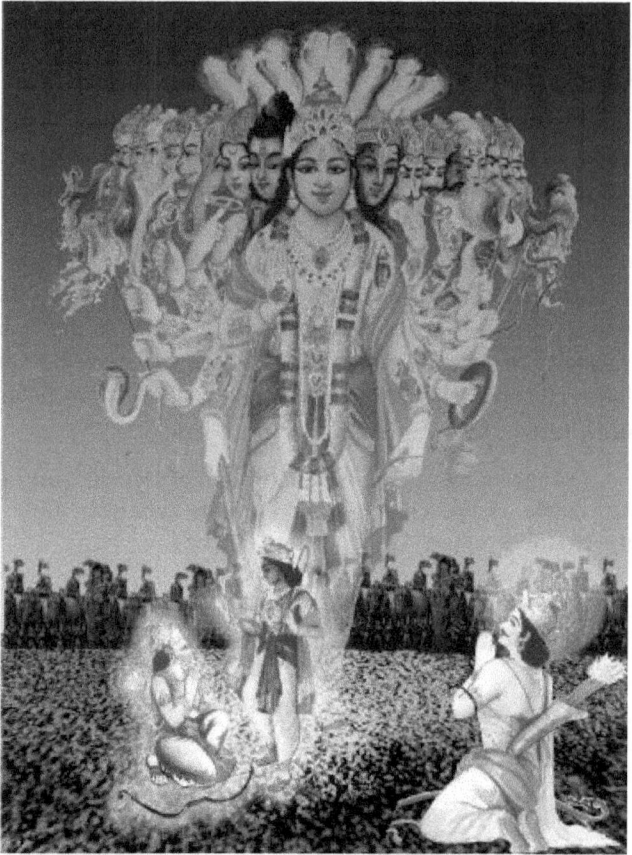

Terri Stokes Art

This is recalled by Arjuna because it was the single tipping point in the discourse with Krishna. It was not explanations and counterpoints, which caused Arjuna to abandon his natural stance, which was to avoid a civil conflict. It was the vision of Krishna's infinite control, and his supernatural majestic form.

Arjuna knew that it was the demonstration of psychic power, which caused him to cooperate with Krishna. It was not devotion or relationship with Krishna. Arjuna was devoted to Krishna as much as anyone else, but the relationship was in contrast with Arjuna's love for others. At the time, his affections for his seniors in the Kuru family, outweighed his love for Krishna. As a practical matter, Arjuna could not commit violence on behalf of Krishna. It pained him to apply himself as disciplinary force to members of his clan. But when Krishna showed his influence over the situation, and demonstrated that everything was under control, Arjuna realized that being opposed to Krishna, was not in Arjuna's interest.

Acting in opposition to Krishna had consequences. Cooperating with Krishna caused the devotee to receive resentments from Krishna's opponents. But since Krishna is the Supreme Person, and has the total responsibility even for Krishna's enemies, it is sensible to absorb Krishna's influence.

Indeed, O Keshava Krishna, what your noble self explained previously out of affection, know that all of it is forgotten by me. O tiger-like person, that is due to my having lost touch with that level of reality. (Anu Gītā 1.6)

It is astonishing that anyone could, within the same lifetime, and not so long after, forget a discourse directly from the mouth of God, a tailored instruction with immediate application.

The mind stockpiled the information as a memory, but only as one which was out of reach for the devotee. Was this Arjuna's negligence? Was it due to the nature of the mind, due to the way the psyche is designed?

Arjuna knew that he was endowed with the explanation of the *Bhagavad Gītā* and with the vision of the workings of the Universal Form. And still, he could only vaguely rehash the incidence.

O great person, my anxiety is present for those valuable experiences to be bestowed again, since O Mādhava Krishna, you will soon be going to your city Dvārakā. (Anu Gītā 1.7)

Contact with the Universal Form of Krishna, and remembrance of Krishna's philosophy and ideas, may serve the purpose of having the association with Krishna. Arjuna felt that Krishna's absence would be counteracted, if there was ongoing access to the philosophy of Krishna, and the perception of Krishna's influence, which is all-pervading.

It seems that in Krishna's physical presence, Arjuna was relieved of anxiety. But Arjuna was uncertain of his confidence in Krishna's physical absence. The Universal Form has physical application, but it is a supernatural embodiment. One cannot understand it, if one does not have supernatural perception. Knowing that he lacked the continuous psychic view of the form, Arjuna wanted to view it again, so that he could make an indelible imprint in his mind.

Then as requested, Krishna replied to Arjuna. After embracing him, Krishna, the person of vast energy, the best of the lecturers, said these words: (Anu Gītā 1.8)

At first Krishna was cordial with Arjuna but as we will hear in the following verses, Krishna was disagreeable with the request for a repeat of the experience.

O son of Pṛthā, what was revealed to you by me is the unmanifest perpetual principle, the actual format of righteous duty, all the dimensions and the eternal reality. (Anu Gītā 1.9)

The basic thesis of the *Bhagavad Gita*, the teaching curriculum, is that of *karma* yoga, the application of yoga expertise to cultural involvement of physical bodies. Since there is the person component in this creation, the interaction or behavior from one person to the next, is cataloged both by Nature and by God. To understand how to act with the least unfavorable consequence, someone should know the laws of Nature, and the censoring influence of God.

Krishna revealed the format of righteous duty, as well as the dimensions, the eternal reality, which supports whatever is temporary, and the unmanifest perpetual principle itself.

How is it that Arjuna could forget the information and revelation?

Your loss of awareness and loss of dimensional contact with that is really disagreeable to me. Indeed, you are a person with a degraded mind. You are faithless, O son of Paṇḍu. (Anu Gītā 1.10)

Krishna did not approve of Arjuna's inability to recall the teachings and revelation. Somehow Arjuna shifted to a low plane of consciousness. Krishna addressed Arjuna as a person with a degraded mind (*durmedhāḥ*). Somehow due to being out of touch with the supernatural level of the Universal Form, Arjuna lost confidence in extra-dimensional worlds. Krishna expressed a dissatisfaction with this.

Surely, the system of righteous duty expounded in my lecture is the way to easily accomplish the spiritual reality, but my recollection of that speech is an impossibility. (Anu Gītā 1.11)

The discourse of the *Bhagavad Gītā* was a spontaneous conversation. Some say that it was planned, and that Krishna arranged the fate, so that Arjuna would be emotionally weakened, just for the purpose of having Arjuna plead with Krishna for a solution, which Krishna gave in the form of the *Bhagavad Gita*.

However, these statements of Krishna in the *Anu Gītā* proves that speculation to be invalid. It was a spur of the moment conversation. It was not contrived. Arjuna was in an emotional whirlpool. That happened because of his natural existential stance as a limited being. Unless he insists of himself, he cannot remain on the plane of consciousness, which gives one access to the supernatural realms.

Because the conversation was spontaneous, Krishna said that he could not reproduce it. He could give an overview, and some details, but to do so verbatim was near impossible.

Arjuna is a limited self. Krishna is the Supreme Self. It follows that the Supreme Person cannot be at the beck and call of any limited being. The God has relationship with every limited self, but that does not mean that a limited someone can adjust the relationship, to induce God to lecture on selected topics.

Surely, that Supreme Spiritual Reality described by me previously was experienced by the application of a yoga technique. Now I will speak on the basis of ancient history. (Anu Gītā 1.12)

Some devotees try to establish that Lord Krishna has no interest in yoga. Many devotees believe this. Yet, many events from the life of Krishna prove that yoga like other aspects of human life, are of interest and are used by Krishna. *Yogayuktena*, or by application of yoga technique, was the method used in the display of his Universal Form.

Mystic power was involved in presenting the apparition, and in giving the description of the unmanifest perpetual principle, the actual format of righteous duty, all the dimensions, and the eternal reality. Krishna, the physical chariot driver for Arjuna, was in touch with the realities, but to make them visible to Arjuna, the exercise of yoga penetration was required.

Arjuna was not concerned with the mystic skill of Krishna, as to if Krishna used that or did not. Arjuna wanted only to see the apparition again, and hear of the wonders of Krishna penetration through everything in the physical world.

Krishna, however, refused to use his mystic powers. He would help Arjuna to recover the memory but only by citing ancient history, where the subject of the challenges of life was explained.

Definitely, by adjusting your intellect to this, you will achieve the highest dimension. Listen to what is said by me, O best of those who support righteous behavior. (Anu Gītā 1.13)

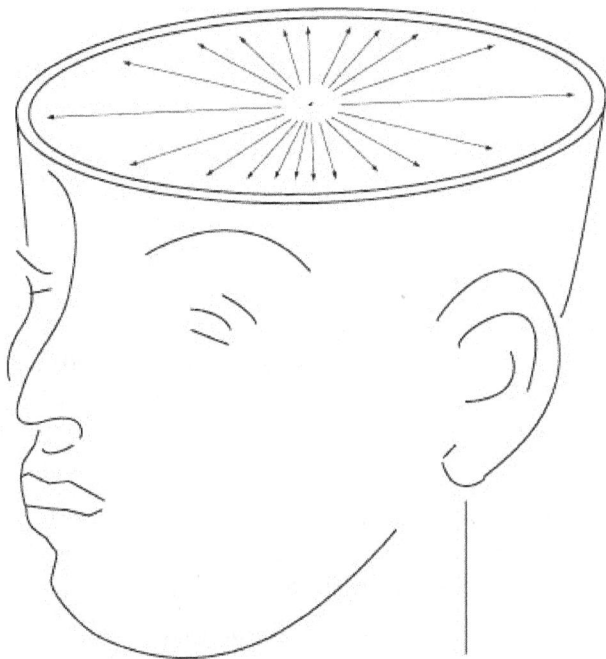

energy being drained away from core-self
by outward-bound sensual energies

This new method is that of adjusting the reformed intellect to the facts of reality. It is *buddhimāsthāya*. This is an important hint given by Krishna to Arjuna. Applied to the circumstance, it means that if a devotee got a revelation from a divine personality, as well as lengthy explanations about the different levels of reality, and if still that devotee cannot retain the impressions and education, he may resort to intellect adjustment. To do this he must get accurate information from a siddha perfected being or from a divine personality.

Requesting the repeat of an apparition is not a good idea. This is due to the fact, that during a lifetime, such a vision is usually given once only. Beyond that, the method is to bring the intellect in compliance with the laws of Nature, and the situations of the divine beings.

O subduer of enemies, it so happened that a ritual ascetic from the celestial regions visited us. He was difficult to locate. Being from the dimension of the Creator Brahma, he was duly honored by us. (Anu Gītā 1.14)

Whether on the physical level or the lower astral regions, it is difficult to find a person who is native to the dimension of the Creator *Brahmā*. If somehow one meets such a yogi devotee, one may press him for the information which one could use to compress the intellect, bringing it into submission so that its interpretation of events is consistent with reality.

When this is done, one will begin to perceive the Universal Form of Krishna, and adapt the lifestyle, so that one's acts reflect the preference of Krishna.

O best of the Bharatas, listen to what he said, as he was specifically questioned by us in a way that was in conformity with the divine world, and with due consideration. (Anu Gītā 1.15)

A siddha yogi qualifies as someone whose opinions and decisions spontaneously match those of the Supreme Being. This is because his intellect, gives accurately assessment of situations. The intellect is a precision psychic analysis tool which must be calibrated for the proper interpretation of events.

The ritual ascetic said: O Krishna, you asked methodically of the lifestyle which results in liberation. Being merciful to all living beings, O exalted person, you inquired of that which shatters delusion. (Anu Gītā 1.16)

At the end of this physical life, one is confronted with what will be hereafter. At that time, whatever was done will be summarized, in the form of one being ushered or transited to some psychic dimension. One will be with some of the attributes which one felt, and was recognized by, when the physical body was alive.

The *Anu Gītā* concerns this matter of *death You!* or the death of the physical body which was known as you. What is the lifestyle which will result in liberation, so that one can exist in an environment, which has no counter energies, which result in physical or astral discomfort?

I published a commentary on the *Anu Gītā* under the title of *Anu Gītā Explained*. Was that sufficient? Why did it occasion me to compose this second explanation?

The *Bhgavad Gītā* is also concerned with actions during the physical life which would result in a grand existence hereafter, or at least in a promotion for higher opportunity to study existence in the next birth. The *Anu Gītā* however is confined to the instance of the destinations hereafter, and the lifestyles on the physical side, which either frustrates or results in a desired and cherished existence, somewhere, somehow, hereafter.

O killer of Madhu, I will answer your inquiries appropriately. Being attentive, listen to what is said by me, O Mādhava Krishna. (Anu Gītā 1.17)

This lecture was so appropriate, and was such a clarification about physical and subtle reality, that even the God, Krishna, felt honored to hear it.

An educated ascetic named Kashyapa, who was proficient in sensual austerity, and who was the best of those persons who mastered righteous lifestyle, approached a well-trained ritual ascetic who was conversant with righteousness and understood the repeated transmigrations. (Anu Gītā 1.18)

For this study it is best that the student be proficient in sensual restraint and cultural settlement. The *siddha* perfected yogi, whom Krishna addressed initially, cited two other persons, one of which gave the lecture which will be narrated.

Kashyapa knew something about reincarnation, and the laws of existence which govern that. *Kashyapa* was proficient in sensual austerity. He mastered the skill of righteous lifestyle, and still he needed information from *siddhas* who were in a higher category.

Kashyapa took training from an unnamed ritual ascetic who was conversant with righteous conduct, and who thoroughly understood how one is victimized by repeated transmigrations. What are the rules by which a person assumes an embryo, lives as a physical body, experiences the death of it, lives on hereafter, and then again assumes another embryo, or goes to a psychic dimension permanently?

That well-trained ritual ascetic was in full knowledge about the acceptance and relinquishment of a body. He had boundless capacity for knowledge and experience. He was versed in whatever was of value or essential in the world. He was a person with deep insight into the aspects of enjoyment and misery. (Anu Gītā 1.19)

Kashyapa's teacher was the ideal limited self. His rendition of reality would be useful, because he was not the Supreme Being, who would show actions which could not be enacted by a limited personality. This teacher was a self whose experiences could be realized by another limited person.

To understand death, someone must be versed in the process of how a person accepts, and then loses a physical body. The person's capacity for knowledge and experience should be vast. He must have deep insight into the enjoyment and misery which a limited being encounters, and is subject to.

He knew the truth of birth and death. He was the expert on merits and faults. He perceived the elevation and degradation of the souls. He knew the objective of the embodied souls in terms of their anxiety and cultural work. (Anu Gītā 1.20)

Kashyapa's teacher had a mind which directly perceived the operation of the dimensions, the introduction of a lifeform in its parents' bodies, the development of that form after its birth, its growth to maturity, its deterioration in the elderly years, and its death.

During the life of a body, merits and faults are committed by it. Some of these were inevitable. Some happen because of ignorance and stupidity. Even positive actions may be done involuntarily. Some are committed willfully.

According to the lifestyle, a person becomes elevated or degraded in one or two aspects; social interaction and inner sense control. Someone may exhibit sense control and be a socially misfit. Some other person may be socially capable, and exhibit awkward sense control. Expertise in both areas is required.

Being a perfected yogi, he moved around as a siddha, a liberated soul. He was tranquil. His sensual energy was effectively restrained. He was effulgent and splendorous like spiritual reality. He roamed everywhere as desired. (Anu Gītā 1.21)

This teacher of *Kashyapa* transited to many dimensions. He was effulgent and splendorous like spiritual reality. He was self-satisfied because of integrating many experiences when touring through the planes of the psychic world.

Since his sensual energy was effectively restrained, he was not distracted to enjoy any specific person or place. That allowed rapid rating of the different locales.

It should be that before the death of the physical body, someone should know what is available hereafter. Each person should have a plan of preference, about where to transit after losing the identity as a physical someone.

If the idea is non-existence, no preparation is required. If it is existence somewhere, somehow, the lifestyle should be such that it facilitates that, and makes that the likely outcome.

This teacher of *Kashyapa*, toured the dimensions to satisfy his curiosity about what was available. He knew the means of transit, the behavior, and sense control, which was the prerequisite for access to the subtle existence.

He knew the technique of psychic passage. He moved with the siddha perfected yogis who could disappear and who roamed everywhere like a wheel. Kashyapa having heard of his knowledge of the essential truth, desired to see him. (Anu Gītā 1.22)

If there is an afterlife, if even there is no such psychic place, if only there is birth as a baby, and then again somehow, there is birth as a baby again, with no intervening spacious existence, then one should master the technique of psychic passage. One should do so while the physical body lives. It should not be left to chance to experience what will be the situation hereafter.

Whosoever has the experience about the afterlife, should be consulted so that one may get hints about it, and develop interest in researching it. As birth is individual, so is death. Hence the collective security one feels as part of a family, city, or nation, should not foreshadow that death is individual, and should be checked, and rechecked.

That roaming ascetic moved with those siddhas who sometimes sat together or assembled in solitary places. He went as by chance, going about unattached just like the wind. (Anu Gītā 1.23)

People congregate, some associate, some avoid the company of others. The tendency to have friends and family is universal. It is suggested that yogis forgo the need for association. They should practice alone. To be successful in self-realization one must internalize, recognize the constituents of the psyche, and bring the inner factors to order.

Still, there is need for association with, and avoidance of some human beings. It is always in a yogi's interest to associate with those who are more advanced. Hints about difficult practices and unknown techniques, may be shown either by description, or by psychic demonstration of a teacher.

At a certain stage, when one becomes a siddha, an advanced yogi, one will move with those siddhas who sometimes sit together, or assemble in solitary places. At that time, one will travel by chance, and will remain unattached like the roving wind.

Such a yogi checks on these conditions.

- status of ordinary people who have no interest in anything psychic

- movements of souls as they transmigrate from an old or damaged body to another

- observation of the progress and methods used by beginner yogis

- estimation of the risk of taking another physical body for the purpose of teaching advanced yoga

- consultation with higher entities in various dimensions in the astral world

- meeting deities if permitted by those beings

- studying the attractive power of the psychic Nature

- designing a schematic for final escape from the cycle of birth and death

Then that best of the well-trained ritualists, Kashyapa, being intelligent in his own right, approached the wandering yogi. Being a person who was eager for righteous lifestyle, Kashyapa, in submission, with full prostration, fell at the feet of the ascetic, who felt Kashyapa's great devotion. (Anu Gītā 1.24)

If somehow one gets the association of a *siddha*, it would not matter if that person used a physical body or only used a subtle form. In either case the challenge is to get effective techniques and success-blessings from that personality. It is not, however that one can demand of that ascetic, that he/she should offer this, or that method, or grace.

There is a feeling one may get, when speaking to an advanced person, where one becomes confident that he/she can bless, or award one with instant advancement. This is problematic for the teacher and student. In the first place one should go to an ascetic for advice and recommendation. But one should also realize that it is likely that the instruction will be unpalatable, and may seem impractical.

The feeling that a great soul should instantly cause one to become advanced, is itself a cause for the reluctance to make efforts for spiritual improvement. Thus, when the teacher suggests that spiritual practice be done, the disciple may experience a negative response. That causes reluctance for the practice.

In amazement, seeing that wonderful person, Kashyapa, the foremost of the trained ritualists, submitted to that great spiritual master who exhibited exemplary conduct and sacred knowledge. (Anu Gītā 1.25)

Kashyapa will question the teacher but in a way which is not challenging, for the purpose of gaining insight, and learning of the teacher's experience, which *Kashyapa* did not have, but which would render an introduction to other realities.

Asceticism is one achievement. Non-self-destructive behavior is another. A person may exhibit extreme ascetism and be a social misfit, where he performs actions which are detrimental to one and all.

It is also a fact that people who master morality as it is defined in their religious text or legislature, may be awkward when it comes to inner ascetism. Their reliance on moral reputation makes them insensitive to mysticism. The snag for them is that when ascetism is applied to the inner psyche, its results may not be obvious, which means that no credit will be given for it. And when the results of inner ascetism become visible through some physical alteration, people may dislike it, which will bring social pressure to bear on the ascetic.

Some ascetic masters do not exhibit exemplary conduct. *Kashyapa* was fortunate to be in touch with a guru whose social behavior and spiritual disciplines were in order in their particular spheres. It does happen that a spiritual master may be versed in a particular yoga discipline and be off-key and downright deviant for social behavior.

O subduer of rebels, Kashyapa was dear to the self and pleasing to the teacher. He was educated and exhibited appropriate conduct, pleasing behavior and timeful activities in reference to the teacher. (Anu Gītā 1.26)

Even though *Kashyapa* was the ideal student, this does not mean that an awkward person should not seek help from a great teacher. Every human being has the right to approach the teacher, even the misfit students. However, one should admire *Kashyapa* and any other ideal student. From his behavior, one may learn what to aspire for in becoming the idea disciple.

Thus, being satisfied and pleased by the disciple, the tranquil spiritual master who experienced the highest perfection, spoke. Hear of this from me Janārdana, maintainer of the living beings. (Anu Gītā 1.27)

Whatever the guru told *Kashyapa* was so genuine, that it was repeated by Krishna to Arjuna. Even though Krishna is the maintainer of the living beings, still the ideas expressed attracted him, who felt that it was the right discourse for someone like Arjuna, a person who lost track of the teachings and revelation of the *Bhagavad Gita*.

Anu Gītā is an essential reading for all persons who read or heard the *Bhagavad Gita*. It completes what was presented initially to Arjuna, which he forgot, because of enjoying himself after the victory at *Kurukshetra*.

Bhagavad Gītā includes a detailed instruction on how to better utilize the social situation in this world. *Anu Gītā* deals with the directions of how to better situate oneself from a preferred destination in the psychic world, the realms of the hereafter.

O dear one, by their various aspirations and actions, or by yoga practice, pious activity and isolation, people go to the world where bodies quickly die or are situated in the celestial places where the lower deities reside. (Anu Gītā 1.28)

If we begin someone's history in the hereafter, in a psychic realm, there are two movements possible. One is to become conscious as a lifeform in the physical world. The other is to remain as a resident of a psychic domain. We can assume that anyone who has a lifeform came from a psychic existence. That person became a physical being as an infant in some species of life.

Everyone else who exists somewhere, must be in the psychic existence either waiting for physical assumption of a body here, or remaining as a psychic being in some subtle or supernatural environment.

It is vital that we admit that one can exist and not be aware of oneself. This means that existence does not necessarily support objectivity in every case. If one's existence shifts where there is no objectivity, one will be unaware. That means that one will lose track of the self.

As far as time is concerned. That has value if there is memory as a reference and support. As soon as one has no access to memory, time track is lost. That is another limitation of awareness.

In none of these locations is there endless happiness; none of those places have eternal residence. Again and again, there is demotion from the highest dimension which one attained with difficulty. (Anu Gītā 1.29)

According to the *siddha* perfected yogi, who ventured through several dimensions, and who heard from other advanced beings, the situation here and hereafter is uncertain.

He claimed that in none of the physical or astral locations is there endless happiness. None, he said, has eternal residence, something which is what everyone who has a physical body, is after.

As for those who aspire for and attain higher astral locales, they should know that there is demotion from the highest dimension which one may attain with difficulty.

There are celestial beings who remain in the higher astral situations. Rarely are they demoted. But even for them there is risk, as for example when those psychic layouts are demolished.

Due to my performance of social crimes, I got the result of awful and tortuous states of consciousness. This was due also to improper cultural activities, desires, and delusion. (Anu Gītā 1.30)

As for the hereafter, a human being attains a situation there in some dimension, mostly based on the social behavior. It is not based on one's view of one's right or grievous actions. It is based on the layout of the psychic realms, and how one is attracted to one, or the other, according to the vibration cultivated, while one lived in the physical world.

The spiritual teacher cited his experiences of living in the physical world, and performing social crimes. He remembered that he got the result of awful and tortuous states of consciousness. That, he said, was due to improper cultural activities, desires, and delusion. This happens because of a failure to understand the workings of Nature. It is also due to an overestimation of one's ability to influence fate.

Instead of observing, learning, and adjusting to the way Nature operates, one may instead feel that one can influence Nature to render desirable outcomes. The way Nature packs her conveyor belt of circumstances relates to Nature's way of spreading events.

Again and again, I endured death of a body, and yet again and again, I endured birth of a form. I consumed various types of food. I had many parents. I sucked on different types of breasts. (Anu Gītā 1.31)

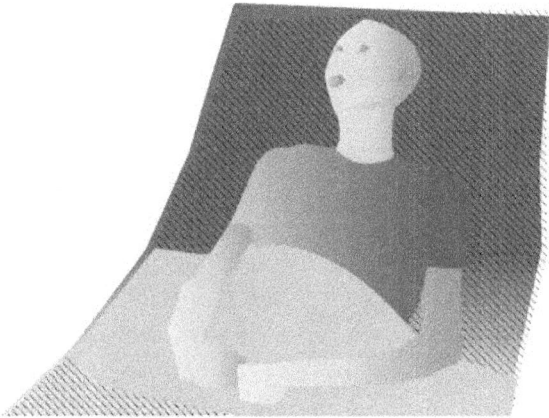

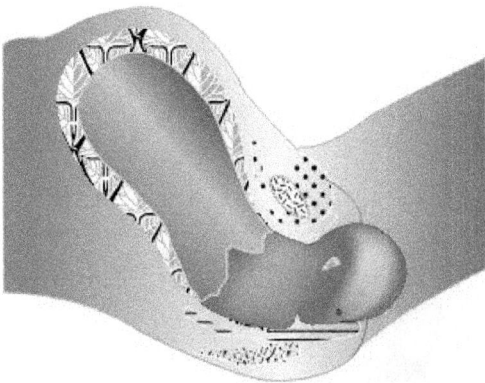

death You!

This teacher recalled his past lives. With that knowledge, he drew informed conclusions. Most human beings do not recall past bodies. And certainly, the selves in animal forms, lack the perception.

For the humans, who have no past life self-evidence, the idea of pre-existences is rejected or believed. It is by meditation that one may come to terms with this information of *Kashyapa's* teacher. By transcending awareness of physical things, one may develop psychic feelings, which afford one the ability to sort psychic objects.

We can share in the experiences of others, not just humans but animals, insects, and other life forms. We may do that by observing their situations, which give them advantages and disadvantages, when compared to our individual situations. The physical body is itself a location, a habitat, or realm. Some self in an insect body experiences that form as a mento-emotional environment.

To follow the ideas of *Kashyapa's* teacher, we may assume that the corePerson persists after the death. In his report, he endured repeated incidences of death of various bodies. He went through births of numerous forms. According to the body type, he ate various foods. And needless to say, he had many parents who nurtured his forms. In mammalian forms he sucked on different breasts.

For some readers, this information may trigger intuitive understanding of Nature's recycling actions which are psychic, rather than physical events. It may for others cause astral insight experiences, where one finds oneself to be a certain person or animal in a previous birth. One may relive that former life and have an understanding of who one was and where one was located.

I experienced different kinds of mothers and fathers in various species. O faultless person, a variety of pleasures and miseries was endured by me. (Anu Gītā 1.32)

There is a repeat of incidences when someone transmigrates in the same species or in various species, in a linear, or complex shuffle, from one birth to the next. Eventually there is an intuition which dictates how one should behave. This guiding force is based on the many experiences one endured in the bid for survival of each lifeform one inhabited.

Eventually one develops a sensitivity, whereby one intuitively knows, which behavior to adhere to, and which to avoid. This is based on the pleasures or miseries yielded by the indulgence.

The soul acts as an auxiliary power supply for the psyche. Its radiation is used to support the lifeforce production of psychic and physical energy. According to how an experience complements the aura of the soul, that is how the event is tagged intuitively, as desirable, or undesirable.

According to social position, there is interaction between souls. This develops into attraction or rejection of one person to another. Over time these relationships leave an imprint of liking or disliking another person. This instinct causes irrational treatment of someone. Or it may cause appropriate emotions to arise.

Time and again I was separated from those who were dear to me and then was forced into association with those whom I disliked. After attaining wealth by difficult means, I had to endure its loss or confiscation. (Anu Gītā 1.33)

It is not what one imagines life to be. It is how Nature constructs, enlivens, and concludes circumstances. At best, an ascetic should put aside his ideas, and study Nature's methods and achievements. Then the yogi will have opinions which are theorems of Nature's formations.

One becomes attached to pleasing circumstances. One expects that these will be prolonged. When Nature shifts from a desirable situation, one becomes terrified. This could be avoided if one trains the self to be flexible, even towards unfavorable events.

The accumulation of wealth causes one to adopt views, which if Nature does not endorse, produces anguish and criminal behavior. Then one is put into difficulty for violating the laws of the government and Nature. But there is also theft of one's wealth, or confiscation by governments. These events are painful to endure.

Terrible insults in the excess were endured by me, from people of greater status and from relatives as well. Unbearable painful horrors were suffered by the mind and body. (Anu Gītā 1.34)

In physical existence, due to length of time one must remain as a body in the environment, one must endure insults from people of greater status, and from those of lesser class, if they are levered into a social position, where it would be difficult to subdue or resist them.

Someone may carry a resentment from a former life. It may or may not be justified. It may activate a negative energy, which when hurled would cause emotional, or physical injury. Sometimes a spouse or a child will feel resentful. That person will speak in a way which is painful to bear.

The log of painful horrors which are inflicted to someone is beyond reconning. It is an ocean of difficulty. It assails people wherever they go. Observing this, a yogi realizes that Nature does its accounting, which is different to what the individual limited self hopes for.

I endured horrible indignities, vicious deaths, imprisonments, and miserable conditions. I was sent into hellish conditions and was painfully punished in the realm of the deity who judges hereafter. (Anu Gītā 1.35)

We are certain that in this physical world, even in the most primitive societies, there are courts where people are condemned and assigned punishment. These are legislative systems where the rules of law are enforced. Some laws which make no sense to one set of people, are standardized by other groups.

We also know that in the astral world, during our dream experiences, one may be harassed by others, even wounded temporarily by someone. Thus, the possibility of hell hereafter is credible. Someone somewhere may bear a grudge or may have a violent urge towards one's person. This is credible.

The idea that there is an astral court where departed souls are judged and punished, is not difficult to visualize. In this world, there are many courts in numerous countries. People, regardless of guilt or innocence are subjected to incarceration, or some type of restriction, or even capital punishment. Hence it is reasonable to conclude, that on the astral side such situations exist, where one could be confronted, and then be arrested by some astral beings, who are part of a government. As physical prisons are real places in our current experience, astral hells are real as psychic

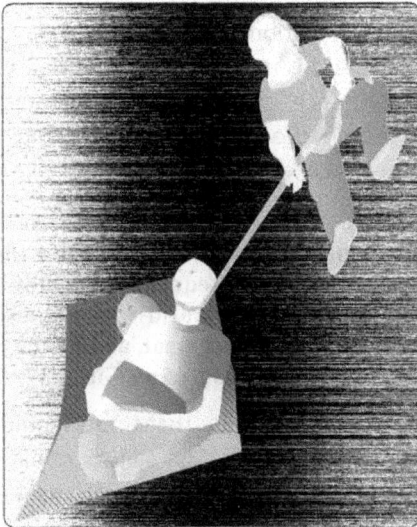

locations.

Old age and disease constantly assailed me. The disasters were more than sufficient. In this world, the psychosis which arises from the perception of dual conditions was felt by me. (Anu Gītā 1.36)

As soon as one emerges from the womb of the mother, one is threatened by growth and disease. Growth is desired. In fact, it is an involuntary urge which is supported by ingestion of nutrients. The constant alterations being made, which are illustrated as growth of the infant body, are a format of elderliness or of progressive decay. Hence growth compliments disease even though it presents itself as a promise for sexual maturity.

The physical problems are one reality which confronts every living being. However, there is another challenge, which is the psychosis, which comes from being subjected to dual conditions of sensuality. There is yet another aspect which is neutral feelings, where it is neither desirable nor undesirable. That may present boredom or other depressed states.

Disagreeable conditions are inside and outside the psyche, such that there is nowhere to focus, where one would permanently experience only pleasurable states. It is all-surrounding in the physical and psychic territories. How does one get to the place where only pleasurable sensations happen?

Then, it so happened, that an overwhelming disgust and a depression was felt by me. Subsequently, I totally abandoned the fatiguing operations of this world with its miseries. Then being conversant with that detachment, and by the favor of the self, I attained spiritual perfection. (Anu Gītā 1.37)

Kashyapa's teacher suggests that there should be a favor granted to the self by the self. The self must itself act in its interest to terminate its needs for the excitements, which flip into distressful conditions and distraught feelings.

The trigger for this courtesy was an overwhelming disgust felt in the psyche. That converted into a deep depression. That in turn caused the self to mature, into the action of abandoning the fatiguing operations of this world, with its miseries.

Devotees of Krishna should note, that in this case, there is no mention of a direct act by Krishna. The devotee himself/herself must experience the overwhelming disgust and the resulting depression. It must be convinced by the experience that it would forego supporting the attachments, which the self has for Nature's displays, which occur outside and inside its psyche.

Kashyapa's teacher, through numerous meaningful experiences, attained liberation by the grace of his coreSelf, with the cooperation of its adjuncts. Here the analytical organ, the sensual energies, the senses themselves, even the recall ability and the kundalini lifeForce, each of these turned to support the detached coreSelf, which earned its exemption from helpless attraction to Nature.

I will never again be involved here. I observe the worlds. From the time of my perfection to the time of the end of these beings in the creation, the auspicious destinations attained by the self will be noted by me. (Anu Gītā 1.38)

On the basis of his coreSelf's resistance to the presentations of Nature, *Kashyapa's* guru declared that he would never again be involved in this physical, and psychic procurement of experience, through sensual intake. Something happened to cause his entity to be detached from Nature's operations.

The question arises, as to how there can be change in what was declared to be changeless. If there is a spiritual self which will endure beyond the physical body, and if that self is changeless, because it is part of the absolute background of this world, then how could this ascetic pronounce that he was once involved here with urges and fulfillments, and then he lost that drama.

This teacher said that at this time, his activity was to observe the worlds, the physical and psychic dimensions he transited into. He would note the auspicious destinations he accessed.

To our surprise, this teacher admitted that even though he was liberated, it was only in the sense of having detachment from the operations of Nature in the mundane spheres. He was not released into a sublime environment as of yet. He knew that he would remain in the timebound places for some time, at least until the time of the end of these beings, who currently comprise this cosmos.

O best of the well-trained ascetics, having obtained the highest perfection, I will go to the highest dimension. Then again, I will go even higher. I will definitely attain the level of exclusive spiritual existence. You should harbor no doubts on this subject. (Anu Gītā 1.39)

It is informative that the condition of liberation is a lengthy process. It entails transfers from lower to higher places, on and on, until the yogi reaches the level of exclusive spiritual existence (*brahmaṇaḥ*).

The ascetic would transit to the highest dimension, which is accessible from this physical place, but he had information that such a place was only the highest which was accessible from here. Once the person shifted upward, he was informed of higher realms.

What *Kashyapa's* teacher had was the determination and intention for elevation to become situated in what was higher, then see the reality of yet higher places, and be qualified to shift upwards again.

Those who feel that the transit from here to the highest dimension, should be completed at the time of death in one giant translation, are unrealistic, and function from the assumption, that one is equipped with the transport means to the spiritual world. The evidence from this teacher disproved that.

In the first place, many people who believe in a paradise hereafter, have not experienced that place. Obviously, it is not a physical location. It must be psychic or spiritual. Hence its access is not like travelling to a place on the earth. Hence, one should be reserved about what will be attained hereafter.

I will never again return here to the world where bodies quickly reach their end. I am pleased with you. O person of great insight, say what I can do for you. (Anu Gītā 1.40)

Relationship reciprocation was active in the nature of Kashyapa's teacher. This showed by the teacher's pleasing mood, and willingness to provide testimony about the dimensions. He declared that his existential content was such, that there remained no attraction to positive or negative features of physical existence. Whatever pull he experienced before, no longer was active. His coreSelf was indifferent to the excitements it craved before.

This is a developed resistance to the influence of Nature. It happens after many life experiences in various species. Eventually something special happens. He explained this before.

- *Then, it so happened, that an overwhelming disgust and a depression was felt by me. Subsequently, I totally abandoned the fatiguing operations of this world with its miseries. Then being conversant with that detachment, and by the favor of the self, I attained spiritual perfection. (Anu Gītā 1.37)*

The time is now! Express what you are eager to know. Actually, I am aware of the reason you contacted me. I will go shortly. Thus, I informed you. (Anu Gītā 1.41)

Concerns about the earth, about participating in its history, about making an impact, and introducing improvements for oneself and others, diminished in the being of this teacher. He lost even the compassionate interest for humanity. There was a short period left for serious students to consult him.

Fortunately for us, a record of the discourse is available. The gravity of it is enormous. By the grace of time, even today, thousands of years after, this information is presented.

I am very pleased, O great soul, with your mature behavior. Inquire as much as desired about whatever subject is of interest to you. (Anu Gītā 1.42)

This clarifies that the compassionate aspect of this teacher, was activated by its encounter with a submissive person. As a treasure of transcendental experience, *Kashyapa's* teacher was tight-lipped, except when in the presence of a worthy disciple. This percolated the spiritual information to one and all, even to people who were not as advanced as *Kashyapa*.

I think you are very intelligent. I greatly admire you. O brilliant Kashyapa, by your insight, you recognized me. (Anu Gītā 1.43)

The availability of this information about the possibilities, hereafter, is due to the yogic perfection of the teacher as well as to the proper attitude of the student who is *Kashyapa*. Relationship is vital.

A disciple who is insubmissive, who underrates the teacher, who does not respect the master, is unable to absorb whatever benefit one would derive. Even if the teacher speaks to him, and opens the door to the teacher's experiences and conclusions, still that disciple would be unable to absorb the grace energy, which one must have to put the teaching into practice.

Krishna, the son of Vasudeva, said: Then gently grasping the feet of that perfected mystic, Kashyapa asked questions which were difficult to answer. The best of the advocates of righteous lifestyle spoke of all those matters. (Anu Gītā 2.1)

One should keep in mind, that this is the answer to the question about what to do, if one forgets the *Bhagavad Gītā,* and does not recall the description of the Universal Form of Krishna. For Arjuna, this is the replacement for his lack of recall of the *Bhagavad Gītā* and more important, it is for him the invaluable replacement for the apparition of the Universal Form.

Just imagine how important this information is, that it is on par with the vision of the Universal Form of God. It is wonderful, fabulous, amazing, that Lord Krishna delivered this to Arjuna, and facilitated this to us, by having *Vedavyasa* deliver this literally to humanity in the *Mahabharata*.

The *Bhagavad Gītā* is vital. And yet, when asked to repeat its information and manifest its apparition, Lord Krishna flatly refused. He presented this as the replacement glory. This focuses on what is hereafter. Because of our assumption as physical bodies, we are familiar with this side of existence. What we lack is insight about the hereafter.

It is not how to fight a battle. It is not how God can assist if one is on the right side of a conflict. It is not even about God's intervening power into human affairs. What is it?

It is about the fact that when all is said and done, correctly or incorrectly, one will not be permitted to continue as the present physical body. One will be compelled to transmigrate, to shift to another psychic plane, either for a limited time or forever. Hence, one should prepare for that shift. That is the pressing issue.

Kashyapa said: How does the physical body deteriorate? How is a new one acquired? How does one who is in the trouble-ridden course of haphazard transmigrations escape from the puzzle? (Anu Gītā 2.2)

A yogi should study these questions carefully. These are the only matters worth investigating. The truthful answers are the only solutions worth contemplating. In the end of this life, one will be shifted to some other dimension, and must live in that environment. If it is a nice place, one is lucky. Otherwise, one will be miserable. What can be done to secure transit and accommodations in a paradise?

Even for those who feel that paradise is unwanted, even they need to peruse the possibilities hereafter. Even those persons should have some preference, and should figure if Nature will accommodate their needs.

The physical body deteriorates through a growth process, which is conducted by the genetic potential, which was derived from the parents during the gestation period. Initially this growth action was positive. It caused the infant form to grow to maturity.

Being fused into a body, how does the self become released from it? And how after being released from one, does the self become another? (Anu Gītā 2.2)

The mystic perception is that a self is fused into a body, but the materialistic view is that a self is its body, particularly its physical one. However regardless of what one believes or experiences, the end of the body is certain. Each person attests to it, because of the evidence regarding the deceased relatives. Even though the parents of the body seem to be the producers of the infant stage of the body, still those people will be nil in the nick of time.

If there is a psychic part to the body, then another story, another history, begins when the body dies. That would be a psychic one. But what is the process, whereby that psychic remnant is released from being the physical system.

If there is a psychic remnant, which survives the death of the physical body, what happens whereby that psyche becomes another embryo in some other species of life?

During the life of the physical body, the self considers itself to be that body. When the physical body dies, what identity surfaces as the psychic remnant? And again, when the psyche miraculously becomes an embryo, how does that happen? What participation of the psychic remnant is necessary?

Using the presumption of reincarnation, where it is accepted that a physical person has a remnant identity which survives its death. How does the self become another self, another infant of new parents? Why does the self not recall the existential changes?

How does a human being experience his or her sublime and degrading acts? And conversely, where do the actions manifest for one who is without a material body? (Anu Gītā 2.4)

What are the psychological tools, which relate the impact of a person's socially acceptable or socially disagreeable acts. How would someone know if Nature will react violently, or agreeably, to his exploitation of its resources.

It should be considered that if someone is deceased, that spirit or ghost remains linked to his/her actions, committed before the death of his/her body. How does Nature, or a supernatural agency, serve that person the liability or credit, for his/her previous faulty or noble acts?

Thus, as requested, the perfected yogi answered those questions in sequence. Hear from me what was said, O Krishna, descendant of Vṛṣṇi. (Anu Gītā 2.5)

This is a reminder that this conversation took place between an inquiring person, *Kashyapa*, and a perfected *siddha* yogi, whose name was not given. Krishna questioned another *siddha* who cited this story to the *Yadu* family members. After the battle of *Kurukshetra* when Arjuna and his brothers ruled the *Kuru* kingdom, Arjuna requested a repeat of the *Bhagavad Gītā* discourse, and a show of the supernatural persons and powers in the Universal Form of Krishna. Krishna refused to repeat the explanation and apparition. Instead, he repeated what was explained by a siddha.

The perfected yogi said: Certain actions performed here result in longevity and fame. All such effects are exhausted when the individual acquires another body. (Anu Gītā 2.6)

There are many jerks and twists in the staccato performance of a psyche, as it is played, in life after life. Each life is interspace by a death sequence, which comes to an end sooner or later, as the circumstances are conducted by fate.

Life is reduced to the actions which are performed, but which result in longevity and fame. There is an energy which continuously scans the consciousness for the experience of good health and prominence.

No one is allowed to be perpetual as a physical body. Even the environment constantly undergoes change in some rapid or incremental rate. As soon as a body reaches maturity, it begins to deteriorate. The idea of Nature is to cease the accumulation of longevity and fame, the two aspects which someone craves.

One lives the life as a physical body. One is confronted with its fatal damage. At death, one is left as a psychic remnant somebody, but one is not permitted to enjoy the success one amassed, by using the physical system. The account is logged in the annals of Nature on the psychic plane, but one is not allowed to carry it over physically in the next physical body. Instead, only the psychic effects go with one to the next body. Those effects will remain as they will not have an influence, if one is not positioned in the new life, for support by the environment.

The psychic effects live on, but these are not surfaced, except through certain physical conditions, which accommodate the individual's destiny. To make matters worse, the individual is unlikely to recall the past life activity, which produced the psychic effects which he/she feels intuitively.

With the longevity, that self-destructive, empowered person performs contrary acts. Due to this, his intelligence malfunctions and he becomes positioned for degradation. (Anu Gītā 2.7)

Actions which someone performs, either voluntarily or involuntary, carry reactions for the actor. According to the willfulness or circumstantial pressure which drove the person to act, the levy of the actions varies. Nature tags the affair and keeps memories from multi-dimensional perspectives. It uses that live photography to sponsor future involvement but it does so without regard for the comprehension of the involved entities.

One person may intuitively know which parameters are used by Nature for the manufacture of an event but others may have no idea. In fact, another person may have a totally incorrect understanding, which makes sense to him/her even though it has no relevance.

If death is discussed in this book, if death is the subject delineated, why is there so much information about life, about what happens during the life of the physical body? The answer is that *death is life continued*. Such that life in turn is death continued. The sequence of a life, then a death of that life, then a life again, followed by a death, is a multidimensional staircase in the scope which is called existence.

Each individual who is known as a physical body, is empowered by fate. Even to cry loudly, a newborn infant must be equipped with the weapon of voice, so that its crying will urge its mother to nurse it. That is power but it is awarded for limited purpose by providence.

There is not a single living physical body which does not have some type of power which was rendered into it by fate. Even a dead body which is regarded usually as a dead person, has some power as allowed by fate. However, the teacher of Kashyapa tagged most entities as being self-destructive, such that good health which shows as longevity, is misused, as the body is used to commit contrary acts, which offends the operations of Nature. Due to this, one's intelligence supplies incorrect conclusions. Using those parameters, one slides through the formation of the event which caused the degradation.

A healthy body is good but one must be careful in its usage. Otherwise, one is likely to commit actions which convert into undesirable outcomes. A healthy body is not a privilege to do as one pleases. It is an indication that if one maintains the body in a healthy way, that is preferred. But for the events one constructs or participates in, those require adherence to the methods of Nature. If one offends Nature, even if the body is healthy, there will be negative consequences.

Despite mental clarity, bodily energy, and opportunity, that person who has no insight about the spiritual self, eats when it is too late and thus acts in other contrary ways just as if he were someone who was against the self. (Anu Gītā 2.8

It is interesting that this teacher explained that even the diet used is important. Stated precisely, the time of eating, even, has to do with the life one will enjoy or endure hereafter. Even an aspect as trivial as eating, has effects hereafter. How so? Because the physical actions during a life, emit psychic influences which alter the condition of the person hereafter. The physical body is directly an influence on the subtle form. When that subtle body has no physical parallel, the influence from the physical side stays with the subtle body as an embedded habit.

One should understand and be clear about it, that mental clarity, bodily energy, and opportunity which is in one's favor, does not mean that one has insight to make decisions, which are in one's long-term interest.

Someone can be logical and precise, and also make self-destructive decisions. Or that person may act in a way which is unbeneficial to all concerned. A person may get the opportunity to act in the local or global interest, and due to having a stunted insight, he/she may further endanger the situation.

If one does not understand the relationship between the physical body and the psychic one which is interspaced into it, one is likely to act in a manner which subjects the self to lower awareness. It makes sense that one should act for self-preservation. However, one must have special intelligence before one can do so consistently. One should remember that even though there will be a psychic remnant self which survives the physical body, still the condition of that subtle body could be degraded by the physical activity.

He indulges in many harmful practices. He consumes in excess or insufficiently. (Anu Gītā 2.9)

Someone who thinks that he knows how best to act, but who is contrary in reference to the laws of Nature, will indulge in harmful practices. His lifestyle will cause him to consume in excess or insufficiently. This is due to his careless regard for the responses of reality. Even in trivial actions, like food consumption, he will make mistakes such that over time, he develops habits which will condemn him to ill health in the body.

The idea that someone is not his body, not his physical casing, does not mean that the person should ignore the actions of the body. If one acts carelessly with no regard for the way Nature will react to one's behavior, one will be put into many distressing situations, where the idea that one is not the body, will do nothing to alleve the trauma which one is subjected to.

The complete view is that the coreSelf is not the physical body which it must identifies itself as, and yet, that self should act responsibly because the reactions of actions of the body, reach the coreSelf, and cause it to be subjected the pleasant and unpleasant events

He takes spoilt or improperly combined foods which are incompatible to one another. Or he takes heavy foods or again takes that before the previous meal is digested. (Anu Gītā 2.10)

Irregular diet happens because of inattentiveness either by the parent or child. As an infant one is born into a social format of parents, relatives or guardians who introduce one to a specific diet. One is helpless at that stage.

When one gains adult status, this happens because of growth of one's body. Then the responsibility for meals is transferred to oneself. However, even then one is conditioned to use, abuse, or even reject certain foods. It is likely that one may make dietary decisions which cause ill-health.

The value of any diet is that it yields psychic energy which affects the subtle body. Even though food is physical, it has a subtle emanation which affects one psychologically. If one is unaware of this, one will eat according to the dictation of the sense of taste. That may eventually lead to ill-health for the physical and subtle bodies.

He indulges in physical exercises in excess or he cohabits sexually as a regular practice. Due to always craving actions, he suppresses bodily urges to evacuate even when he becomes conscious of the need. (Anu Gītā 2.11

The two factors, food and sexual intercourse are essentials for most adult bodies. As Nature would have it, one eats. From that food sexual hormones are produced. These produce urges for reproduction, which is possible only through intermixture of sexual fluids of a male and female human being.

For every mouthful one eats, a portion of it is extracted into the human body. Some of the nutrients are contributed to the reproductive organs. This in turn cause sexual urges so that the conclusion is a pregnancy.

Nature has the idea of reproduction of the species. With that there is expression of sexuality, which has with it pleasure. It is not just any pleasure. It is the most acute pleasure which one may indulge in without special chemicals or ascetic practices. This pleasure is so attractive, that once it is experienced in the adult stage of a body, a person craves it. As an act in itself, sexual intercourse becomes a habit.

Addiction to physical action causes positive and negative habits to develop. This makes one reluctant to take restraining advice. That in turn hardens one's resistance to good counsel. One establishes a lifestyle which makes one insensitive to the urge for evacuation. That causes constipation.

That produces a nagging energy in the mind. This alert may be ignored because of attending to matters which are either urgent, or which are imposed because of events in the lifestyle. The pressure from constipation negatively affects the subtle body.

He eats fruits which are excessively juicy and indulges in sleep during the daytime. He eats that which is not ripe or cannot be digested in due course. That causes the person to be anxious, angry, and faulty. (Anu Gītā 2.12)

We are affected by what we eat and by when we eat. It is not that one can eat anything at any time, and not have adverse effects in the long term. A human being should observe the effects of particular diet, and note the optimum times for eating. Then he should adjust his lifestyle accordingly.

The environment has a part to play in how food is digested and excreted from the body. As the form ages in its elderly years, the organs become less and less efficient at their functions. This should be noted and actions taken to optimize one's health.

The idea that one is not the physical body, and that one is not affected by the operation of it, is a logic which only simpletons will approve. Not being the body in no way changes the relationship that the psychic part of a person has with the body, which is its physical parallel. Instead of denying one's identity with the body, it is better to accept the familiarity with it, and then adopt a lifestyle which promotes its optimum and efficient condition.

If the mind becomes anxious, angry, and faulty, that will handicap the coreSelf, because it relies on the conclusions made by the intellect, about which actions to perform, and which to neglect. If it does not get information about situations from the senses, the coreSelf cannot on its own make decisions in an informed way.

For better or worse, the coreSelf relies on the intellect which in turn is dependent on the senses. That is how information about the environment is derived. Disclaiming the intellect in no way causes the core to do the operations of the intellect. It remains dependent on the intellect for conclusions.

From aggravating the flaws in the body, he acquires disease which ends in death. And thus, he may try to commit suicide by hanging with a cord or some similar activity. (Anu Gītā 2.13)

The responsibility for the health and wellbeing of the physical body lies with the parents during the infant years. That concern shifts to the person himself/herself during the adult years. From day one, the body has glitches. Nature manufactured everything in this creation with flaws. However, one should not adopt a lifestyle which aggravates or increases the incorrect biological and psychological designs.

Physical and mental disease will happen. A sane person should live so that these inconveniences are kept to the minimum. Since in the infant years, one's lifestyle is created by parents, they are responsible. As soon as the body grows into adult stage, the concern shifts to oneself.

By logic, one can understand that he/she should act in a non-suicidal way, but due to massive ignorance, and due to not knowing everything about how to safely conduct a body, most human beings make repeated mistakes, and are hard set to continue with a faulty lifestyle.

One is at a disadvantage in this world. Why? Because one does not have full information or insight about the operation of the physical body. Due to having only some correct deductions, one cannot make perfect decisions in every event. Now and again, one behaves in a way which is conducive to one's wellbeing. Overall, we must learn by observing the body, and getting information from others, who somehow gained understanding, about how best to use the body.

Though it is part of the scope of experiences which one may have in this existence, suicide is not a solution to the problems. Its value is the realization that killing the physical body of oneself or anyone else, does not achieve the death or diminishment of the psychic self.

Whatever problems someone was confronted with, which brought him to take his life, those headaches remain after he killed the physical body. A successful suicide results in physical absence but it does not remove the psychic presence. The person remains as a psychic being. He/She continues with the same outlook it had before losing its physical tool for social participation. That self survives with the problems. The individual must continue to exist even though it prefers not to.

From these causes and effects, there is deterioration in the body of the living creature. Therefore, regarding the living being, understand it as it is, as I will describe. (Anu Gītā 2.14)

The inefficient use and resultant deterioration of the body, causes physical and psychological painful conditions, which are detested by most entities. There are some people however who are masochistic by nature. They crave painful conditions of existence.

The body will deteriorate. It does have a maximum capacity for self-damage. It comes from nature with faults which no man can correct. And yet, if possible, one should behave in a manner which does not increase the ailments. This means that one must manage the body, and maintain its situations for optimum health.

This is relevant hereafter, because the condition of the physical body is mimicked by the subtle one, to such an extent that the subtle body adopts the healthy, or unhealthy condition of the physical system.

An unhealthy physical body inefficiently uses the energy of the subtle form. That results in the subtle system being exhausted. One will have to live as the subtle form hereafter. Its condition during that time, may be similar to that of the physical system before it died.

Impelled by heat in the body, urged by the force of air in it, which penetrates every part, all energies of the life force are thereby restricted. (Anu Gītā 2.15)

The bio-physical energy of the physical body is affected by the heat and air in it. This energy is the lifeForce. It is conducted through the entire body, or it may be obstructed with dire health consequences.

Since there is an ongoing exchange between the physical system and the subtle one, and since the physical one is predominant, one should observe the condition of the physical body regularly. One should do whatever can be done to repair damage to the physical system.

The issue is the subtle body. Since it is affected by the physical one, the condition of the physical apparatus should be monitored carefully. This however should not become an obsession. It is a practical matter based on the subtle body's tendency to mimic the condition of the physical one.

When the physical system dies, the subtle one which is the psychic remnant of the person, will continue. Even though it can be damaged, even though it can suffer from exhaustion, where it has to sleep, or have its objectivity suspended, it cannot die as the physical one does. Still the subtle body's inability to be killed, does not include it being unaffected by the physical body, when that form is alive.

It is only when there is no allied physical body, that the subtle form is free from having to mimic a physical system. However, it carried with it the impressions which it received from the last physical body, and it continues to mimic a healthy or unhealthy condition hereafter.

Being very forceful, the heat in the body becomes very impulsive. It penetrates all vital parts of the living being. (Anu Gītā 2.16)

The heat in the body is required, but it can be disordered such that too much or too little, may cause death. Access to repair an overheated or frozen body is limited. This is because one cannot easily dissect and inspect the body. Even one's body has inner parts which were never seen and will never be seen by the self.

Imaging devices enable physicians to visualize some inner parts of a body, but even then, there are parts and processes which cannot be diagnosed.

Eventually there is a point in each body, where the individual concerned, or anyone else, can do nothing to stop the body from dying. The urgency of life is death. When dead, the urgency of existence is to become physical again or to be involved in another dimension.

No matter what, no matter who he/she is, this life will terminate in death. It behooves every person to ponder this. If there is something one can do to figure what will be the condition hereafter, one should by all means adopt that behavior during the life of the body.

Then the individual spirit being fully afflicted, is displaced from the perishable body. When the vital organs deteriorate in every way, the entity relinquishes the body. O best of the trained ritualists, know that the psyche suffers terribly. (Anu Gītā 2.17)

Some persons die suddenly where the physical system is damaged irreparably. These people were not afflicted for weeks, months, or years, with injuries by a mishap. Some others suffer from a damaging impact for a short time, for days or weeks. These may not have prepared for death.

However, the displacement from the physical body, leaves the person with only its psychic existence. If the person was unprepared, he/she will be traumatized to be restricted to a psychic existence, and to have no physical control.

Being that death is inevitable, and there is no evidence that there was an exemption from it, it is reasonable for everyone, even children, to prepare for it. One should consider that death can come at any moment.

There is nothing a person wanted to complete, which is so urgent, that Nature may not deprive the person of his/her body. An example is the composition of this book. The writer feels an urgency to do it. And yet, he cannot be certain that Nature will honor those aspirations. Nor should he be offended, if Nature decides to produce circumstances which abruptly kills the body, which is the very means of producing this literature.

It is approved for Nature to interrupt the completion of this. My position is to use the opportunities provided by Nature. It is not to dictate what Nature should or should not do. We should take hints from Nature and work within its format. When there are no opportunities, one should not be alarmed. One should not panic. One should not demand.

If perchance the body is killed unexpectedly, one should mentally be in acceptance of fate. One should not regret the incidence nor feel that something is lacking or missing, because one did not complete obligations. It is just fine, because at any stage, the activities in this world will be expressed. Even if there are no human beings left to impact history, time will traverse the scape of existence. Actions, either grand ones, or atomic movements, will transpire. One should be at ease with this.

Whatever energy is unfulfilled, whatever urge is not gratified, whatever craving one did not satisfy, those premises for action will remain in dormancy until there is opportunity for their circumstance. One should be confident of this.

Some spiritual teachers say that for the spirit, there is no suffering. They posit that the spirit is untouched by whatever afflicts the physical body. This teacher of *Kashyapa* disagrees with this. He stated that when the vital organs deteriorate in every way, the entity relinquishes the body. At that time and even prior, the psyche may suffer terribly.

Questions arise.

- Is the person affected by physical circumstances?
- Are traumas which happened when the physical body was present, impacting the subtle form?

The answers to these queries are resolved when we consider that there is a coreSelf but it is involuntarily linked to adjuncts. This linkage causes the transfer of energy in downward and upward directions, where the higher one may affect the lower one, and the lower one may affect the higher one.

It is preferred that only a higher principle should affect a lower one and that the reverse should not occur. However, that is not the reality. The use of the coreSelf's interest by its adjuncts, causes some awareness on the part of the core, where it experiences, shadows of the trauma, which its adjuncts are subjected to. These may be pleasant or unpleasant experiences.

It is only if the core would be isolated from the adjuncts that it would not be affected. However, such disconnection is not within the immediate power of the core. Hence it is in the core's interest, to be as detached as it can possibly be. That would afflict it with the least energy withdrawal.

All living beings are forever disoriented by birth and death. O best of the trained ritualists, they are observed being displaced from the material bodies. (Anu Gītā 2.18)

A limited being does not have the upper hand. Whatever controls this situation, whether it be a supreme individual or massive cosmic energy, that alone remains as the Ultimate.

At any stage the Ultimate may shift the situation in one's favor, or it may cause ruination. Whether it is a personal, or mere energetic authority, is not the issue. What is important is to know that at any time, a limited being, oneself, could be erased. We are already familiar with ourselves, to know that the conscious phase of self, is only part of the self experience. There is an unconscious phase. We do not have absolute control over the shift from consciousness to unconsciousness, nor from unconsciousness to awareness. That other person or reality who/what controls that operation is the Ultimate.

Birth or death means the emergence in one environment, and the departure as well. Neither is controlled by the limited self. There is a pretense that one may be absolute, or that one may become absolute, but that is illogical and is totally improbable. The fact is that one is disoriented by the movements of Nature in her physical and psychic aspects.

What happens is that one discovers oneself as an embryo which is a visible beginning. This happens with one having no memory reference. And without that, one is left as if one is identity-less, as a mere start of a limited awareness. From that stance one is pressured to make something out of that reference-less beginning.

The teacher of *Kashyapa* explained that he had the vision for mystic penetration, where he viewed the shifting through existence of some limited entities. He observed how they became identified as physical bodies, and then were displaced from the formations. This happened involuntarily, with superficial input from the entities.

They enter wombs as well, and suffer violent pains in the vital organs. It is observed that the human being is repeatedly subjected to agony. (Anu Gītā 2.19

Gautam Buddha concluded that this situation is without exception a trauma-saturated place. His view may be contradicted because most people find that if trauma is defined as what is unpleasant, then only some experiences are traumatic. And if trauma is defined as all psychological shifts, then yes, the situation is challenging.

But some people find pleasant situations to be desirable. They do not agree that the entire experience of the cosmos should be rejected. Buddha however disagreed. His argument was that the pleasant desired experiences carry the flip side of displeasure, which must be experienced at some time. Hence, he stood his ground in condemning the cosmic existence.

What to do? Each individual should analyze and draw conclusions for himself/herself. It is a matter of trying to enforce those ideas from one's limited leverage. Buddha proposed a *nirvana* attainment, which is complete exemption from the ravages of this existence, from its total presentation. Hence the question arises, can the cosmic situation be controlled by any limited personality? Each should research this for himself/herself.

However, there is another proposal which was shared by the teacher of *Kashyapa*. He suggested that despite the pleasantries afford to the individual, still, one is subjected to gestation, and suffer violent pains in the vital organs, both while in the womb, and when one is expelled from it. We are repeatedly subjected to agony, that is reason enough to find a way out.

A human being suffers when the limbs are broken, and again distress comes from cold water. The composite energy of the five elements is felt. From cold there is agitation in forceful air which moves distressfully in the body. (Anu Gītā 2.20)

Each entity should self-observe its response to the conditions it is subjected to. There are situations which are enjoyed or rated as preferred. These however do not counterbalance the psychological or physical drama which is endured, which one can neither resist nor be indifferent to.

The body itself, as it is experienced as one composite self, yields pleasure in one instance, and pain or anguish in another. Somehow, one should estimate this. One should derive an assessment to see if this existence is worth the while. This does not mean that one can immediately exempt the self from this. If such a reclusion is possible, one must discover the method of doing so. Since transcendence is abnormal, it would require extraneous physical and psychic efforts to achieve it.

Some people report transit to supernatural places where only a blissful existence is possible but these persons usually return to the earthly existence. Their departure from here was involuntary, which means that they did not initiate, and then control the transit. These are the challenges for those who want to achieve transcendence.

The in-breath and out-breath are situated in the five elements which compose a body. The air goes upward and downward but it is finally freed from the body while causing pain. (Anu Gītā 2.21)

At death, the vitality provided by breath, comes to an end. The ingestion and expulsion of air terminates. The body is declared dead. Conversely, at birth, the hiss of breath through the body is regarded as survival of the fetus, with no help from the mother's breathing energy.

Once the breathing starts, its intake is scattered in every part of the body, such that if any part is deprived, that area does not function properly. However, when the entire form is shocked with termination, the self relates to that as pain. That is the rupturing of the connection between the physical form, and the subtle support for it. This subtle collective continues existence, and is used to attract another physical form, or to become established as a psychic existence, which does not require physical responses.

It is observed that without breath, one gives up the body. Being without bodily warmth, without breath, without vitality, the consciousness is displaced from the body. (Anu Gītā 2.22)

Rarely does anyone ever give up the body. Due to innate attachment to physical history, and fear of pain, most entities cling to a diseased or damaged body, until it dies and the person experiences a lack of relationship with it. This is when the person discovers that he/she cannot in any way motivate the body, and cannot in any way be the body as its controller, through the exercise of willpower for movement.

Even though some people commit suicide by taking actions which kill the body, those persons do not control the way, the psychic self is disconnected permanently from the physical body. There is no guarantee that anyone who kills a body, will control the events which occur to the psychic portion of that dead form. Stated simply, the psychic maneuvers which occur when a body dies, are for the most part a natural process, just as birth of an infant occurs by so many natural developments, which no human being can dictate.

Death means that the consciousness of a self is displaced from its physical body, but how that occurs is beyond the power of any limited somebody. However, what can be done by someone, is that he/she may study the movements of Nature, to understand what will happen. Then one can introspect, to discover which parts of Nature's actions one may regulate.

The death zones are present in the psychic world. One can research these in meditation and astral projection. Then one may discover how one can go to a place which is to one's liking. The easy option is to ignore the fact of one's upcoming death, except that the normal result of making no effort to understand the psychic terrain, is to be recycled back into the physical world as a baby, which suffers and enjoys as it did in the previous life.

Thus, the personal body, being totally detached from the spiritual level of existence, is said to be dead. Even with the same psychic energy, the soul cannot perceive the sense objects which the body procured previously. That soul was itself productive of the vital energy which was produced from food consumed by the body. (Anu Gītā 2.23)

The declaration of death is made on the physical and astral sides of existence. Its announcement on the physical plane is made by others. The deceased entity cannot directly speak of it on the physical planes. In the astral world, however the deceased person can announce his/her condition as being that of a mere psychic person. The meaning is that the physical person self is no longer an actor on the stage of history.

Despite being the remnant psychic force, which is the remains of the composite person who was identified as a living physical body, the astrally projected self loses the sensual access which was developed for it, when its physical body lived. It no longer hears, touches, sees, tastes, or smells physical objects. It finds that the physical world is not registered bluntly to it. The deceased person has senses, but they are not ushered through the bio-electric nervous system of a living physical form. This is experienced as deprivation. This feeling may bring with it a deep sense of loss. It may foster regret.

As soon as the physical body lacks vital energy, it is regarded as being dead. The psychic contents of the person no longer support its nervous system. The physical system becomes unresponsive to the psychic force of self. Breath ceases. On a grand scale, deterioration begins.

That eternal individual soul works here on earth using a material body. Know that whatever ingredients gather together become emulsified in certain organs which are the vital parts, as explained in the authoritative books. (Anu Gītā 2.24)

To understand the physical existence in terms of personality, one must focus on the psychic content of self. The background which supports the physical maneuvering is psychic energy. To calculate using the conventional idea of a physical someone, we must agree that the full physical self cannot be transposed to transcend death. Only a portion of the full physical person can be shifted. That would be the psychic remnant which is translated elsewhere when it no longer can motivate anything on the physical plane.

That psychic remnant which is shifted from the physical level and which can no longer register itself as the full physical person, may feel undone, removed, and disfitted, when it discovers that it can no longer impact history. Its psychic actions, though subtle, no longer are amplified physically. Its ideas cannot be converted into physical actions directly. It lost its physical placement.

Some ascetics feel that the self is actionless. That whatever it is, it is not capable of moving an object. It cannot move itself from place to place. They attest that it is locationStatic. However, when regarding the self in the conventional way, the experience is that the self moves, is moved, and within limits moves certain other objects. It is not cosmic, where it can move a universe, nor move things with comic authority, but it can move, and cause a limited range of objects to be relocated.

In deep meditation, one should realize this. One should see how energy which radiates continuously from the coreSelf flows away from it and causes motion in and with its psyche.

The compound which is the living physical body, acts as a whole in the complex environment which is the physical world. Each self of the trillions of psychic unitSelves, energizes its body as it is permitted by the living condition of the form. There is movement inside the body, as the body remains stationary or acts to shift itself, or anything else, which it can handle in the environment outside the body.

Then with the deterioration or damage of those vital organs, the life force is aroused. Quickly entering the center of consciousness, it restrains the bodily awareness. Then that soul, though conscious, is without bodily awareness. (Anu Gītā 2.25)

The living physical body is a complex bio-electrical mechanism which has two power sources. One is its chemical reactions which result in it having a lifeForce. The other is the ever-producing radiant energy from the coreSelf. These two are the batteries for energetic activity.

When the chemical reactions which provide actionPower become disrupted, the vital organs become damaged. That results in regional or total failure. The lungs no longer process fresh air properly. The heart no longer maintains its hydraulic activity. This results in death of the physical body.

Despite the malfunctions of the vital organs, the radiant power of the coreSelf continues uninterruptedly, but the physical system is unable to use that continuously supplied energy. Hence the physical body becomes rigid and dies.

Apart from the radiation from the coreSelf, the subtle body generates psychic lifeForce. At death, this power can be at its optimum or minimum. It will be there on the psychic side when the physical system is finished, but it may be in a weakened condition. Over time, after death, on the subtle side, it will become rejuvenated. As a sick physical body may resume its healthy condition over time, so the energy of the depleted or sickened subtle body will become reenergized in the astral world after death.

The physical system is similar to the psychic one but only to a limited degree. The subtle body cannot be killed as the physical one is subjected to deterioration and cessation of movement. But the subtle system can be exhausted, even though it would regain its energy over time, and will not die. Before the subtle body becomes totally exhausted, it will go into an immobile state where after a time, it will become rejuvenated. This happens by an osmosis energy exchange, where the psychic contaminants are slowly replaced by energetic subtle nutrients.

When the physical body becomes irreparably damaged, when it is terminally ill, the lifeForce makes an attempt to collect the parts of itself, and to retreat into the center of consciousness. The coreSelf for its part notices this, and appeals to the intellect analytical psychic orb, for a report on actions which would reverse the illness. Someone may consider the condition as the end of life, while another may think that there is a way to reverse the condition.

However, noticing that there is no response to regain a healthy state, the lifeForce and the coreSelf come to a state of desperation, and look for a way out, a process for safely, and with the least pain, abandoning the physical body. Of course, releasing oneself from a dying body is rarely accomplished by any limited self. Instead, the body dies. Then there is release from it. For some this is a dismal and unwanted condition, because those persons would like to remain as physical persons with the privilege of having roles in history.

A few persons welcome the disengagement from the physical form. Some turnabout to discover what is available in the psychic world. Usually, those ascetics experience a boost, or upgrade in consciousness, as soon as the disconnect with the physical system occurs. They go to higher astral zones or to supernatural or spiritual places.

The inherently conscious being is depressed by a dulling awareness, while its vital organs are still in a malfunctioned state. That individual soul being support-less is affected by the status of the airy energy in the body. (Anu Gītā 2.26)

In any extreme illness, even those which do not terminate in death, a depressive emotion is experienced. This dulls the consciousness of the person. Because the coreSelf supports the psychic mechanism of the self, and due to the fact that the core is not supported by the lifeForce in turn, an unhealthy condition is experienced as discomfort by the self.

The reduction in efficiency of the chemical power in the body, causes an increase extraction of energy from the radiant self. This in turn is interpreted by the self as unwanted discomfort.

Before it can be totally exhausted, there is an involuntary disconnection of the coreSelf from the lifeForce. This is experienced as unconsciousness, where the core is temporarily disconnected from its psychic environment, the subtle body.

Then it makes a loud harsh sigh of breath, which quivers the unconscious body. It quickly transits out of the unconscious body. (Anu Gītā 2.27)

The disconnect between the psychic self and the physical one, is a subtle maneuver which is conducted by a jerk action of the lifeForce. There is a **snig** sound which is made when this happens. That may or may not be heard by the dying person. It depends on where the levy of focus is applied at the time of the break.

This final displacement of the subtle body from the physical one, is not controlled by the coreSelf. Just as the impregnation of an embryo is not controlled by the limited self who is that new body, so the departure of a subtle body from a dying physical one, is not under the command of the core. For that matter, it can happen that the core is not aware of the disconnection. It is also possible that a core may not ever know of the disconnect, and may continue existence in some psychic place, with no recall of the physical life lived.

Those who are conscious and coherent at the last moments before death of the physical body, may make a harsh sigh of breath, where that quivers the unconscious body. The lifeForce with its accessory powers, with the intellect, the sense of identity and the core, then move quickly and transit out of the unconscious body. But this is not controlled by the coreSelf. It is an involuntary process. It is experienced during fearful incidences when someone is in dangerous situations, except that then there is no completed disconnect. The victim is left with the fear of death only, the trauma of being put into great pain.

Being permanently displaced from the body, that individual spirit exists being enveloped in the psychic effect-energy of its actions. Being stigmatized by such, it has the energy of its spiritually uplifting, and socially rewarding acts as well as any criminal effects. (Anu Gītā 2.28)

The subtle body is a collective just as the physical one is. As there are parts to the physical form and also organs in it, so there are operational junctions and orbs in the subtle body. Ultimately the most important psychic item is the coreSelf. However, that alone cannot operate a subtle body. It needs the functions of adjuncts like the sense of identity, intellect, memory, and kundalini lifeforce with its sensual devices.

There is no question of the coreSelf directly operating the subtle body or psyche. This is because the level of energy of the core is different to that of the vibrational content of the subtle body. This makes it necessary to convert the power of the core using several adjuncts.

It is untrue that the subtle body is the coreSelf or actual spiritual person. It is not that. The subtle body is a bodyContainer which houses a coreSelf, adjuncts and accessory energies. These collectively are a psyche.

Along with the psychic machinery, the psyche has the energy of its spiritually uplifting, and socially rewarding acts as well as any criminal effects. These move about in the astral existence after the disconnection from the physical form.

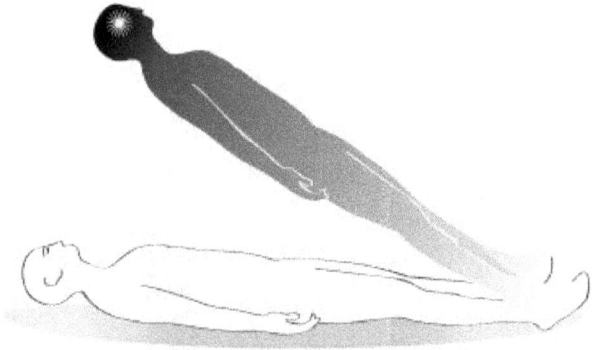

spirit fused into astral body,
which is displaced permanently
from the physical body at death

A ritually-trained ascetic who is endowed with knowledge, who heard from authoritative sources, is known by his characteristics as one with socially-commendable acts or by what is the opposite. (Anu Gītā 2.29)

A yogi may have a good or bad reputation. It is based on his/her social responses. People will rate him/her in terms of his/her relational demeanor. According to the time, place and occasion, a yogi is served reactions from acts in past existences. He/She should brace for this and should not react as if the impositions of fate were out of place or inappropriate.

As soon as one enters any dimension, forces of attraction and repulsion become sensitive. These cling to or are repelled from the yogi. These assists, resists, or are neutral, in respect to what is desired by the yogi. If one does not give way to fate, one will be inconvenienced and will be victimized by the all-surrounding energies.

As in darkness, those with vision see the changing aspects of the firefly disappearing, now and again, so are those with insight perception (who perceive psychic reality). (Anu Gītā 2.30)

Once one becomes a physical body, one's psychic perception is funneled through physical senses. It is a task to extract the psychic senses from the physical ones. Because of the compelling force which fuses the psychic energy through the physical body, even the yogis must do sensual energy retraction practices, to pull the insight energy from its reinforcement of physical perception.

In the darkness of the mind, a yogi should meditate to sort the coreSelf and its adjuncts. He/She should wait in the mind for psychic perception to develop. He may accelerate the process by deliberately restraining the mind from its outward going pursuits.

When the sensual energy which naturally courses outward is retracted, there is an accumulation of psychological power which causes insight perception.

Thus, with divine perception, the perfected yogis see the individual soul, as it is displaced from a body, or as it transits from the astral world to attain another form, or as it enters the womb. (Anu Gītā 2.31)

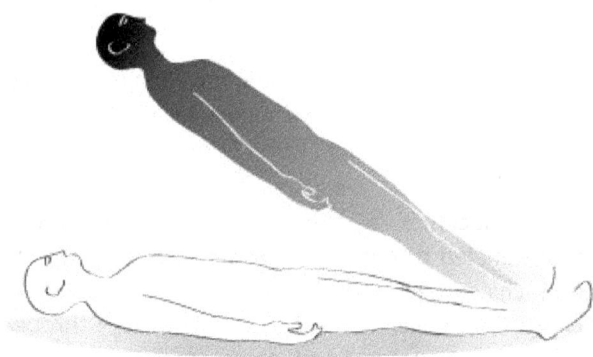

astral body leaves dead physical form

astral body is attracted to romance energy of future parents

astral body fuses into father's feelings

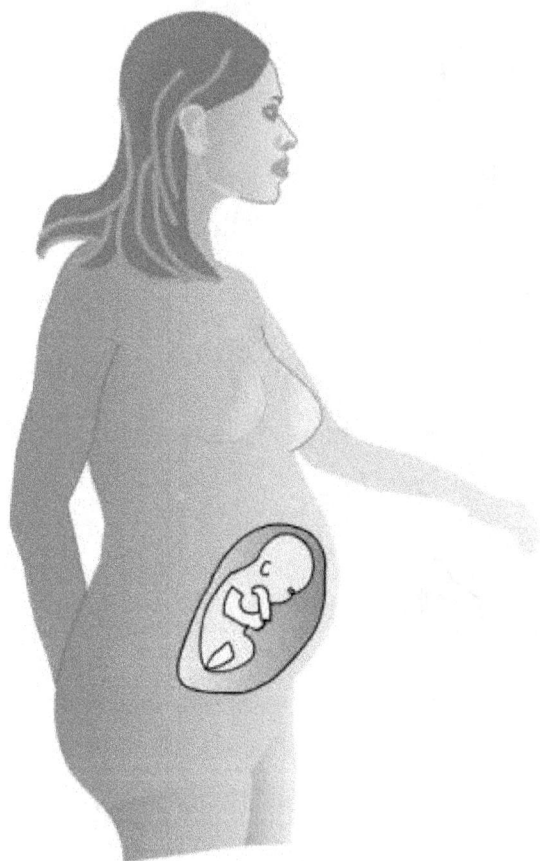

mother becomes pregnant
with compressed astral body
which was fused into father's semen

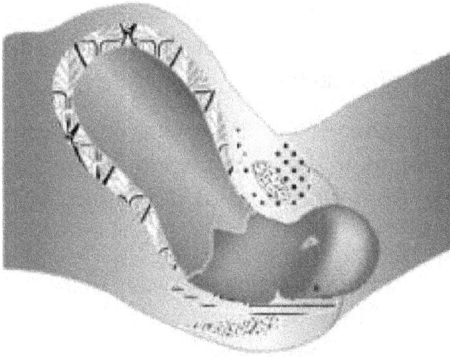

new body which is astral body
and matter which was attracted to it
is separated from mother's form

For the study of the hereafter, three information are required.

- the subtle body's condition while there is a physical form

- the subtle body's condition when there is no physical body

- the subtle body's conversion into being an embryo

The dream experiences are the first indication that there is a psychic component to the self. When in dreams, the self disengages from physicality, one should be observational and should make an effort to identify with and operate the subtle body.

Dreams are involuntary but during their events, one may assume some control over the subtle body. One may learn about the dreamscape dimensions, and establish a preference for where one would like to exist hereafter, when the subtle body no longer has the physical one as its physical identity.

Where does the dream body go when the person assumes himself/herself as the physical body? Is the dream form interwoven into the physical system as only psychic energy? How can one be aware of the dream body when one functions as the physical form?

Hereafter, when there is no physical body, does the dream body live on, in the dream world, where it moves from place to pace, from dimension to dimension, as it did while dreaming?

The conversion from being a psychic being only, with no physical form, and then becoming an embryo, how does that happen? Why does one not recall the conversion step by step?

The *guru* of *Kashyapa* explained that with divine perception, the perfected yogis see the individual soul, as it is displaced from a body, or as it transits from the astral world to attain another form, or as it enters the womb.

After death one of two attainments are possible.

- remain as a psychic being with no physical counterpart

- convert into being a physical being by becoming an embryo

It is hardly likely that one will permanently convert into being a psychic presence with no physical body. One will experience the self as a psychic being for a short period, then one will be attracted to the means of becoming physical. That process occurs spontaneously with one being attracted to potential parents.

Some deceased people, whom I know, were determined to remain on the psychic side of life. Their desire in this regard was due to fear of illness if they again become an embryo. However, this fear in itself, even though it is powerful enough to delay someone from becoming a child again, cannot make the delay perpetual. In time, by natural attraction most entities who remain in limbo in the astral zone, will be attracted to new parents, and will again become a physical person.

It is possible however, even though it is rare, that a yogi may translate permanently into being a psychic being, just as the teacher of *Kashyapa* was. A yogi may shift upwards to astral zones where deities reside. In those places the configuration of the subtle body is such that it has no need to be part of physical history. It does not feel the need for physical completion of its desires. Ideas for physicality like having physical buildings, ideas for family leadership like being a father or mother of children, do not arise in those higher dimension bodies. A yogi who transits to those higher places, may escape from the force of involuntarily becoming someone's child.

Concerning this, it is perceived according to the authoritative texts that there are three regions. This earth where the creatures live is the world of social action. (Anu Gītā 2.32)

Different teachers relate different regions, but regardless, this earth, where the creatures live, is the world of social action. This is *karmabhūmi*, the location where one may perform physical actions which are ascribed as history. Somehow, someone feels a compulsion to make a mark in the world.

Most of the people who died, have either assumed an embryo, or are in the process of acquiring one. This course does not depend on the individual. He/She is involved but not as the primal schemer. As straws float in a stream, and are carried here and there by the currents, so the limited selves are conveyed by Nature through her domains.

In time, all embodied souls having committed socially-acclaimed or socially-condemned actions, get elevating or degrading experiences in reference to previous performance. (Anu Gītā 2.33)

The physical action location is a reactive environment except that the reactions are timely in the sense of a cosmic solution. This may make sense to a limited self, on occasion. Being with little or no insight into the causal circumstances which wedge an action, someone cannot calculate the returns from an action accurately. Thus, his/her response to any situation is likely to be haphazard and untimely.

How does one know if an assault is a fresh attack, or a blister of an offence one did in the past? When should one be active or passive? Who should be excused? Who should be punished?

How does one make contact with the calculating basis of this reality? How does one determine correctly what is appropriate or inappropriate?

Those who commit socially-unacceptable acts here on earth, transit to hell hereafter on the basis of the same acts. Being wasted, those faulty human beings are regularly tormented in hell. It stands to reason that freedom from that place is very difficult to attain. Thus, the individual spirit should protect itself from that fate. (Anu Gītā 2.34)

Because there is a psychic underbasis to the physical existence, each physical action has a psychic counterpart. That register mixes with other psychic factors, which when boomeranged into the physical world causes unexpected events to manifest. But there is another scene, which is that the physically based psychic energy, and the other psychic reality, become entangled and produce both physical, and psychic hellish conditions.

These situations, some of which are desirable, and some undesirable, become manifest into one's perception, as they are released by fate. Some can be ignored. Some can be neutralized. Some must be endured.

By all means, a yogi should study the connection between hostile acts committed, and their returns, in the form of hell on earth, or hell hereafter. He should avoid unfavorable returns. His pattern of behavior should be such that its content does not aggravate Nature into penalizing him with hellish conditions.

But regarding their ascent, the entities being elevated, reside in their attained realms. Listen attentively. I will describe the truth of this. Having heard this your intellect will be steady. You will have the best information and will be decisive about social actions. (Anu Gītā 2.35)

One should do whatever brings good fortune not just immediately but in the distant future. One should live as if one would exist eternally, so that events committed now will result in favorable circumstances in the distant future, even if these events manifest millenniums, after they were enacted.

Assuming that time is perpetual, and that one will be somewhere, somehow, in one of the multidimensions, one should be ready to transmigrate at any moment but having done what was auspicious in the long term.

No matter where one goes, one will be involved relationally with others. That will occur. Hence one should not be a social irritant. All the same, one should not be a social addict, someone who is socially needy, and is a nuisance. One should keep a respectable distance from others, but should be willing to serve, if there is the opportunity. Whatever one does should be rendered with value and quality. One should not be a meanie.

Those which are the regions of all forms of the stars, the orbiting moon which shines on the earth, the self-effulgent orbiting sun, all situated in their realms; know these as the locations attained by those who perform socially-beneficial acts. (Anu Gītā 2.36)

As on earth, there are hellish conditions, tolerable situations, and heavenly delights, so in the cosmos there are various types of realms. Many of these are transparent subtle dimensions which our physical senses fail to appreciate.

Some such places are horrifying to the senses which one would assume if one traversed there with full sensual perception. Some are similar to the earth in regards to solidity and gravitational atmosphere. Some others are superior places which are beyond one's wildest dreams. In some elevated places, the pleasure felt is so acute, as to be near intolerable. And so, there are hellish locations where the discomfort is unbearable.

The attainment of the stars, the moon or the self-effulgent orbing sun is not the physical access of these places. Currently we have that physical access in part because we use starlight, moonlight, moon tides, and sunlight.

Besides the physical use of these heavenly bodies, there is their psychic features. Even the earth has psychic dimensions which we sometimes access in dreams, and which are similar to, but dissimilar to what we know about it physically.

To prepare for death, a yogi must free himself/herself from the physical assessment of perception. This must be done in reference even to the earth, such that in dream experiences, we can become familiar with the other dimensions of this earth, which are accessible through astral travel.

Still, if one insists on using the physical reference, and one cannot break free from it, because of not getting sufficient transcendental experience, even then, one should study what happens in dream experiences on the earth or in the earth, so that one can understand how one may exist in the psychic manifestation of this planet earth, being there in social and environmental situation with others, or being alone. One should be prepared to live in the parallel dimensions which are near but not identical to the earth, places where one meets others and interacts. One should notice what is different about the other earth dimensions. For instance, currently we have automobiles on earth. Some drive using engines and tire traction. Does one find that this is necessary in the use of cars in dreams?

What about distance?

Is distance perceived in the same way on the psychic earth, as it is on the physical planet?

After the consumption of the energy of pious acts, they are repeatedly demoted. There in the celestial regions, there is distinction as well, regarding high, low, and median status. (Anu Gītā 2.37)

It takes energy to act, but energy is also generated by an act. This is the binding condition. The energy used in creating activity is mixed with reactive forces which spring into being because of the initial activity. That combination is used by the time factor to produce more reactive energy. That may convert into immediate repercussions. Or it may transfer into a dormant condition, which will come alive somewhere, somehow, in the future.

The accumulation of pious acts resides on a psychic plane of consciousness, and is used by fate to shift the actor to a heavenly world hereafter, but only for the time value of the piety. As soon as the pious benefit is expended, the person sinks to a lower plane. That is experienced as disappointment. Thus, the conclusion of a pious act on earth, is a heavenly condition which when it is expended, results in depression, with a feeling that heaven must be earned again, by getting an opportunity for more pious acts.

When one arrives in heaven hereafter, and if it was possible because of socially pious activities in the last body, one should rate the duration of stay in that desirable place. However, in the majority of cases, the pious persons in heaven become so preoccupied with the enjoyments, that they have no idea that the sojourn is limited. It will trail out. Abruptly, one will be translated downwards to a psychic plane from which one can again become a physical being on earth.

One will have the urge to be pious again. To fulfill that, one will look for opportunities to do good to others and to have the means to help others, in a way which fate will regard as worthy of upliftment, when one is deprived of the physical body, which is itself the means of generating pious credits.

Apart from the concentration of pleasure in a heavenly world, there is a social environment with others, some who have more piety, some who have a similar quantity, and some who have less. That is the subtle tension in those celestial places. Anyone who cannot tolerate those gradings, is immediately displaced from heaven. He/She finds the self to be removed from there, and to be in a psychic environment where it is possible to develop an embryo, where one can work again to generate piety, in the hope that when one goes to heaven, one will be in the top tier of pious individuals. Such is the social tension.

Even in the celestial world, there is no contentment after one sees someone with greater effulgence and splendor. Thus, details of all courses of soul transit were described by me. (Anu Gītā 2.38)

The competitive nature of a human being is reactive on earth and in the heavenly places, such that even in the celestial realms, one feels out of place when in the presence of anyone, who attained heaven by pious acts. One does not compare oneself to the deity and his/her assistants, but only to those who have an earthly pious condition, as their basis for being there. This is because pious earthlings are honored by the supernatural people in that heavenly place.

When one sees how someone else is honored with more finesse and appreciation by the permanent denizens of heaven, one feels undone. One develops an instant resentment to the honored earthlings. This causes a darkening of one's subtle body. A greyish energy is seen in it. That makes one feel uneasy and out-of-place.

Instantly, with that energy content of the subtle body, one is shifted to a lower plane, where one is attracted to relatives and friends and to the sexual circumstance which affords one the opportunity to take an embryo.

We can estimate the situation where even in the celestial world, after a person sees someone with greater effulgence and splendor, there is no contentment in his/her feelings. One feels undone, dissatisfied as it is, with only one thought in mind, which is to be a human being again, and to carefully act so as to be the best of the pious individuals. One becomes determined to be a religious man/woman of impeccable character and deeds.

The aspiration to go to heaven hereafter, and to do so on the basis of socially accepted acts and even hidden activities which benefit one and all, has its downside. Hidden in it is the motive to best all other persons, such that in heaven one will be honored beyond compare. That flaw is ever present. It has to do with the expression of pride, something which torments even the most pious being. But if the aspiration for heaven is flawed and innately so, then what should anyone aim for?

Regarding the production of the embryo, I will tell you of that after this. As I explain this to you, listen with rapt attention, O trained ascetic. (Anu Gītā 2.39)

Once the stay in heaven runs its course, the snag is to join the queue of departed ancestors who must become embryos. Why does that have to be, the gruesome passage through the mother's body? In heaven, one does not take birth through a woman's passage. One does not die as a physical body. There, birth means the mere appearance of a psychic body. Death means the de-energization of it. There is no birth and death as with a physical system.

A limited being is subjected to this. He/She neither can create nor put an end to this. That is a discontent which one must deal with.

There is no elimination of the energy of auspicious or inauspicious social acts. Obtaining bodies in sequence, the activities express energies in various environments in sequence. (Anu Gītā 3.1)

The idea of ending the psychic impressions of auspicious or inauspicious social acts, is illusion only. One cannot destroy the current display, nor the past ones which were or were not converted, nor the future ones which will be formulated and enforced. A limited being has no chance to displace or eliminate the energy of pious or impious social acts. All of it is present at any given moment, with some being inoperative for the time being, and others being in the play of consciousness.

No one can eliminate the energy of what is done which is good or bad by someone's estimation. Whatever peels from an act, survives intact. It influences the future. In fact, Nature uses it to sponsor and condition the future. As one attains a body, circumstances are created which services or frustrates the actor who is a limited personality.

As during the bearing season, a fruit-bearing tree yields much fruit, so meritorious acts which are done with a pure mind supply ample benefits. (Anu Gītā 3.2)

A meritorious act carries a value according to the mental condition during its performance. The same physical action which has a higher or lower mental or emotional motive, will have a corresponding value. The existential weight of the act varies according to the promptings for it, and its method of execution.

Some returns from an action done using the physical body, may reach the actor hereafter in a higher or lower astral place, or it may surface in part, or fully, in another physical location.

Faulty acts done with a corrupt mind, produce corresponding results. With the mind before it, the self manifests social activities. (Anu Gītā 3.3)

In every case, the mind is before the self, as the medium between the self and the physical world. The mind should be guarded. It is the translator. The self is so sublime that it cannot directly maneuver the physical body. For any impact on the physical world, it must operate its relationship with the mind

As nature would have it, the self is afflicted by the information which is transported to it by the mind. Hence it is sensible for the self to position itself for optimum relationship with the mind. The communication between the mind and the self is such, that faulty actions produce resulting trauma for the self, who may or may not escape the anguish.

With the mind before it in every case, the self indulges. Some of this is voluntarily and some involuntary. Thus, to monitor the communications, the self should be as detached as possible.

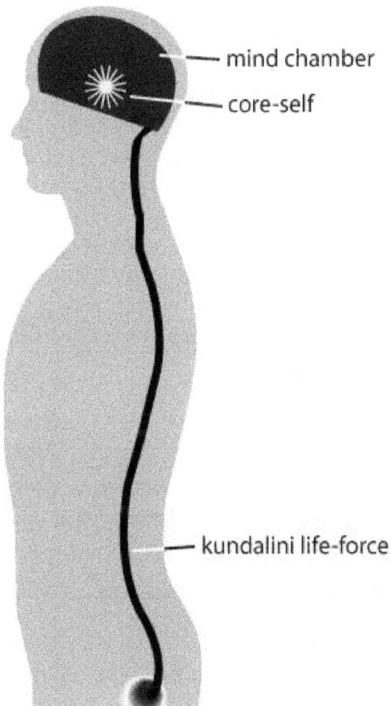

mind chamber

core-self

kundalini life-force

Being possessed by the energy of action, the person is overwhelmed by anger and lust; like that, it enters the womb. Now hear my explanation of this. (Anu Gītā 3.4)

The energy for action is present on the psychic and corresponding physical planes. The handicap is that some psychic motivations include a need for physical completion. That means that the person is prompted to complete his/her psychic actions on the physical level. This means mandatory physical presence which is serviced through acquiring a physical body.

If someone can act psychically and not have the need to complete a corresponding physical motion, that person would exist on the psychic level and not be a physical being, not have to acquire and operate a physical body which is short lived, and which is subjected to birth through parents, and death with painful experiences.

The physical level has frustration as an integral part of it. That includes anger and lust, which are involuntarily activated, if circumstances do not fully endorse, and support the manifestation of a desire.

Being fused with blood and semen, entering the womb of a woman, it becomes the psyche which was produced from the effect-energy of its pious and despicable acts. (Anu Gītā 3.5)

There are many individual souls on the psychic level of existence. For that matter, there are trillions of them. Most exist in a state of limbo, waiting for physical opportunity. As soon as there is a physical energy match with the psyche of an individual, that person feels unified with the energy, and becomes a form of that energy, which consists in part of the effect-energy of his/her pious and despicable acts.

Before becoming a physical person, the individual is a psychic feature, which contains its potential based on its pious and despicable acts. Hence his/her tendencies and their potentials remain the same, and are expressed in the new fetal environment, in the infant form, in its youth, maturity and elderly condition.

No individual can fulfill all urges, and their potential expressions, in any given physical lifetime, but the remnant condition is retained. That transits with the personSelf into whatever hereafter situation, it is shifted to. Some of it is expressed and fulfilled there. The rest is held in reserve to be activated at a future time and place, where the environment can accommodate it.

Due to subtlety and the unmanifest texture of the being, it is not permanently fused with anything anywhere. It obtains a body which is based on spiritual energy. Thus, it is always a spiritual reality. It is the reference of all creatures. By it, the living beings exhibit symptoms of life. (Anu Gītā 3.6)

The coreSelf is a speck of spiritual reality, but it is subjected to affiliation with lower factors. According to its power, it may resist some influences. Because it is a different spiritual something, it is not permanently fused with anything anywhere in the psychic Nature. Yet, its temporary affiliation is challenging for it. The union between the coreSelf and its adjuncts is not easy to dissolve. It occurred involuntary. The self has no diagram of its situation.

In one sense, the coreSelf is the centralized primary power source but from another view, it is merely that for its psyche. Its concerns are not cosmic. It is not responsible as the massive power supporting all other realities. In so far as the self is the primary power source for its psyche, it is responsible to energize its adjuncts in a way which is conducive to its wellbeing.

This applies to each lifeForm, not just the human being, except that the humans have more leverage, because they use more refined adjuncts, and can leverage some influence in the psyche.

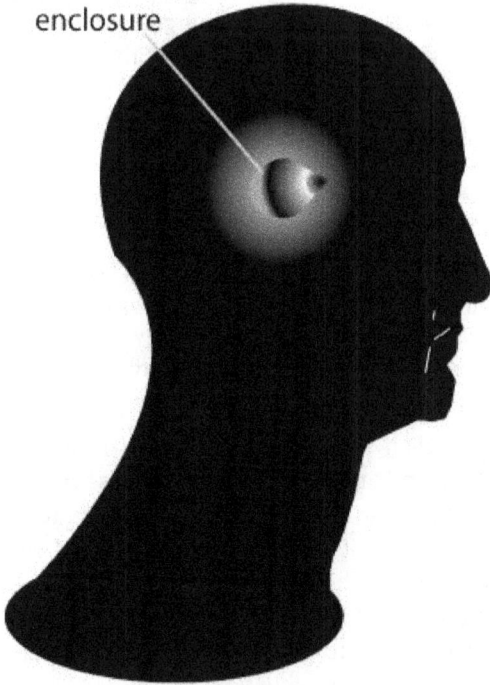

sense of identity enclosure

I-self enclosed by sense of identity

isolated
attentive powers
(sense of identity)

segregated
core-self

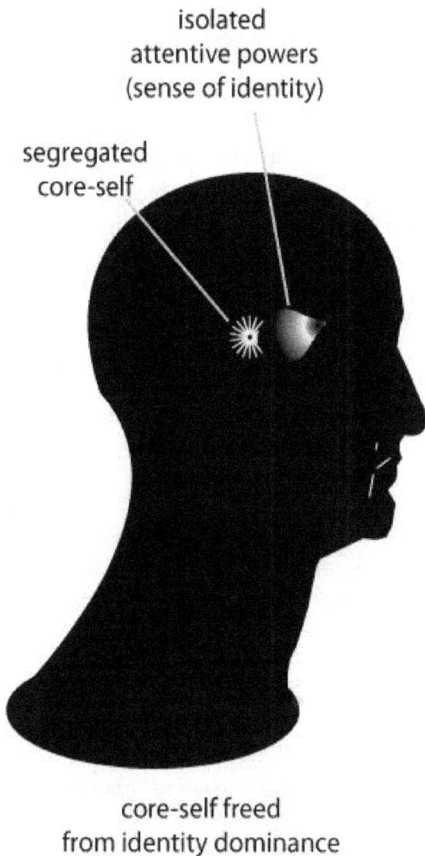

core-self freed
from identity dominance

The individual spirit's energy is diffused into every part of every limb of the fetus. It accepts the body's composite consciousness. It simultaneously resides in all locations where there is distribution of breath energy in the body. Then the fetus being conditioned by consciousness, moves its limbs. (Anu Gītā 3.7)

It is mysterious how a psychic person could be a physical body. The process of the gestation and birth of a baby, when regarded as a biological development, is explained without psychic reference. The mystery is featured when there is discussion about the possibility of a psychic self as the background factor.

The consciousness in the body is spread through each living part of it, but there are biological functions which operate in a way, where they appear to be independent of any psychic power. Hence it is necessary to accept, or to deny outright, the existence of a psyche which though unified, will separate from the physical apparatus at death.

The psychic energy, in conjunction with the biological apparatus, operates through the body by the spread of consciousness on the psychic plane, and the spread of electrical energy on the biological level.

The coreSelf is a radiance, an individual brilliance, which continually and everlastingly radiates spiritual energy. Its consciousness of what it is not, depends on how its radiance is spread through and can related to other realities.

The sensitivity of a self is directly related to how that person is connected to whatever it contacts in some environment. When a self is relaxed, it may expand its conscious reach to get some idea about other psychic or physical objects. Otherwise, when a self is tense, it may reach the situation of other factors.

The connection between a self and someone or something else, determines how that self will be affected by the other person or object. Even though it radiates continually, its objective grasp on its existence, and on anything else, varies, so that it may be aware, or unaware of itself or anything else.

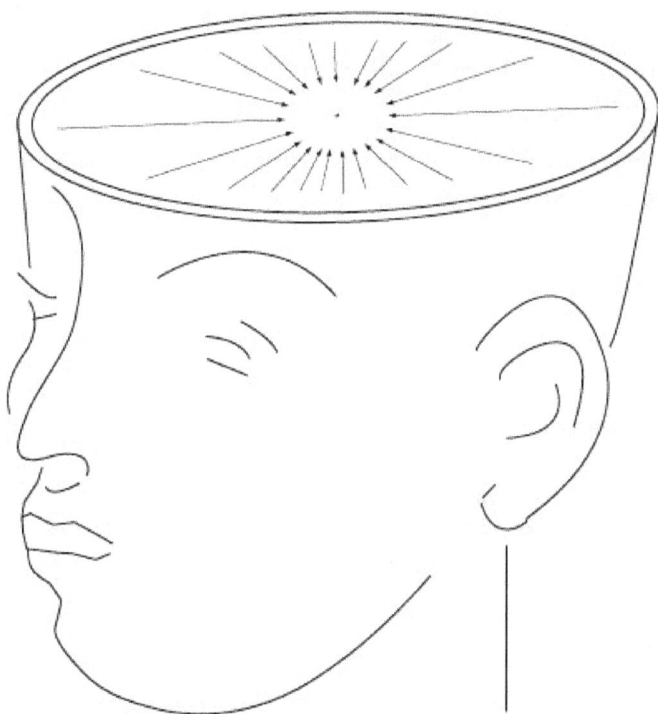

attention energy retracted into sense of identity

As molten iron which is poured into a mold, takes the form of it, so you should know that as being similar to how the individual spirit enters the womb. (Anu Gītā 3.8)

The radiance energy of a self is constant and does not vary in self-power. However according to how the self's radiance is accepted or neglected by some other person or thing, that is how the self is felt. Its influence varies. Its susceptibility to another influence varies as well.

According to how a disembodied self is attracted to its future parents, that is how it is induced into the psychic energy of those people. This causes a fusion of the aura of the parents with the radiance energy of that self. It is however with the subtle body of the self, with its psychic containment.

When unified with the parents' psychic energy, that other self is converted into a lusty influence, which becomes sexual energy in the parents. Then an embryo develops where the psychic energy conditions the nerves of the fetus to be responsive to it.

As fire penetrates a ball of iron, heating it, so you should comprehend the presence of a soul in a fetus. (Anu Gītā 3.9)

The radiant energy of a self is subtle. As fire is gross in reference to heat, so the physical body of a self is obvious in reference to the radiance of that self. The coreSelf is not its physical body, but all the same, it is essential to the life of that body. The liveliness of the physical form depends on the presence of the radiance of the self.

A disconnection of the coreSelf from the physical body causes instant collapse of the physical form. This is due to the inability of the form to derive energy from the ever-radiant self.

As a blazing lamp illuminates a house, so consciousness gives feelings to bodies. (Anu Gītā 3.10)

The physical body is as good as the feelings which inhabits it. As soon as there are no feelings in the physical body, its behavior is terminated. It can however have feelings in some parts, and still be functional to a degree.

In so far as it has feelings, that is how much consciousness it displays. From the physical perspective, the existential radiance of the core is amply demonstrated, if the physical body is in optimum health. Otherwise even though the radiance is perpetual and constant, still it appears from the physical plane, that the self is reduced. That is because the rating is based on physical condition.

For as long as one rates the condition of the person on the basis of his or her physical body, one will think that the physical condition is the essential situation, even though it is not.

The effects of beneficial or degrading activities which the individual soul performed in previous bodies, must be endured by necessity. (Anu Gītā 3.11)

The beneficial or degrading acts of an individual are logged by Nature, which uses the resultant energies to construct new circumstances in which situations are created, which draw the entity into participation. The route of this is to cause an entity to be involved so as to neutralize some desire energy.

None of the energy which is contained in the universe escapes from it. Whatever one does is logged. Wherever one goes is noted. Nature is mathematically efficient. It accounts for every particle, method, and mix.

Then that (effects) is exhausted and again other effects of new actions are accumulated. This continues for as long as the righteous lifestyle which situates the person in yoga and liberation is not integrated. (Anu Gītā 3.12)

Three types of individuals are involved with Nature.

- one who is fully expert at righteous lifestyle
- one who is partially aware of righteously lifestyle
- one who is resistant to righteous lifestyle

Righteous lifestyle alone will not cause anyone to become liberated from having to be an embryo. For that one must be a functional righteous person and also master yoga.

Righteous lifestyle by itself serves as a foundation for gaining opportunities in the future, where one will get further offers for birth in an aristocratic or wealthy family. Eventually after taking such births, one will become a person with primary influence.

Regarding this, I will tell you of the righteous lifestyle, by which, the soul becomes happy, despite its revolving through births in rapid succession one after another, O best of the human beings. (Anu Gītā 3.13)

The admittance is that even though the coreSelf is transcendental to its adjuncts and related facilities, still, that core is affected by the operations, which its psyche are involved in. This admittance is denied by many yogis and philosophers who pretend that since the coreSelf is transcendental, it cannot be affected by its adjuncts or any related equipment and influences which it encounters.

First one must honestly do meditation to see the distinction between the core and its adjuncts. One must then isolate each adjunct to test to see its influence, and the lack of its relationship with the core. One must check to see how the core is affected. It is not beyond the range of influence. If the core was influenced at any time, its infallibility must be denied. Something that is partially remote is still within the influence.

The idea of total non-affectation of the coreSelf is fantasy only. The issue to contend with is that of the least possible affectation. One must research, and know about the righteous lifestyle by which the self becomes happy, despite the fact that it has no absolute control over its transits through many births, in rapid succession one after another, here, there, or everywhere.

The mere idea that the coreSelf found itself in this creation, and got a hint that it should seek release from the trauma it experiences here, is proof enough that the core is not an absolute principle to itself. There are other controlling factors which were not controlled by the self but which make actions which put the self in jeopardy. At best, the self should act for its maximum exemption from trauma.

Contributions, vows, sexual isolation for attaining the spiritual plane, keeping social rules according to traditions, sensual restraint, tranquility, and social compassion to all creatures, (Anu Gītā 3.14)

...proficiency in self-restraint, not being cruel, ceasing all attempts to take the wealth of others, not acting deceptively, or speaking dishonestly to any living being here in this world, not having deceptive thoughts towards any creature, here in this location, (Anu Gītā 3.15)

...serving the mother and father respectfully, ceremonially regarding the deities and guests, ritually honoring the spiritual master, expressing empathy, being clean, always tightly restraining the senses, (Anu Gītā 3.16)

...being a cause for auspicious activities; that is defined as the conduct of those who are sincere. These produce the righteous lifestyle through which the people are always protected. (Anu Gītā 3.17)

While it sojourns, or is subjected to movements in this type of creation, there is a combination of external and internal behavior, which is optimum for the continued elevation of the self. Since the coreSelf is not absolute, it should figure a method for the least friction with physical or psychic phenomenon.

Contributions should be made to others. The mere idea that a person endeavors to find the cause of this existence, is indicative of that person being an inquiring self. This individual should assist others to whom one develops a fated relationship. However, one should not feel that one can really change this creation, nor bring it to an order which will remove all disparities. It is important to help others but that should not become an obsession. When one meets a person in need, if one has excess, or enough, one should be kind to that other person. Still, it should not become a habit that one seeks the needy, and makes it a habit to be a contributor.

An ascetic should make practical **vows**. He should not boast of achievements nor make declarations that he will do things which are fantastic. Mostly the vow should be made between the self and itself, or between the ascetic and his spiritual advisor. Regardless of the pledge, it should be practical. It should not be excessive. Little by little one should pledge to improve the external and internal behavior, so that in time, one may improve the relationship with the internal and external environments for the detachment of the self.

It is required that one should **develop sexual isolation for attaining the spiritual plane**. This should not be a radical movement which is sudden, not well considered, and which one will not maintain over time, because of not having the sensual strength to do it.

No matter where one goes, no matter whom one meets, no matter what one says or does, one is faced left, right and center, up, down, and median, by the need for sexual intercourse. It is everywhere in this creation. It is an all-pervasive power.

The opinion that one can completely transcend sexual desire is a huge fantasy. In fact, the mere idea that one is present in a physical body, is proof enough about one's origin. Only by sexual actions could one attain such a body. There are millions of living selves in the astral world, psychic beings, who would instantly become physical beings, if each were afforded the opportunity to be an embryo. It happens through one facility which is sexual performance. The urge for it is absolute in this creation.

However, one should do everything possible to develop sexual isolation, because otherwise it will not be possible to switch one's essential interest, and locate the spiritual plane of existence. One should not turn one's nose against sexual intercourse, but all the same one should not become familiar with it. One should not abuse it. One should regard it as sacred. It was the means of getting the body through which one can strive for liberation.

Those ascetics who have sexual access should study the course of it, as to its power over oneself. One should develop a healthy respect for sexual feelings. One should know how the process of birth happened, with Nature using one's spiritual radiance to power its creative schematic of one's embryo, and how after some time, Nature decided to cause parturition of one's fetus body from the mother's womb.

This research develops into an understanding of how death takes place, and how one is recycled through material existence in one or the other species of life, with one's spiritual radiance as a prominent power supply.

An ascetic should **keep social rules according to tradition**. If he violates social stipulations, it is likely that he will be penalized. That may affect the spiritual practice. Even though many traditions are useless in the long term, and some actually deter spiritual advancement, one should observe rules, which if violated, may cause one to be inconvenienced.

The value of a social activity depends on the focus of the actor involved. Materialistic persons give a high levy or worth on physical participation. Even though a yogi may act side by side with someone, the yogi's value for the activity should be minimal, where he/she does not focus on it as sharply, and as value-laden, as someone else. That frees the yogi from heavy reactions which will come in the future. Others will get a different return from the same action.

Sensual restraint is required. If there is no checking and rechecking of the sensual force in the psyche, the yogi will commit actions which are impulsive, but which will result in unfavorable events.

Everyone was issued as a physical body with urges, but a yogi should detach himself from most of the compulsions which arise in the mind and emotions. Every desire which arises should be censored. Even flash events which are so powerful and rapid, that there is no time to restrict their manifestation, should be curtailed. By meditation one can learn how to restrict even the most compulsive habits.

Tranquility is the background on which one could reserve time for considerate actions. If one is easily agitated, one will commit many actions for which one will become depressed, or will regret when their reactions manifest. Tranquility can be cultivated in meditation.

When one sees that one has little impact in this creation, and that whatever one achieves here, will be scrubbed by the time factor, one may be humored, and gain humor by seeing that one is insignificant.

Social compassion to all creatures is a requirement. It is a general attitude not a slogan. It is not aggressively implemented. In fact, a yogi/yogini should be isolated as much as possible. Otherwise, the compassion will cause unwanted involvements with others, which will become distractions, and which will utilize the valuable time, which a yogi should use for practicing meditation and psychic investigation. One should not become obsessed with expressing compassion for others, but if fate confronts one forcibly, one should act with compassion, but without becoming liable for the kindness one gives to others, which causes them to commit actions which fate itself demurs.

A yogi should be **proficient in self-restraint**. That takes practice in meditation with application to social life as one advances. Self-restraint begins with willingly observing moral stipulations. One should train oneself to debar the self from certain social pleasures. With this, there is a power struggle in the psyche between the urge to gain an enjoyment, and the need to comply with a social pressure, which dictates that one should not commit a behavior, which is socially unacceptable. This applies to simple matters like not urinating in public. It extends to big social issues like not having sexual intercourse, when it will be considered to be morally reprehensible. These however are reliant on social pressure to help one to complete these restrains.

Greater effort is needed for internal restraints which are a struggle between the coreSelf, and the inherent urges in the psyche. These are powerful urges which force the self to abandon desire for elevation. In meditation, a yogi must discover and curb the inner urges, which he/she finds difficult to regulate. That is not a social struggle with society. There is no reward from society for compliance in that case. It is merely a battle within the nature of the self. It is the effort to bring the senses to order, and to excavate deep rooted habits, which obstruct the elevation of the self. That is a psychological battle.

A yogi/yogini should **not be cruel to others**. One should step away from being in a superior social position, from which one can hurt others or exploit them. Whatever is to happen in this existence will take place, with or without a yogi. One should understand that one is dispensable.

This situation will proceed with or without the individual yogi. He/She is unnecessary. Nature awards importance to someone at its convenience. If one agent is absent, nature may proceed and may complete its mission without that individual.

Always remember that a yogi should be involved to the smallest degree. Even then, he/she should avoid situations which will bring unfavorable returns, which will be enforced by providence. There is no need for arrogance on the part of a yogi.

Even though Nature may offer opportunities, where one can exploit, and have leverage over others, one should resist by **ceasing all attempts to take the wealth of others**. An advanced yogi is not offered opportunities for exploitation. This is because Nature senses his resistance. Novices in spiritual research are regularly given opportunities to take advantage of others.

Some novice yogis extract the confidence of others by brandishing beliefs, like for instance, an idea about going to a heaven of a deity after death, or like the idea of attaining liberation in blissful existence, or in nothingness when the body is no longer the self, and is a dead object.

These activities are sordid. They bring unfavorable returns which the novice yogi cannot dodge, because these are enforced by the inscrutable powers of Nature. Self-realization is not about convincing others. It is not about saving someone else. It is not about assuring others. It is about researching the span of the spiritual self, and getting its identity energy in order. Others may be assisted in this quest, but the main thrust is self-discovery.

A yogi **should not act deceptively, nor speak dishonestly to any living being**. The best social posture is to be isolated. This is because inevitably if one is socially involved, there will be social circumstances, which will force one to omit facts, and even to deny what one knows to be the truth. This happens because of the nature of this world. This is why as far as possible one should reduce the social involvements.

In circumstances where one feels that it is necessary to be duplicitous, one should know that there will be a dire reaction, which one will be confronted with in the future. Understanding this, one will as a matter of self-interest, keep the social involvements to a minimum. One should avoid persons in whose association, one finds that one cannot maintain full honesty.

Understanding that the events in this world are weaved with honest and dishonest relations and that one cannot change this, one should discipline oneself, so that one's association with others, is the minimum. It is not a matter of full out truth in all times and places. Even honesty carries hazards. Someone may be hurt by one's full admission. That will yield resentments which one will have to absorb from the offended person.

To **not have deceptive thoughts towards any creature,** one must reduce the possibility of self-survival incidences. That can only be done if one reduces contact with others. In this creation the situation is that one lifeform eats the other. That is the efficiency of this place. No individual or collective agency of any sort, limited or unlimited, has up to this date changed the deception which is inherent in the moment-to-moment operation of this place.

For survival, even vegetarians commit violence. The plants themselves commit violence on each other and on tiny creatures in soil. It is not possible to avoid deception. What can be done is reduction of our survival needs, and the corresponding curtailment of the struggle for survival.

By all means, one should **respectfully serve the mother and father.** The institution of parenting was established by Nature long ago, even before the human species emerged on this planet. It is necessary to have it. A yogi should honor the ancestors primarily by begetting children, but he should not indulge in sexual excess. Even though society gives its permission from privacy between a consenting male and female, the yogi should not over indulge for pleasure's sake.

One should study how sexual indulgence consumes one's attention. It is a major distraction because it consumes one's attention, and causes one to divert from inner self research.

In some way, somehow, a yogi should **ceremonially regard the deities and guests.** This does not mean that for every yogi, there should be elaborate rituals and pronouncements for deity worship. Some yogis may do so in small ceremonies. It depends on his/her circumstances regarding the amount of time and the wealth available. For deity worship, one must be trained in the procedures. If not, one should hold short routines consistently and with obeyance.

One may **ritually honor the spiritual master.** That depends on the suggestions of the authority. Some spiritual teachers do not require the formality. Some outright discourage it. These usually expect honor in the form of compliance with regular practice of the meditation and behavioral methods prescribed.

On occasion, one should **express empathy to others** but not as a mission in life, only when fate puts one in a circumstance where one feels the necessity to be involved with someone else. A yogi should reduce association so that he/she can find time for practice. There is sufficient incidence for involvement even if one is isolated, such that it is foolish to make it one's purpose to empathize with every and any person whom one encounters.

A yogi should **be clean**. His/Her surroundings and body, external and internal, should be maintained. Even when in isolation, a yogi should not live with disregard to basic cleanliness. All the same, a yogi should give more priority to internal cleanliness of the body as compared to external appearance. But if the yogi has to attend functions and greet visitors, he/she should be dressed appropriately. External bodily cleanliness is necessary if one attends religious functions and give speeches. A yogi who does this will spend more time bathing and dressing to suit the traditional requirements, while another yogi who is isolated, will spend more time doing the austerities and meditation which supports his individual practice.

An ascetic should **always tightly restrain the senses**. Even if to please someone, he must indulge in sensual gratification, that yogi should within the psyche, curtail the greedy attitude of the inner senses, such that they are effectively curtailed, even though he/she appears externally to be indulgent.

It happens that someone may invite a yogi to a function. That host may serve the yogi a sumptuous meal and stand over the yogi, to be sure that he eats every bit of it. The host may even ask the yogi about the deliciousness of the food. In such a situation, even though the yogi did not enjoy the meal, he will be circumstantially forced to pretend that the meal was enjoyable. He may even act with enthusiasm while eating the meal, even though the fact is that he did not like it.

This is why it is necessary for a yogi to curtail association and to be restrictive. If one fails to do this, one will be drawn into self-destructive indulgences for which one will regret.

A yogi should **be a cause for auspicious activities**. But in so far as such involvements consume valuable time which could be used for more spiritual advancement, a yogi should avoid becoming known socially. The more a yogi becomes popular, the more there will be time-demands. This will reduce spiritual practice and cultivation. There is a way of causing auspicious activities without becoming occupied with others in charitable or religious institutions. One should note that any association with anyone who is not a strict ascetic, is a danger to one's spiritual progression.

A righteous lifestyle which fits the definitions of proper behavior given by Lord Krishna in *Bhagavad Gītā* is required for a yogi. No limited being is free to do whatever he likes. One should curtail vicious activity, avoid bad situations, and sincerely practice yoga as explained by Krishna.

You can see those qualities always in those who are saintly. In them it is definitely situated. On inspection the ideal behavior produces righteous lifestyle, which is inherent in those who are saintly. (Anu Gītā 3.18)

Even if a yogi is isolated, even if he is miles and miles away from civilization, in a location where no one is likely to find him, still he must deal with psychic proximity to others. Physical remoteness does not guarantee psychic isolation.

Thus, in every respect, a yogi must monitor his physical and psychic proximity. For a novice, physical distance from others is sufficient but for the advanced yogi, awareness of the psychic reach is necessary. He must monitor subtle contact. He must be sure that thinking access is restricted.

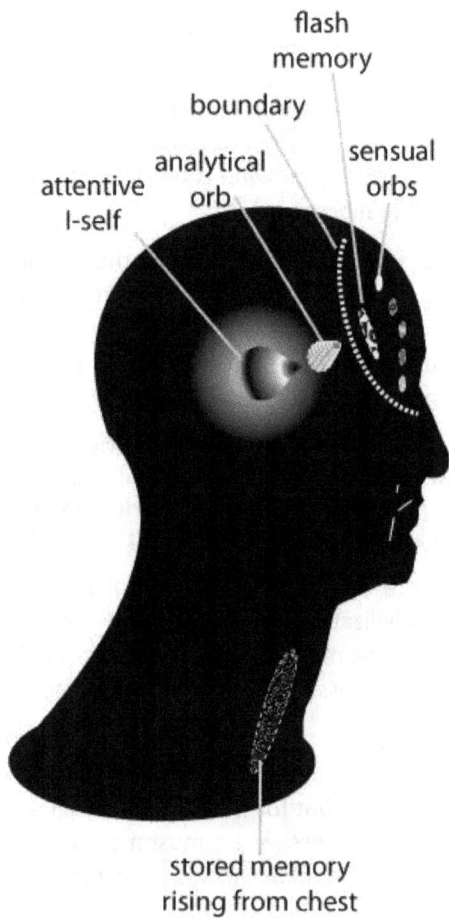

flash
memory

boundary

sensual
orbs

analytical
orb

attentive
I-self

stored memory
rising from chest

stored memory
controls mental process

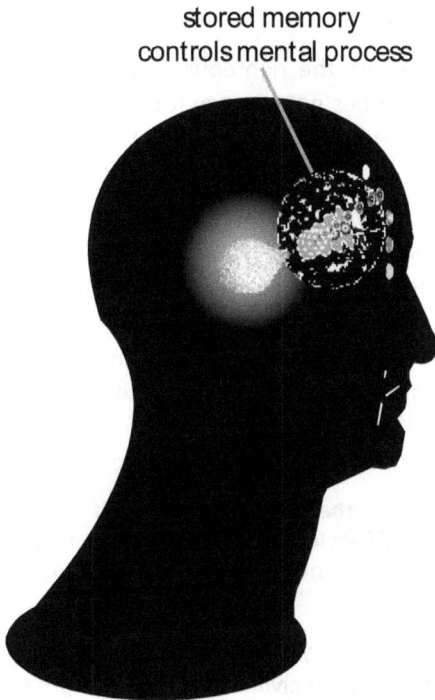

Among them is embedded the lifestyle which is the perpetual form of righteous conduct. Whosoever aligns the self to that does not obtain an unwanted destiny. (Anu Gītā 3.19)

The life which one lives is itself the result of past encounters. It is a basis for the life to come. Whatever one does now, will play a part in where one resides hereafter. If rebirth happens, it will occur with Nature using energy from one's current physical activity. One should not be careless but should know that righteous conduct is worth the endeavor. In time, that energy will sponsor a preferred future.

Thus, when society is deteriorating, it is the recommended behaviors which keep the situation on the course of righteous lifestyle. But the yogi, the liberated person, is rated above this. (Anu Gītā 3.20)

Even though the righteous lifestyle is preferred, a yogi, unlike others, does not operate it to gain enjoyment. The yogi functions but with inner detachment. He does not work for a good future in the physical world, or for a heavenly outcome hereafter.

As a practical matter, a yogi works for the benefit of everyone, but he does not have a keen interest in enjoying a future outcome hereafter. Yogis should not become criminals, and should not be careless, thinking that it does not matter if one is socially destructive or not. The yogi should contribute for the welfare of world, but with no urge to enjoy the circumstances which this existence displays.

Regarding the person who with regularity has the righteous lifestyle, deliverance from haphazard transmigrations occurs after a great span of time. (Anu Gītā 3.21)

Righteous lifestyle is what promotes and sustains the better part of human civilization. But that does not mean that it is the most rapid method for attaining liberation. It promotes a good lifestyle with the best that Nature can offer any limited entity.

Detachment from even a righteous lifestyle is what will cause an entity to act in a way, which results in liberation from having to take a physical body. Over time, if someone becomes expert at righteous conduct, he/she will figure that a righteous lifestyle will result in one getting more opportunity for the same, but not for becoming liberated from material existence, nor from its psychic parallel.

Thus, the living being is destined with the effects of actions which were performed previously. All such effects are the causal basis for his arrival here in an altered state. (Anu Gītā 3.22)

The physical life is part of the course of existence. So is the psychic life hereafter. One must understand how they are related. After physical life, there is psychic existence. Usually, that is followed by a new phase of physical life, which in turn is always followed by psychic life.

Physical life results in two outcomes.

- psychic life followed by a new phase of physical life

- psychic life followed by the same or by another phase of psychic life

Irrespective of variations in outcome, physical life is always followed by psychic life. There may be an interlude after physical life. At that time, the deceased person finds himself/herself in the psychic existence with confusion or clarity. From that state someone either continues in the psychic environment with confidence or becomes an embryo.

One's present and past actions have some effect on the outcome one experiences in the afterlife. It does matter if one behaves in a manner which Nature approves. One cannot guarantee that one will be liberated. One cannot know for sure if a deity will free one from this place. Since Nature will judge one using its own standards, which will or will not tally with one's expectations, one should learn how Nature responds. Using that parameter, one should act to be the least aggravating person in the creation.

By what force was it transformed to be a material body? There is doubt in human society about this. I will now mention the subtle cause. (Anu Gītā 3.23)

The psychic energy which is native to a particular coreSelf, remains with that entity, while it functions through or as a physical body, and while it relates through or as a subtle form. Even while a physical body is alive, the entity experiences itself, in some dreams, when it remembers instances of itself which functions with abilities which were used on the physical side. It has other dreams in which it functions with qualities, which it does not recall from the physical events

What controls the availability or absence of parts of its psychic energy? Why can it use certain tendencies and relational energies on the physical, or astral level, at some times and then during other events?

After producing a body for himself, Brahmā, the father of fathers of all creatures, created the cosmos, the three-partitioned world, with animate and inanimate beings. (Anu Gītā 3.24)

The existence of this, the here of it, is that it is a locale which is evident to our senses. Is it a distortion? Are our senses apprehending this with incorrect references?

The mystic who taught *Kashyapa*, stated that *Brahmā* was the father of fathers, who created the three-partitioned world, this cosmos, with animate and inanimate beings. *Brahmā* produced a body for himself and flashed this cosmos into existence, with animate and inanimate beings.

Then from that creation, he produced the life force energy potential of all embodied selves. By that all this is pervaded. It is known in this world as the supreme potency. (Anu Gītā 3.25)

First there was nothing for a reference for this, then there was *Brahmā*. He produced the lifeforce energy potential, a mystic potency, which enlivened everything and endowed the spiritual selves with a sense of existence and purpose.

That which is here is alterable; the other is immortal and unalterable. All species of the three worlds are paired one by one, singled, separately. (Anu Gītā 3.26)

The physical body is designed for detecting what is obvious. The senses pursue what is evident. Subtle objects are difficult to detect. The species are urged by internal energies which are polarized for reproduction. Usually there is one coreSelf who is the primary occupant and consenter in each psyche.

The father of fathers, Brahmā, having first created his own body, produced all other living beings; the stationary and the mobile ones. Such is the information, which was heard from the ancient authorities. (Anu Gītā 3.27)

This is cited as information given by ancient authorities, prior to the time when the mystic ascetic related this to *Kashyapa*. He accepted what he heard from previous teachers, that the father of fathers, was *Brahmā*, a god who created his body, and then produced the other stationary and mobile lifeforms.

Regarding this, the cosmic father Brahmā designed the spread of time, the social activities of all creatures and also their return to act in the physical world after death. This information about previous births, is consistent with the experience of one who is wise and who perceives the spiritual self. (Anu Gītā 3.28)

To pry into origins, one must look backward to understand how this creation manifested. Was it produced by a god, or by natural progression, or by a combination of someone and natural progression?

Time commands this, as we experience, but time varies as to its rate in whatever dimension it regulates. We experience varying attitudes, and runs of time, in different subtle places during dream experiences. Even in the physical world, we may experience different stretches, with rapidity, or deceleration of time.

By using mechanical or atomic clocks, we know that there is a standard for time. Yet we are afraid of time because its scope is beyond us. The rating of our lifespan is intimidating.

The social activities of the creatures have a familiar pattern, but we are at a loss to fully explain how actions are motivated. Even when it is not in their interest, the entities rarely can resist motivation. That means that their relationships are impulsive.

Despite *Brahmā* being the creatorGod, and the living entities being micro-personalities, they do not share in the god's original power. *Kashyapa's* teacher declared that the transmigration cycle of being a physical person, then losing that experience, then being a psychic person only, then again being someone physical, was a situational creation of the *Brahmā* deity.

Everything I explained was proper and fit for expression. The wise one always sees with deep insight the inconstancy of pleasure and pain. That one perceives how social actions are related to species degradation as well as to the body which is a perverse aggregation. (Anu Gītā 3.29)

To understand death, one must understand the formation of life. The secrets of death are exposed in the subtle part of life. As soon as one turns away from life and pries into its psychic framing, one will perceive one's death situation.

While one lives, death is present as whatever one does on the subtle side of life. The blank space one experiences in memory, when trying to access what happened before the formation of one's embryo, is itself a perception of death.

A being should relax his/her hold on physical events. He/She should grip psychic reality, and wait for clarity regarding that. At death, one will be forced to relinquish the focus on physical life. Hence there is no reason to keep stressing physical history, something which one must relinquish at the death of the body.

He remembers that every bit of happiness is really a distress. He will transit beyond this frightening vast span of haphazard transmigrations which are difficult to undermine. (Anu Gītā 3.30)

Whatever happiness there is, which is based on physical existence, is an introduction to unhappiness. This is because such happiness cannot endure. The quality of physical reality is that it will convert to something else, either shortly or in the distant future. At that time, whatever satisfaction it provided will disappear, leaving the enjoyer to assume some other state.

The happiness yielded here will not endure. That is the flaw of it.

A yogi should discover the frightening vast span of transmigrations, which he traversed in the past. Many of these voyages were completed in ignorance, whereby in the memory research, they are found to be a gap of existential space, after which some recall of other lives are sensed, and may be deciphered.

A yogi must estimate his many births, which were followed by death of the body, then there were short or long spans in the astral existence, which were concluded by adoption of an embryo of some sort, either as a human or some other species. Then again, there was a lifespan in some species, where it was felt as necessary to behave in a certain way, as channeled by the particular lifeform. Over and over and over again, this happened with each lifetime being disrupted by termination of the form, which one identified with as oneself.

Though harassed by birth, death, and disease, he knows the life-force energy potential. He perceives a similar consciousness-energy in all psyches which are reinforced with awareness. (Anu Gītā 3.31)

The promise of the lifeForce energy is that of eternal life, but in this situation that cannot be delivered. It is a bright light which shines in this existence, but it is an empty promise, because it is not an eternal electricity in its current format.

In this world, it is the excitement which sponsors sensual suspicion, but all the same it flashes in and out. It flickers in this physical life, and in the astral situations. Knowing the lifeforce, a yogi no longer relies on it, and no longer is eager to use it. He/She does not trust it to fulfill what it promises. It is misleading in every respect. It has fresh tricks at every step.

Then, becoming disgusted with all of this, he searches for the passage to the supreme location. I will speak to you factually of this information, O best of the human beings. (Anu Gītā 3.32)

Being promised so much excitement, being disappointed, feeling depressed over and over, after many births, a yogi/yogini feels a deep-seated change, where the irresistible lure for pleasure, converts into a message which describes the promised experience to be what it is, which is a farce presentation which must end in distress. From then onwards, seeing the truth of it always, there is no strong urge to pursue what is offered. This existence which before was a motivator for participation, becomes something bland from beginning to ending. For that one yogi, everything changes as his perception deepened. It penetrated what was seen before. He recognizes the excitement which lured him before, as a mere strand in a fabric of hurt. He lost interest.

O best of the educated persons, concerning the eternal imperishable location, learn from me, O educated ritualist, as I describe everything about it. (Anu Gītā 3.33)

As far as life after death is concerned, the ideal situation, the environment which would be most acceptable, is one which is eternal and imperishable, where deterioration does not occur, and where every emotion is of a blissful quality. If there is such a place, then one should learn about it, discover it and endeavor for permanent residence in it.

The highly qualified ascetic said: A person whose mind is without thoughts, who is calm, who is absorbed in one cause of an effect, which is the cause of a previous effect, he being detached, is without psychic agitation. (Anu Gītā 4.1)

The hunt for meaning is essential to anyone who considers, that what he/she is currently as a physical body, will be abolished shortly. If one is a temporary something, it is important to measure the past self, the current one, and the future one which will be concluded.

Is there something left to survive the conclusion? On what level will that something manifest? Looking backward, can one tap into the origin of the self? The current vantage has the value of investigation into the origin, and insight into its continuation.

One who is the friend of everyone, who is with everyone, who is level-headed, a controller of the senses, whose nature is devoid of anger and fear, who subdues desire; that person is liberated. (Anu Gītā 4.2)

For anyone who feels the necessity to investigate the termination of the physical person that he or she is, a certain attitude is required. A psychological posture is needed, one from which one can always reach to touch origins, and go forward to meet the end of the physical system, and the edge of the psychic situation hereafter.

The sensitivity for reading the events before birth, as well as the events after death, must be developed during the life of the perishable body.

To be that sensitive, one must be the friend of everyone, but without becoming involved with everyone. One should have a friendly attitude without aggressively, and motivationally, pursuing friendship with everyone. One should be sure not to indulge with everyone, because that will interrupt forces of fate which may inconvenience oneself and others. The technique is to be friendly with the least possible interference, so that one is not a glutton for emotional exchanges with any or everyone.

One should be ready to support someone. One should be level headed, and be a controller of the senses. One should be relational without being positioned with anger and fear. Unto oneself, one should subdue desires, and not be aggressive for fulfillments.

Somehow one should be neutral to the reactive energy in Nature. This will allow one to make decisions which will free one from social complications, and give one the insight in how to act, so that there is the least cording of oneself with physical fate.

Nature uses one's involvement interest to tie one to her future displays, such that attempts to free oneself from being a mandatory actor in physical history, become ideas only, and are never published in the practical sense. A yogi should turn his existence sideways, so that the full brunt of Nature's magnetic force does not hit him/her head-on, because that will force the yogi to take more physical bodies, with no control over what happens, and merely as a functional stooge of history.

One who relates to all beings the way he regards the self, who is self-controlled, pure, who is modest, without pride, that person is free from every faults. (Anu Gītā 4.3)

The behavior during the life of the physical body is part of the calculation about the events, which will occur hereafter. There is a relationship between the psychic situations one will encounter after the body dies, and the life one lived while the physical system was operational.

The interaction between physical history and psychic situation is ongoing. There is constant feedback between the two realities. Hence one should not act carelessly but should be economical in terms of how much involved one should be as a physical actor.

One cannot tell how fate will raft anyone, or as to what it will sink. Since providence has the upper hand, one must be careful to respect whatever there is in the physical or psychic existences. Fate can use anything to disable or decommission someone.

Humility is a permanent situation for any limited being. If it is avoided and not embraced, the person will be flooded with pride, which sponsors arrogance, which in turn causes one to act for self-injury.

One is no more special than anyone else. Even when one is endorsed and empowered by fate, even then one remains as a limited being. One should not assume that the boost to one's ability is a permanent installation. Even if it is, it does not make one an exemption from being disciplined or reduced by fate. After all, any empowerment, all by itself, is valueless if it is not supported by time and circumstance. It can be peeled from relevance suddenly and unexpectedly.

Concerning both life and death, enjoyment and pain, acquisitions and deprivations, likes and dislikes, that person is liberated, who responds to these dualities all the same. (Anu Gītā 4.4)

The operation of energies is interpreted differently depending on the sense perception of the psyche of the individual observer. What is pleasant to one person may be unpleasant to another.

There are persons in every species of life. Due to the facilities which each species affords, there is a prejudice from which each species type rates the other. To some extent the judgement is justified because there is limitation of person expression, due to the sensual outreach of the various bodies.

When one becomes liberated from species prejudice, one resists the dominance of the senses, such that life and death, enjoyment and pain, acquisitions and deprivation, likes and dislikes, are not regarded as reasons to differentiate.

He favors no one. He neglects no one. He responds neutrally to dual conditions. His self is free of passionate emotions. He is liberated in all respects. (Anu Gītā 4.5)

If one is to be a neutral observer, a certain frame of mind, an underbasis of detachment, is required. One should help whosoever Nature presents for assistance. And yet personally, one should favor no one, nor neglect anyone. One should respond neutrally to dual conditions. The self should be free of passionate emotions. When they are felt, the coreSelf should not grasp their pleasure.

The person who is without enemies, who does not favor relatives, who regards no one as his child, who is detached from the benefits of righteous lifestyle, income, and lusty emotion, who is not stimulated by desire; that person is factually liberated. (Anu Gītā 4.6)

There are two types of liberated entities. One is obvious because he/she remains detached from the society of humans and barely participated even in the upkeep of the body. This person seems to have no interest in social conditions, nor in achieving anything in the physical world. He/She has a discouraging energy which smothers all interest in society. Some persons who demonstrate such extreme detachment fake the tendency for some time. Eventually they become exposed, and are condemned in society.

The other type of ascetic who is liberated, participates in social concerns, and seems to be involved, but he/she is detached within his/her psyche, to the extent that the impact of involvement does not make a deep imprint in the mind. For this person, physical actions are superficial only, and yet, it appears meaningful to one and all.

This person is without enemies. In the mind and emotions, he does not compete and has no urge for exploiting others to gain anything. He does not favor the relatives but he does not hesitate to act as a relative and to reciprocate as one would. He knows that people who are not related could be related in the future in some other life, or may be related in some past life. He feels familial urges with persons who are not currently related. He recognizes that those sentiments are based on previous life relationships, which converse presently as subconscious familiarity.

This person regards no one as his child. He deals with his biological children aptly but also knows that the parental authority shifts from person to person as one transmigrates, where someone who is someone's infant in one life, may be that person's parent in some other life. Nature switches the roles at its convenience.

This covert ascetic is detached from the benefits of righteous lifestyle, income, and lusty emotion. He senses that these impulses and actions, are stimulated by desire, which is a complex energy, which one should be detached from, and should not be controlled by.

The person who is not fanatical about righteous lifestyle or about deviant social behavior, who neutralizes the effects of actions performed in the previous lives, who is spiritually pacified by virtue of smothering the evolutionary urges of the present body, who is indifferent to dual conditions; that one is definitely liberated. (Anu Gītā 4.7)

Liberation is an internal posture which is maintained even when the yogi is involved socially or is active in isolation. A yogi should prefer to commit to a righteous lifestyle. He/She should not be attached to, and should not promote deviant social behavior. When acting in the socially approved way, he should not be fanatical. He should not become proud. His posture should be such that it neutralizes the effects of the action performed in previous lives, the energy of which was used by Nature to construct current challenges.

Every body of every creature encloses urges which are spring-loaded. These are activated into compulsion when they detect circumstances in which they can be displayed. This urge energy arrests the psyche. It forces the coreSelf to render permissions for self-destructive acts, and for complications which that self cannot sort.

Seeing the compulsions arising in his psyche, a yogi smothers the evolutionary urges of the present body. He is indifferent to dual conditions, and does not become agitated when he feels motivations for contrary or approved antics and motions.

A person who is without social activities, who is not expressive of desires, who regards the world as being like an Asvattha tree, without perpetuality and being always symptomatic with the delusion of birth and haphazard transmigration, (Anu Gītā 4.8)

Once he sees that his position in this physical situation is invalid, the yogi no longer commits himself sincerely to the development of this world. Being that this situation will be washed away in time, a yogi does not feel that his part in this is substantial. When all is said and done, the wind down of time will terminate as the total death of everything which was, is and will be in this natural world.

The yogi must understand, that even though this creation will be terminated, and that is its mandatory outcome, still for the time being, he/she should act responsibly, and should treat others with care. The yogi is not the supreme controller. He cannot guarantee for himself liberation from this. Hence, by all means he should act in a way which will bring positive returns in the future. There is no sense in being vicious to others, especially since such interactions may result in unpalatable returns in the future.

The soul will not die when the physical body is killed, and yet one should not assault any creature. By all means one should avoid a violent posture, and should not become responsible, for permanently displacing someone from his/her physical form. One should not act in a way which will result in grievance to anyone.

There are many compressed desires in the psyche. These will bud as soon as corresponding events happen. A yogi should gage the expansive, compulsive, and corrosive power of a desire which is yet to manifest. If possible, he should squelch it in its minute non-manifested form.

This world is like an ashvattha tree. It has roots tunneling downward and upward. It feeds on whatever is within reach. Any attachment to anything is a pore through which the compressed desires may begin their expressions. In that the coreSelf acts as a battery to partially power the spread of a manifestation. This proves to be fatiguing to the perpetual self. That self is a radiance, but the wanton use of its spiritual power is taxing for it.

Though it is not perpetual, the physical world draws energy from the radiant everlasting coreSelf. That self provides spiritual power, but if it withdraws itself by being detached, the self will feel the fatigue which it is forced to indulge in. Birth, shifting while alive, transmigrating when the physical body dies, then again taking birth, this is done by the swinging action of Nature. The coreSelf should note this situation. It should institute a viable plan for exemption from the interchange with the mundane energy.

...a person whose intellect is always in a detached application, one whose penance is the detailed observation of personal faults, one who is liberated from psychic bondage, that one is liberated in a jiffy. (Anu Gītā 4.9)

The hold of the intellect onto the coreSelf is done through another more essential adjunct which is the sense of identity. This identity energy is fused to the core on all sides. Due to the natural attachment between the sense of identity and intellect, the core is subjected to the relationship variations which the sense of identity has with the intellect.

If the core could in some way, monitor and regulate its susceptibility to the sense of identity, it would be detached from the machinations of the intellect, because views and influences are transmitted from the intellect through the sense of identity, and then pass into the coreSelf as energy waves or flashes.

Over time, a yogi develops the insight about the arrangements between the coreSelf and its adjuncts. He must study the relationship between each adjunct. It is not how much he can command a function but rather how that function best operates with the least victimization for the core.

The final penance is the acute observation of the interplay between the core and its adjuncts. This is internal research which occupies every second of the yogi's time. It is a switch in the use of the critical energy of the self, where originally that was focused outwards towards others. Now it is inFocused, and is fully preoccupied with disciplining the core and its relationships with the adjuncts.

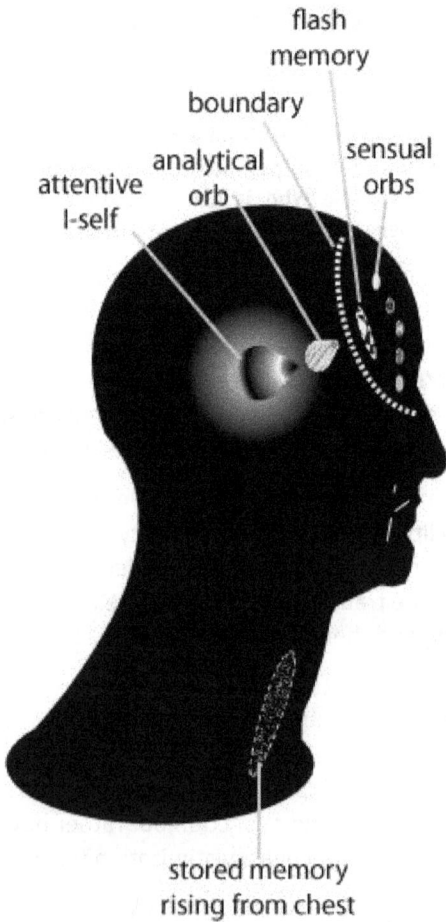

flash memory
boundary
analytical orb
sensual orbs
attentive I-self
stored memory rising from chest

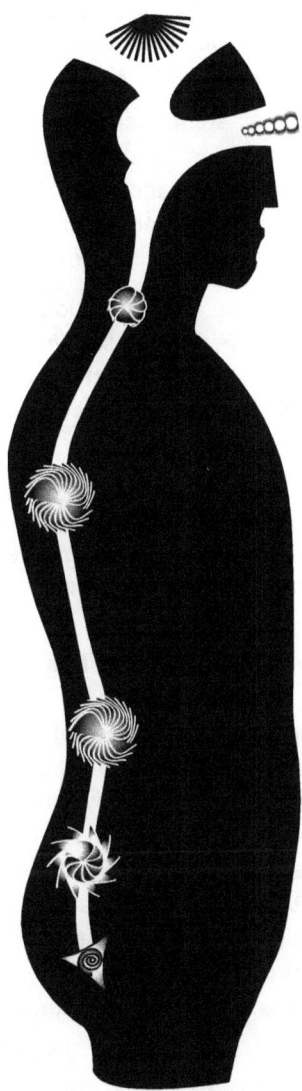

Without fragrance, without flavor, without a surface, without sound, without possessions, without color, without education, when the self observes itself in that way, it is liberated. (Anu Gītā 4.10)

The coreSelf will at some point in its quest for self-realization, make the decision to strip itself of adjuncts and functions, see its bare format and know its dimensions, its expressive force, and absorbent needs. It turns the spotlight of pursuit on itself, like a light which shines on its radiance.

It will find itself to be in a condition which is without fragrance, without flavor, without surface, without sound, without possessions, without color, without education, just as bare radiance. It must dwell in this nude condition in meditation.

It is not the five sense objectives, or the moods which are related. It is not a form of nature. It is without a cause. It is not a perceptive mood of nature though it experiences the attitudes. The person who perceives that is liberated. (Anu Gītā 4.11)

Regardless of what happens hereafter, the coreSelf must be the same in that psychic condition as it was when it was identified as a physical body. If one is not an advanced yogi, one will pass from the physical body by the method of sickness or disease, and with focus on that bodily condition. Once there is no possibility to be the physical body which one used, one will resort to being a psychic self, the subtle body which was used in dream conditions. That psychic self will be a person in the astral world, which is merely some psychic dimensions, places where there is flickering psychic energy, and no constant brick-like materials, like what is experienced on earth.

There is however another process which is used by the advanced yogi, which is to strip the coreSelf of its adjuncts and their affiliated energies, and to selfFocus on the bare core. This does not eliminate the adjuncts and their affiliated energy, but it does isolate the self from those psychic powers. Thus, when the physical system is no longer in operation, instead of feeling the self as a subtle body, this yogi, experiences the core as a distinct, and separate super subtle reality, which is in an energy space along with adjuncts and energies.

This yogi is liberated from misidentification with the adjuncts. He may or may not use the adjuncts. One or two of them may be retired or disabled by him, but regardless he experiences the bare core, the nude self. This happens when he is on the physical side, still being the physical body, and on the astral side after not being the physical form, which died, and was no longer responsive to the commands of the adjuncts.

The coreSelf is not the five sense objectives. Why? Because it cannot be the object of the five physical senses. It cannot be the focus of the five subtle senses of the dream body. This is due to the fact that the core is composed of energy which is beyond the range of the physical and subtle senses, which are used in the physical and dream bodies. A great yogi rids himself of the impression-seeking tendency which uses the physical body and the subtle form to hunt for suitable sense objects.

Nature has formats, many of them, trillions. Some are physical. Some are sub-physical. Some are subtle. Some are supernatural. But the coreSelf is not a form of Nature. The core is without a cause. Though it experiences the attitudes, it is not a perceptive mood of Nature.

Disregarding through the intellect all intentions relating to the material body and the mind, he gradually becomes proficient in segregation from material nature, just as without fuel, a fire is extinguished. (Anu Gītā 4.12)

The intellect is a psychic adjunct which surfaces in the physical body as the reasoning, concluding ability, the rational faculty. It is a psychic technology but it is realized in the physical body as a tendency which functions to create images, burp memories, rate sensual input and issue compelling conclusions.

When a yogi switches to the psychic side, and regards that plane of existence as primary, the intellect is isolated. Then he understands that it is a psychic orb. It is also a position sensitivity, where frequently, it is not perceived, except as a location in the mind space, in the head of the subtle body.

Nirvāna, which is segregation of the coreSelf from the influence of Nature, is a complex procedure which occurs naturally or deliberately. It is hardly likely that a limited self can sort itself, and segregate its core from the influence of Nature. What usually happens is that a yogi works to severe his connection from selected unwanted influences.

This verse discusses the resistance to, and termination of the influences, which flow to the self, because of the opening allowed through the intellect. When the intellect is disciplined, its susceptibility to sensual energy and the memory, is reduced. The flow of information from the sensual intake and from memories, ceases. This results in a self-condition which the core can introspect into, to get self-understanding.

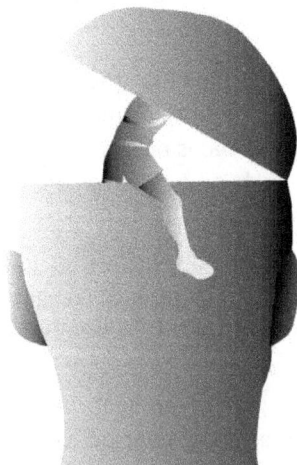

Being freed from all subtle effects of previous actions, he achieves the supreme eternal spiritual reality, which is the realm of spiritual peace and stability, and which is divine and imperishable. (Anu Gītā 4.13)

This location is available now and hereafter. This dimension is also known as the *chit akash*, sky of consciousness. It is wonderful for anyone who attains this place. In fact, even if one has a short window into this place, even for seconds of time, one is blessed.

The aim is to reach this place while the physical body lives. One should do that during meditation. Then at death, one may be transferred there permanently, leaving aside even the subtle environment, even the psychic realms which the subtle body is compatible with.

Next, I will explain the course of yoga practice, which is supreme and which is the best teaching. Having learnt this, the yogis experience the perfected self here on earth. (Anu Gītā 4.14)

Everyone is confronted with the issue of survival. This is because presently, one is circumstantially a physical body which is guaranteed to perish. Denial of being a body, claiming that one is not the physical form, pretending that one is not affected by physical trauma, does not protect one from being subjected to unwanted feelings. Even if one takes actions which kills the physical body, even then one will be left as a psychic person, a soul.

Yoga is offered as the best way to come to terms with what is unwanted. One does so through intuitive and deliberative acts, to shift the sense of identity from focusing on what sponsors the flow of energy between the coreSelf, and whatever would inconvenience it.

I will perceptually transmit this instruction as it is. Learn from me about the dimensional opening through which one transits to the eternal and perceives the self within the psyche. (Anu Gītā 4.15)

At first a yogi gets a peep into the *chit akash* sky of consciousness. This occurs involuntarily. Due to an alert given by the yoga teacher, a student may have a transcendence penetration, and would recognize it, based on what he was told by the guru. Otherwise, one may have a spontaneous experience, and have no idea as to its value, or as to where it provided a portal to.

From this psychological enclosure, there may be an opening to the other place, the *chit akash* sky of consciousness. One should recognize this when it happens during meditation or otherwise.

One must also learn how to recognize the coreSelf. Even that must be taught. Due to being familiar with the operations of the adjuncts, particularly the intellect with its imaging and imagining faculties, one cannot selfFocus. But this can be resolved by getting information from this teacher of *Kashyapa* and from an advanced mystic yogi.

Withdrawing the senses, one should redirect the mind to the core-self. Having done extreme austerities before, one should practice the yoga system. (Anu Gītā 4.16)

The run of energy from the coreSelf to objects which are external to it, occurs by a natural process of sensual expression, either to be reactive with other products, or to self-stimulate internal feelings which are interpreted by the mind as pleasure.

For yoga, this expressive way of existence ceases. The energy of the core, is pulled into the core, where eventually a disinterest in external objects is developed, and a keen interest in the core is expressed. This is the reverse of pursuing feelings through contact with other objects of every type.

Patanjali delineated the yoga process.

yama niyama āsana prāṇāyāma pratyāhāra

dhāraṇā dhyāna samādhayaḥ aṣṭau aṅgāni

Moral restraints, recommended behaviors, body posture, breath infusion, sensual energy withdrawal, linking of the attention to higher concentration forces or persons, effortless linkage of the attention to higher concentration forces or persons, continuous effortless linkage of the attention to higher concentration forces or persons are the eight parts of the yoga system. (Yoga Sūtras 2.29)

yama	**moral restraints**
niyama	**recommended behaviors**
āsana	**body posture**
prāṇāyāma	**breath infusion**
pratyāhāra	**sensual energy withdrawal**
dhāraṇā	**linking of the attention to higher concentration forces or persons**
dhyāna	**effortless linkage of the attention to higher concentration forces or persons**

samādhi	**continuous effortless linkage of the attention to higher concentration forces or persons**

That proficient ascetic, who effectively neutralized the effect-energy from past lives, who was devoid of conceit and deceit, that philosopher, the educated yogi, perceives the self in the psyche through clarity of mind. (Anu Gītā 4.17)

The reduction of sensual interest leads to the last basis for the composite self which is the discovery of the core. As a physical body, the person is a composition of a core, a sense of identity, an intellect, memory, sensual energy and some bio-electric glands and operations.

When the physical body dies, the person is reduced to being a core, a sense of identity, an intellect, memory, and sensual energy. That is the soul, or subtle body, the psyche. It is the sensual energy which is scattered through the subtle body, with the head housing the sense of identity, and intellect. Most of the memory is in the trunk of the subtle body with some files of it being in the head near the intellect.

Whether he is dead or alive, without a physical body or with one, the self is due for an accounting of its reduction as a core. While the physical system is operative, the person should meditate to be its bare self.

If that saintly person could yogically focus on the self in the psyche, then being a person who is obsessed and profiled with that singular objective, he would perceive the self in the psyche. (Anu Gītā 4.18)

It is a dire achievement, a must, that the yogi should isolate the coreSelf, so that his feelings of self are reduced to that core, abandoning the collective as the person. He will still use the collective, and may still function as if he is that. Due to his transcendental experiences, he knows himself as other than the collective, as the inner core. He does not feel undone, because he discovered that he is not the collective, and that he needs adjuncts to perceive certain levels of existence.

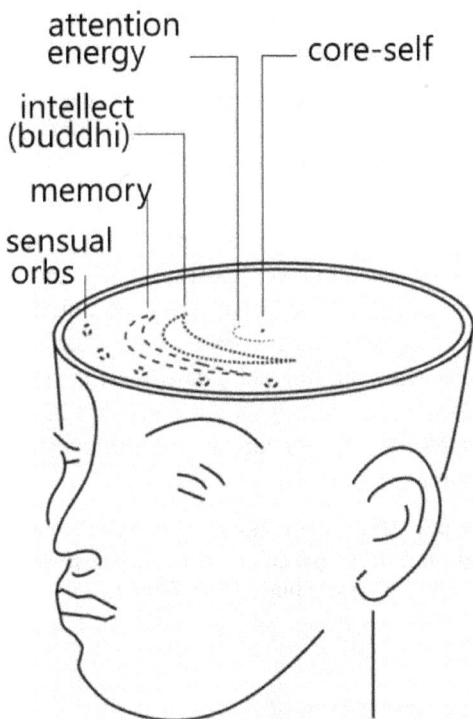

Having total control over the senses, being always proficient in yoga practice, being self-composed, a conqueror of the sensual energies, being like this, that one, being exceptional, being versed in yoga, perceives the self by the self. (Anu Gītā 4.19)

The coreSelf is a subjective-objective principle which is an eternally existence. It is not eternally aware in the objective sense. To study its subjective side, one needs to practice advanced meditation. Then one can perceive the self by itself, to realize its adjuncts, its consciousness states, and its nude condition, regarding what it is capable of, when it does not take assistant from the adjuncts.

As a person after seeing someone in a dream, recognizes that one and exclaims, "This is he," so one who has the proper proficiency in yoga definitely identifies the form of the self. (Anu Gītā 4.20)

When one can repeatedly identify the bare self in meditation, one can keep focus as that self, even when acting as the physical body. Even while using the adjuncts, one can retreat to being the bare person. One does not become engaged fully with the adjuncts, or with what they interlock with. Such a person remains as the core, and does not divest himself/herself as if he/she is the adjuncts, and their complimentary energies.

As one may show straw fibers after extraction from reeds, so the yogi definitely perceives the person-psyche which is displaced from a physical body (Anu Gītā 4.21)

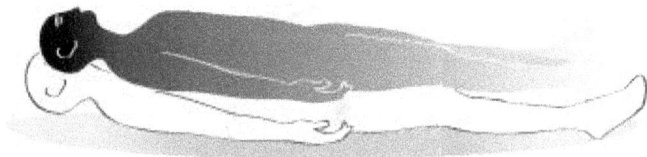

The fibers in weeds are part of the plant's structure. And yet, each fiber can be isolated as one single strand of vegetation or as many strands which are corded to make one stout branch.

When the observing self sorts the components in consciousness, it will discover that there are adjuncts which work in coordination with a core, which has radiance spreading spherically.

The psyche which is experienced as feelings throughout a living physical body, continues to exist when that physical system is damaged irretrievably. The yogi experiences this while being the physical body, and then again when the body is no longer responsive to psychic commands from the self, who was known as the body.

The body is compared with the basketwork grass, and the person-psyche is referenced to the straw fibers. This is an ideal analogy explained by those who are expert yogis. (Anu Gītā 4.22)

The person-psyche is mistaken as the physical body. Hence when that body is finished, there is a feeling of regret and absence. To avoid this, a yogi should accustom the self to its essential core and its adjuncts, but not to the core, the adjuncts, and their accessory emotions and mentality.

While being a healthy physical body, the coreSelf should focus on its spiritual radiance. It should penetrate its accessories, to see how its radiance is spread through the psyche, and contributes to liveliness of the form.

When the body-supported soul deeply perceives the spiritual self through yogic-insight, then nothing is master of that self but it becomes a liberated entity in the three partitions of the universe. (Anu Gītā 4.23)

There must be a deep admittance that the spiritual self is body-supported. That is the fact for the time being. It may be that a particular self can transcend the need for physical body identity, but in general, the reality is that though it is a spiritual self which is sublime, still it requires the use of adjuncts and accessories, which are produced by the psychic and physical Nature.

At first, when there is the insight into the relationship of the coreSelf with anything other than itself, but which it requires for support for one reason or the other, the understanding is that since it depends on those supports, and since the current flow between the core and the adjuncts is sometimes unpleasant, the situation as it was formatted by Nature is unacceptable. The self must work to adjust the connections it has with the adjuncts and sensual energy. This initial quest does not mean that the self can isolate itself completely from the accessories, some of which are mystic features. The adjustment is for the least possible inconvenience to the coreSelf.

However, those great persons who master the psyche, so that it no longer causes distress to the core, are the ones who are liberated in the full sense. They translate to the *chit akash* sky of consciousness. They do not continue to engaged with the disturbing adjuncts. They are not influenced by, nor are induced to indulge in the schemes, and feelings, of the intellect, and lower sensual energies.

One after another, bodies are acquired as desired. Transcending senility and death, the self is neither exhilarated nor saddened. (Anu Gītā 4.24)

The operation of transmigration is not a planned event of a limited entity. It happens spontaneously through a combination of natural and psychic forces. In this way, involuntarily, a limited self becomes a physical body, then it is disconnected from that form by Nature. Following that, the entity again is converted from being a mere psychic being to being a physical person. Then again, this sequence of events occurs as a recurring loop with development and deterioration in tow.

The desire force which causes the physical embryos to develop is a composite energy, with the coreSelf being a primary, or minority cause. There is no guarantee that the desire for a certain rebirth was constructed by the corePerson involved.

One must learn to transcend senility and death, as these must occur, regardless of if it is desired or detested. One must shift from being a physical self to being a psychic presence. With the essential focus placed on the subtle side of the personSelf, one should practice not being exhilarated nor saddened. One should be the neutral observer, with a grasp on what will remain as the psyche, after the physical system becomes unresponsive to a self's commands.

Being proficient in yoga, the person who is a master of his nature, creates for the self a divine psychology which is like that of the supernatural controllers. Having abandoned the perishable body, that person attains the imperishable spiritual world. (Anu Gītā 4.25)

The control which one lacks is self-control, and only to the extent possible, because the adjuncts are not under the self's autonomy. A limited self did not create his/her sense of identity, intellect, memory, and sensual energy. These became available spontaneously as assisting psychic instruments and energy. To master this means to get from those adjuncts, the best possible cooperation which is in the interest of the coreSelf.

The practice of yoga is the method for adjusting the adjuncts for maximum benefit to the core. Once it is realized that the adjuncts are assistant technologies, which must be shed in the long term, a yogi restricts his use of them. This allows for their reform, so that the involvement with the physical and psychic realities, is reduced to a minimum. A yogi realizes that he should disconnect from the adjuncts.

At some time however, either during the creation or at the termination of it, the adjuncts are removed from the fusion with the self. Then the yogi can work on creating a divine psychology which is like that of the supernatural controllers.

Such an expression of self is based on a relationship with a supernatural controller, a divine being. This allows for a selfBody to be developed, to spring into being. This person will be functional in a relationship with the deity. Now the limited self, the deity, and the environment where they relate, would all be of spiritual essence.

**If the world was destroyed, no fear would develop in him.
If all beings were pained, he would not be afflicted by anyone.
(Anu Gītā 4.26)**

The destruction of the physical world, the one which we reside in, the one with the materials which our senses purview, is a threat to our physical bodies. When a yogi successfully transplants his existential interest to the psychic side of life, he/she no longer maintains fear about the continuation of his/her physical existence. The body surely will die. That will be an inconvenience, but the levy of it on the coreSelf will be negligible.

The fear for the damaged to the body, the fear of pain and horror, will be there but it will be the least, because the focus of the yogi on the physical system was shifted.

During meditation, a yogi must remote himself/herself from this physical situation. He/She should get accustomed to the bare coreSelf. Then the self will be accustomed to its nude self with no adjuncts.

The death of this universe is inevitable, but death of this cosmos means alteration on a cosmic scale. It happens in a time medium. A self is left to contemplate what it would be during the death of time. Will the self be suspended until suitable conditions arise again?

For how long can a self exist in an environment which is the ultimate reduction of what this is presently? Will that self have cognition of its situation?

In regards to the horrors and psychosis of happiness and distress, the feelings of affection and attachment, the yogically proficient person is not affected by it. That one is free from attachment and has a mind which is spiritually-pacified. (Anu Gītā 4.27)

The stability required is one of inner repose, where the coreSelf is detached from the workings of its adjuncts. This applies even when the adjuncts operate involuntarily.

The plan for the best position hereafter, begins by the actions taken during the life of the physical body. While being that body, one should act with it with discretion, knowing that it is the psychic version of events which will prevail, and which will result in the most beneficial outcome after death. To summarize the advice: Preparations for the hereafter begin during the life of the physical body.

Weapons do not penetrate this person, nor does death affect this one. Hence in comparison, no one in the world is happier than this person. (Anu Gītā 4.28)

With its adjuncts, the coreSelf survives on the psychic side. It is not affected in the way of dying as the physical body does. However, if it was focused on the physical side during the lifespan, the soul or psyche is affected by the loss.

One should be sure to understand that the unaffectedness of the soul applies in a limited way, and not in every possible abrasion, which may be felt by the loss of physical access.

In so far as death is traumatic and regretful, that applies to someone who did not integrate his/her identity as the psychic remnant which survives the physical body. As soon as one can switch focus to make the psychic events the priority, one may transcend death and not be stymied by it.

The loss of being without a physical body is the feature of not being a direct participant in history. Some overcome this by influencing physical people to act on their behalf. But the value method is to lose interest in physical history, and to understand that one has no purpose in the physical existence. Nature is the complete producer of this situation, with full capacity for monitoring this theatre. There is no reason for any limited being to consider itself as essential or relevant.

When being fully proficient in yoga practice, that person perceives the spiritual self in the psyche, then he feels no special endearment to Shatakratu Indra, the celestial king who did one hundred ritual ceremonies. (Anu Gītā 4.29)

Shatakratu Indra is the celestial king of the heavenly place which a human being may attain after living a righteous lifestyle. Good people are deadly afraid of hell hereafter. Under the shadow of such fear, they aspire for a life of goodness so that hereafter they can live in a paradise which is free from negative experiences.

Nearly every religious sect divulges information about qualifying for a heavenly life hereafter, a place where the follower will be in the association of a deity, and will be free from distress. However, preparations for being qualified for favorable conditions hereafter, must begin during the life of the very body which is destined for death. No matter what psychic environment one may be in hereafter, reaching that level of existence, and staying there for forever, is an uncertainty.

To simplify matters, one should attain self-realization. That should be the focus. At first however one should determine the remnant psychic self, which will survive the physical person that one poses as during the life of the physical system. Once that psyche is acknowledged, and is given priority over the physical body, one should sort it to find the coreSelf.

But one who is attaining the proficiency in yoga practice, should not be discouraged. Hear about this how one whose primary objective in life is yoga, practices trance consistently. (Anu Gītā 4.30)

Because Nature slanted this existence to promote its priorities, many of which run contrary to the spiritual interest of the self, a yogi must be prepared for an uphill battle with nature, where regularly it pursues interest which are against self-realization. It sets itself to use the self for the generation of physical species and their urges. This brushes against self-realization. It causes a self to focus away from itself.

Nature uses the radiant energy of the self to power its operations. That makes the self an extrovert interest which shines the light of the self on everyone but the self.

No one should find fault with Nature because it promotes its urges and their fulfillments as top priority. Rather, one should note this process, and by shifting one's attention to what delves into the secrets of the self, one should make advancement. However, one should take care to act in a way which does not cause Nature to target one, and to make it impossible for one to focus on self-realization.

When thinking of a place which was seen before, one should reside in the city in which the incidence occurred. The mental operations are within the psyche, not outside of it. (Anu Gītā 4.31)

The inner environment is the place. A yogi should *inSelf*. He should *inVision*. He should *inSensation*. He should *inFocus*. The bio-electric energy in the physical body should primarily be internalized. That is the quest of meditation. It is to discover the psychic aspects which collectively are felt as the *personSelf*.

This *personSelf* should be dissected for discovery of its parts, and study of the relationship between the core and adjuncts. At death, there will be no means of operating the physical bodySelf. Only the psychic aspects will remain. Hence it is imperative to know that psychic collective and identify with that as the surviving self. That is the psyche or subtle body which will survive death.

When that is mastered, a yogi should go further to sort the psychic aspects, to single out the coreSelf, to study its relationship with the adjuncts. This should be done during the life of the physical body.

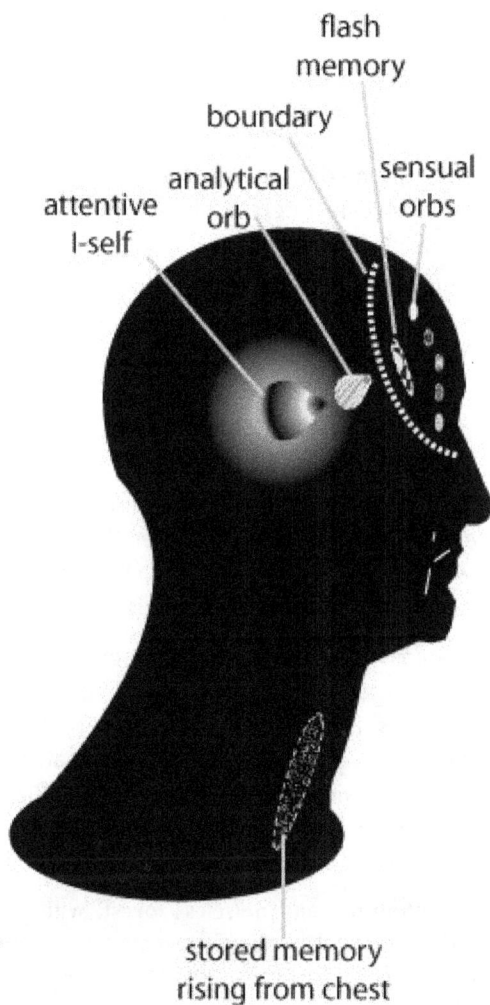

flash
memory

boundary

analytical   sensual
orb   orbs

attentive
I-self

stored memory
rising from chest

Being situated inside the city, he should reside there with his mind absorbed in the exterior and interior features of that place. (Anu Gītā 4.32)

A yogi takes help from more advanced ascetics. And yet the yogi must practice within the psyche to realize how the features of consciousness are positioned. Each yogi must have direct perception of how the mind operates.

As the physical body is situated on earth and is in its atmosphere, so the coreSelf and its adjuncts are in the enclosed space which is the subtle body. This should be investigated during meditation practice. A vast effort must be made to detached the interest of the self from the world outside the physical body.

Meditating in that place, the self sees the whole reality being situated in the body. The mind should not in any way wander outside the body. (Anu Gītā 4.33)

The location of this meditation, its position is within the psyche, within the subtle body, is the feelings within the physical body. The composite of those feelings is itself a psyche, a habitat or living place, an environment. When the yogi focuses into the inners of whatever the self is, with the mind not wandering outside the body, he/she may see the whole reality, the relevance of his/her existence.

The greatness of the universe is one consideration. That there is or may be a colossal deity who is conscious in every part of the cosmos, is another factor. And yet, for the limited self, it is his perceptive ability which is the indicator. It alone is the gage for the individual to recon anything. Whatever it is, whatever potential it has, that alone is the ultimate reference for it. Getting the self to inspect itself is paramount.

In an uninhabited and noiseless forest, while completely restraining the aggregate sensual energies, he should deeply meditate within the body on the whole reality as one object of focus. (Anu Gītā 4.34)

It is required that if one has a deep curiosity about the situation hereafter, one should study the inners of the self. One must venture inwards with as much enthusiasm and curiosity that one exhibits when pursuing external objects of interest.

If possible, the inner quest should be done while one is in an uninhibited and noiseless forest, with the sensual energies restrained from their physical interest. The focus into the feelings should be regarded as high priority.

The teeth, palate, tongue, throat as well as the neck and the heart; on these he should meditate and on what blocks the heart. (Anu Gītā 4.35)

Each part of the psyche should be discovered, analyzed, and categorized in regards to its function, malfunction, repair, calibration, suppression, or elimination.

Hear as it was heard by me, O Krishna, killer of Madhu, what that intelligent student, again inquired about the lifestyle which results in liberation, and which is so difficult to describe. (Anu Gītā 4.36)

This discourse was so valuable that even Krishna, someone who claimed to be the Supreme Person, listened attentively to it. Certainly, lesser selves could gain by reading this. The life of the physical body is a means of attaining salvation. Hence during the life of the body, the research into the psychic universe should be done.

How after repeatedly tasting, does this food become digested in the stomach? How are hormones produced? How is blood created? As for flesh, bone marrow, tendons, and bones, how are these nourished? (Anu Gītā 4.37)

The person himself/herself is the scientist who should investigate the physical body and the psychic format. If one is not ready to do this, it is to be understood that one does not have a deep interest in the range of consciousness which one endures. This is not a fault of any self. But if some self develops an interest in this, he/she should know that with the information shared by the advanced ascetic, the investigation must be completed.

How do these bodies develop in the body (of the mother)? How is strength produced out of the growing human being as the body increases in size? How are the pollutants and excrement removed from the body, being separated from the nutrients? How are non-vitalizing substances and especially pollutants, expelled from the body? (Anu Gītā 4.38)

The natural operations of the body, which are committed as its history, are for the most part done by the lifeForce in the body. This conducts electrical and biological functions for the maintenance of the form. At first however there are involuntary actions such as the expulsion of sperm which accesses the mother's uterus. There is the impregnation of the egg in the mother's passage, the dart into the uterine wall. There is the development of the fetus.

No limited self can say that these operations were commanded or formatted by himself/herself. Nature alone is responsible for this progression which causes the body to come into being.

Once the embryo is expelled into the world, where it must fend for itself, even then most of the operations of its development within its skin are conducted involuntarily.

How is this happening? Instead of living as a body and paying no interest to its function, the self should observe the involuntary operations to understand how Nature conducts the formations.

How does the body derive energy? Despite its frailty, how does it keep living?

How does one inhale and again exhale the vital energy? What is the default location of the self, which is situated in the personal psyche? (Anu Gītā 4.39)

There must be an investigation, into the design and alignment of the components of the psyche. Just as physicians charted the inner and outer parts of the physical body, mystics should map the subtle body or psyche. The most important feature is the coreSelf. Where is it located? How does it participate in the affairs of subtle body?

How, by exertion, does the individual spirit within the body, carry the body? What color and what characteristic does the mind have when it leaves the body? O purity personified, person deserving of the highest honor, you may explain this to me in as detailed a way as possible. (Anu Gītā 4.40)

The individual spirit, the coreSelf, is on a different plane than the physical body. How then is the willpower of the core successfully or unsuccessfully expressed through the physical system? There are so many involuntary functions which are executed, even in the physical body, what to speak of psychic actions. How are these operations initiated and executed?

As fittingly questioned, O Madhava Krishna, that learnt ritualist answered him (Kashyapa). I replied just as I heard, O person with powerful arms, chastiser of rebels. (Anu Gītā 4.41)

There are many mystics and psychics, yogis, devotees, philosophers, and the like. Each may specialize in a particular discipline. *Kashyapa's* teacher was the expert in the details of self-realization as it is applied to surviving death.

As placing property in storage, one becomes the possessor of it, so placing the mind in the body, and restricting the orifices, one should research the self and avoid distractions. (Anu Gītā 4.42)

A person cannot complete self-realization and understanding about the hereafter, if he/she does not intuit the psyche. Even though the natural process is to spend the majority of time seeking items in the environment, still that process does not yield deep insight into the core and the other components in the psyche.

As a person evolves, he/she realizes that it is necessary to introspect. An ascetic takes help from more advanced meditators. With this, he/she must do inSelf research and have that verified by greater yogis.

Thus, being always meditatively absorbed and being pleased in the self, one is soon transited to the spiritual level of existence after becoming perceptive of the life force energy potential. (Anu Gītā 4.43)

A yogi must rate the lifeForce energy potential. Why? Because there must be a reference for figuring the power investment of the core. How much energy from the core is used for maintaining the physical and subtle bodies? What happens if the core's contribution is reduced? What happens if the lifeForce's output is curtailed?

When the lifeForce is efficiently distributed, the coreSelf delivers less energy to the psyche. That allows the core to understand its position better. This allows it to self-introspect even more.

It is not comprehended by the eyes, or by any of the senses. It is by the vision of the mind, that the supreme spiritual self can be perceived. (Anu Gītā 4.44)

The orientation which is natural and easy, is that of using physical senses. The compulsion to use the senses is so strong that it takes special effort to reduce the urges.

The limited selves are numerous. Each must discover itself as an individual spirit. Eventually however there is the realization that there is the supreme spiritual self. That conclusion becomes evident in time. That person is subtler than the limited selves and can only be understood with spiritual senses.

It has hands and feet everywhere. It has eyes, heads, and faces in every direction. The individual spirit perceives when the psyche is displaced from the body. (Anu Gītā 4.45)

The limited spirit, you or me, experiences hands and feet, eyes, heads and faces but not in every direction. Our sensual reach is limited. Even though it has radiance, the individual limited coreSelf only radiates to a limited distance from itself. It is not omniscient.

But there is a supreme self, which has radiance which penetrates whatever else exist. That supreme someone reaches, accommodates, sees, considers, and touches everything in every direction. When one realizes oneself, one gets some idea of the supreme self.

Abandoning the body, that one, using the mind, perceives the self, while effortlessly linking through meditation with only the spiritual existence, just as if the self were smiling at the accomplishment. (Anu Gītā 4.46)

The course of self-realization is completed hereafter but only if it is aggressively pursued during the life of the physical body. To pull away from the body when it is fatally damaged, one must practice detachment from it, and gain experience of the relationship of the psychic components.

A self must put himself/herself into the research about the core and the adjuncts. Then salvation becomes possible. Assistance must be rendered by the advanced mystics, but there must be self-effort applied.

Every bit of this confidential information was explained by me to you, O best of the ritualists. Getting permission, I will depart. You too, my disciple, should go as you wish. (Anu Gītā 4.47)

Thus, it was heard by me, O Krishna, how that student who was a performer of great penance, went as he desired. He is a ritual ascetic who removes uncertainty. (Anu Gītā 4.48)

Krishna Vasudeva said: Then, O son of Pṛthā, that leader of the ritualists, having lectured to me perfectly about assuming the righteous lifestyle which yields liberation, disappeared right there. (Anu Gītā 4.49)

I hope that this was heard by you with singular mental focus, O son of Pṛthā. For while sitting on the chariot, you heard this just the same. (Anu Gītā 4.50)

It is interesting that the *Anu Gītā* was rated to be equal to the information and revelation which is the *Bhagavad Gita*. When all is said and done, the equation about inquiry is settled in the first instance by self-realization, the objective view of the self by itself. Thereafter one may confront the Supreme Person.

O son of Pṛthā, this is not easily integrated by one who is inattentive or dull-witted, or by a person who did not accomplish this experience, or by one whose psyche is habitually corrupted. (Anu Gītā 4.51)

O best of the Bharatas, this which I explained is a secret even among the supernatural rulers in the celestial world. Son of Pṛthā, this was never heard by any other person in this world of short life-span. (Anu Gītā 4.52)

O faultless one, there is no person besides you who deserves to hear this. Nor is it easily integrated by one whose internal psyche has no singular mental focus. (Anu Gītā 4.53)

The information about the self and the superSelf cannot be integrated by any or every one, here, there, and everywhere. It is applicable only to those who put aside external focus and cultivate internal perception. The mere qualification of being a devotee of Krishna is insufficient for imbibing this information, and the experiences which develop from it.

One must be a devotee, and also have the inner spiritual perception, which is not the same as physical sense perception. One must practice in meditation to develop the singular mental focus. That is the method of converting the intellect into a vision orb, which perceives supernatural environments.

O son of Kuntī, the celestial world with its deities is saturated with persons who performed approved social actions. The cessation of these short-duration bodies is not desired by those supernatural officials. (Anu Gītā 4.54)

A self-realized person loses interest in righteous lifestyle but all the same he/she does socially approved acts to honor the course of human society. Those people, however, who think that social life in the physical world is the most valuable sociology, get promoted to a celestial world which is supervised by deities, whose interest is this physical world, because it produces pious entities, and supports orderly reproduction of human beings.

The deities of those celestial places which are attained by socially approved behavior, do not encourage self-realization or the discovery and liberation of the coreSelf. They are interested in physical reproduction through short-duration bodies. The deities themselves have long ranged subtle bodies. They do not as a habit take physical embryos, but they encourage the earth-bound beings, to have the short-ranged bodies.

That objective is the highest, O son of Pṛthā, which concerns the eternal spiritual existence, whereby abandoning the miseries, one achieves immortality and is happy always. (Anu Gītā 4.55)

The earth-referenced heaven, the celestial world which is attained by having a record of righteous lifestyle, is not the focus of the advanced personalities. There are three positions.

- physical life on earth, where socially acceptable acts are performed for the welfare of one and all

- celestial heavenly life in a dimension which is superior to that of the earth, where only piously inclined persons reside, and only for as long as such persons are elevated by the buoyancy of their pious acts, committed during the time of using the last physical body

- spiritual heavenly life in a dimension which is higher than that of the celestial heaven

The **physical life on earth** can be used to elevate one's behavior in terms of socially acceptable actions or in terms of elevation to transcend the natural interest in physical history. If one focuses on pious behavior, one will not have the impetus to investigate the components of self.

Impious behavior is not acceptable in either case, either for elevation to a celestial heaven, or for self-realization, or for attaining a spiritual environment.

The danger of focusing on pious credits is that one may lose sight of the idea of self-realization. Nature does not encourage self-realization, but it prompts a person to act for evolutionary elevation, which is not the same as understanding the self as a radiant core.

The **celestial heavenly life in a higher dimension** has a defect, which is that, after one gains the elevation, by doing socially acceptable acts, one is elevated to that place, but only for as long as the energy from the pious acts is sustained. As soon as that energy is exhausted, one becomes demoted to the earth plane, where one must again strive for righteous conduct, so as to be elevated again.

There are permanent residents in the celestial heaven. Some of these are deities. Some are associates of the deities. They do not have the earth-bound mentality, where they feel it is a priority to be part of the earth's history. They do not have an urge for having a physical body. This frees them from the transmigration curse, which afflicts most of the limited selves, who assume bodies in the physical world.

The **spiritual heavenly life is the highest domain** with eternal environments. One cannot attain this place on the basis of pious activity. This is acquired on the basis of shifting one's focus to the coreSelf, and having curtailed the influence of the adjuncts. This is the most inaccessible place.

Assuming this ascetic righteous lifestyle, even persons from faulty families, women, as well as commercially-minded people, even laborers can achieve the supreme destination. (Anu Gītā 4.56)

The ascetic righteous lifestyle and the social righteous lifestyle vary. The ascetic one results in translation to a spiritual environment. The other, the socially motivated one, is the basis for transfer to a heavenly place in the astral existence, from where one will be demoted, as soon as the energy resulting from the piety is exhausted.

What of the trained ascetic ritualists, O son of Pṛthā, or the well-read administrative rulers who are committed to their approved duties, and who eagerly aspire for the eternal spiritual world? (Anu Gītā 4.57)

This was stated with due reason as well as the process in the practice for attaining this, the results of the accomplishment, liberation, and the conclusion about misery. Therefore, O leader of the Bharatas, there is no other happiness which is superior to this. That is for sure. (Anu Gītā 4.58)

One who is educated, one who is confident, one who is energetic in the pursuit of this, that person with a short life-span, who discards as being meaningless the course of this world, O son of Paṇḍu, soon achieves by these methods, the supreme destination. (Anu Gītā 4.59)

This is all that is to be said. There is nothing beyond this. O son of Pṛthā, one who practices proficiently and consistently for six months accomplishes this yoga. (Anu Gītā 4.60)

Chapter 7
Uddhava Gītā Extract

The following verses, this Chapter 7, are extracted from the *Uddhava Gītā* which is part of the *Srimad Bhagavatam*. These are used because they deal with death. Krishna spoke of this to Arjuna in the *Bhagavad Gītā* discourse but he explained some more of it to *Uddhava*. Consider this.

If they know the process of achieving happiness and removing distress, surely they do not know the yoga technique by which death could be made powerless. (Uddhava Gītā 5.19)

When the information tallies, when the experience is fully sampled, one realizes that the drive from Nature is to coral one into the corner, in fear of distress. One craves happiness but one remains afraid of being subjected to traumatic circumstances.

However, despite integrating that conclusion, one has no idea of how to make death powerless. This is due to the fact that Nature has the upper hand over the manifestation of one's objectivity. At any moment, Nature can suspend the self-knowing part of consciousness. This means rapid loss of memory and the inability to be coherent.

There is a solution to this problem. It is the mastery of yoga practice, the mystic method of studying the operations of consciousness, so as to maneuver or hop from life to life, skipping Nature's method of transferring from life to death.

What thing or enjoyment pleases, when death is near. That which satisfies does not serve the purpose, just as an animal which is pulled to be killed at the place of execution. (Uddhava Gītā 5.20)

Despite being offered ripe grain, luscious grass and cool water, an animal which is being pulled to a place to be slaughtered cannot improve its insecure situation, merely by becoming distracted by the food offered to it.

When death is near, some pleasure for the body has no relevance. After someone develops wealth and establishes a lifestyle which others envy, the opulence becomes meaningless. In fact it is regarded as an insult. In the end, the body is fatally damaged or terminally diseased. There is no worse sight than a wealthy individual who is confronted with certain death.

That which is heard of is also affected, just as what we experience presently, is affected by rivalry, envy, destruction and wastage. The desire for it is hampered by obstacles, just as in farming, there may be no produce. (Uddhava Gītā 5.21)

The stockpile of information consists of memory and current experience. In either case, there is a background of insecurity because of rivalry, envy, destruction, and wastage. Nature is ongoing but it may be posited that it began at some point. Even so, the conclusion is that initially it emerged with the energy of rivalry, envy, destruction, and wastage, woven through it.

The unwanted features cannot be extracted from it. In whatever direction one goes, the negative aspects are present. They were operative in the past, and will wrap and be inserted in future incidences.

One can do the best that one can, and still there will be obstacles, just as in farming, so many unpredictable factors besides the farmer's labor, are necessary for success.

If righteous duty is well-performed, and is not affected by obstacles, then what is the result of it? Hear how that takes place. (Uddhava Gītā 5.22)

If the farmer has a successful crop, it is not an indication that success will be ongoing. In fact, it is not possible for there to be perpetual success in the physical world. Hence the idea that there will be a final condition of permanent happiness is grand delusion only.

The most one will get from living a life where righteous duty was done, is a heavenly state of mind and condition hereafter. If one is facilitated by Nature, so that one performs only righteous acts, there will be a time when the results of such behavior will be reconstructed as circumstances of heavenly life, both here and hereafter. However, one will be challenged by the factor of limit.

Having worshipped the supernatural rulers, the sacrificial performer goes to a heavenly place. Like a god, he enjoys the celestial pleasures which he achieved by endeavor. (Uddhava Gītā 5.23)

Without being under the influence of pious people, who are either physical or psychic, it is near impossible to perform righteous acts. One limited being, cannot sustain his behavior with only righteous conduct. For this to happen, he/she must have assistance from others, especially from supernatural people whose psychic influence may dictate into a human mind, the ways and means of approved conduct.

When after living a pious life, one is deprived of the very body, through which one exhibits the socially constructive behavior, one gravitates towards supernatural people who reside in psychic places on the subtle side of existence. Like a god, one enjoys the celestial pleasures which were achieved by the pious life one lived on earth.

In a glowing flying conveyance, which was acquired by his accumulated good luck derived from past endeavors, he enjoys, being dressed in beautiful clothing, in the midst of celestial women and praised by celestial musicians and songsters. (Uddhava Gītā 5.24)

In the heavenly world hereafter, a good man or woman, is welcomed as a celebrity. The denizens of heaven rate one's performance and praises one for being such a saint. There, one is chauffeured through that heavenly place. With no effort to cause it to happen, one finds oneself to be a pleasure body, with suitable clothing and decorations. Every part of the subtle body one functions as there, has happy feelings in every part of it.

Male and female beings are elevated like this. In some cases, people who were partners on earth, find themselves together as celestial couples who enjoy feasting, making love, and being entertained in the heavenly places.

Those who arrive there without partners find themselves to be paired with a person or with persons who feel perfectly matched.

Sporting with the women, going wherever desired by that flying conveyance, which is trimmed with a loop of small cymbals and bells, the person is happy in the pleasure groves of the celestial people, and is not aware of his up-coming fall. (Uddhava Gītā 5.25)

Though not mentioned, women go to heaven. Someone who performed pious activities as a single woman with no sexual partner, arrive in the heavenly place without a spouse, and is paired with an angelic male as soon as she arrives in the heavenly place.

Women who arrive with a spouse, remain paired with that male person, and have experiences which are pleasure saturated. The partners are greeted together. They enjoy together privately and publicly as well.

He enjoys in heaven until the merits of his good behavior are exhausted. On expiration of that force, he falls away from there, without desiring that, being forced to accept that by the time factor. (Uddhava Gītā 5.26)

The duration of such heavenly life is limited. the sadness of it is that one has no idea that it will end. This is becaue one did not consider its termination while one acted with righteous conduct while on earth.

A good individual who has wealth, and who shares some of it to needy persons, may not recon with time while living as a physical self on earth. This will cause him to postpone assessment of the value of his pious activities, as to their actual worth and duration.

Even if one was the most pious person, still at some point, Nature will disable one, so that one cannot continue generating pious credits. Then if one has the objectivity, one may rate the compound value of the piety one amassed during the life. However, even then, how is one to decide as to the actual value and time worth of the efforts.

Once the rich person arrives in heaven, he/she will be absorbed in the intense happiness within the celestial body, and in the environment as well. Due to this absorption, one will have no idea of when the sojourn will suddenly cease, like a flame which finds that its fuel source is finished.

As soon as the result energy of his earthly pious acts are exhausted, that person whose reputation was extolled in heaven, will find himself/herself to be converted into being a grey colored form in that heavenly place, one that slips away quickly, fading from that place, with no grip on it, like a small cloud which vanishes on a hot windy day.

Or if due to wicked company, he is addicted to irresponsible acts, if he does not control his sensual energy and is lusty by nature, miserly, greedy and is a womanizer, or one who causes injury to other creatures, (Uddhava Gītā 5.27)

...if without scriptural sanction, he kills animals and worships ghosts and spirits, he goes helplessly to hellish dimensions, and enters dreadful mental darkness. (Uddhava Gītā 5.28)

Conversely, one who was irresponsible, one who was a criminal, may be transferred to a hell hereafter. Just as a saintly person transited spontaneously to a heavenly locale, so a criminal may go to a hellish location which is a psychic prison.

Someone may indulge in black magic, where through psychic violence he/she subjects others to physical or psychological harassment. The result energy of the criminal behavior, stays with that person. It causes hellish conditions to be manifest to that criminal as soon as he/she can no longer use the physical body as his existential address.

That person will suffer internally from dark states of mind and mental horrors. He/She will suffer externally as well. One may during dreams during the life of the physical body visit hellish or heavenly places, which exist hereafter. Such experiences should not be dismissed as illusions.

When enduring life in a hellish place, one is released from that environment when the return energy of one's vicious acts is exhausted. Just as the heavenly stay will be terminated when the energy power which caused it is exhausted, so a person will be released from hell hereafter.

Doing through those bodies, activities which result in misery, he again gets another form, there at the same hellish place. What happiness is there for those who perform righteous actions for the sake of bodies which are subjected to death? (Uddhava Gītā 5.29)

As boxed in by Nature, seeing only what it allows one to perceive, a limited entity becomes conditioned to act in a particular way, and with specific prejudices which are inoculated into his/her psyche. Struggling day and night to maintain his/her precarious grip on objectivity, and having little abstract perception, the entity is held accountable for the use of its involvement with its feelings and analytical ability.

What can be done about it?

The least anyone can do is to commit righteous behavior. To do so one must be intuitively good, or be trained, or confined so that one's selfish temperament is effectively suppressed. But even then, this loop of being a physical body, then being peeled from it, then becoming another physical system, is unavoidable. What hope is there in it?

The Blessed Lord said: The mystic skills attend to the yogis who conquer the senses, who complete the required disciplines, who master the life force energies and whose consciousness is linked attentively to Me. (Uddhava Gītā 10.1)

Apart from the ordinary entities who find it unnecessary to do inSelf spiritual research, there are entities who instinctively push themselves to understand the psychic aspects. Of these some do non-speculative research. They are the foremost of the ascetics, and if they are attracted to Krishna, their quest advances progressively.

Just as an ordinary entity is obsessed with his physical body, just as he positions it to enjoy sensations, so there are advanced entities who focus inwardly. They chart the emotions, sensuality, memory, analytical and illustrative abilities. In this adventure, mystic skills are discovered.

The deserving Uddhava said: By what linking of the attention to a higher concentration force, does a mystic skill develop, O infallible Krishna? How many mystic skills are there? Tell me of it. Are You the giver of such skills to the yogis? (Uddhava Gītā 10.2)

The physical skills of a human body are charted by human beings. In terms of history, the world moves on the basis of the skill of individuals, and collections of people in the form of households, village, towns, cities, states, and countries. By focusing on particular physical and superphysical aspects, humans develop methods of exploitation through which inventions are created.

But there are mystic skills, the study of psychic influence on other humans, or within the same person. During the time of Krishna, some persons charted methods of developing mysticism.

Uddhava wanted to know this psychological science, as to the involvement of Krishna, who was declared as the master of the mystic sports.

(Krishna said:) Those who progressed the farthest in yoga, state that there are eighteen mystic skills, and eighteen types linkage of the attention to eighteen types of concentration forces. Eight of these are prominent in Me, the remaining ten are caused by a particular influence of material nature. (Uddhava Gītā 10.3)

Of the eighteen psychological powers, eight are prominent in Krishna, the Supreme Personality. The other ten are caused by saturation of a particular influence of Nature. No mention is given about the limited entities. They are in the trillions, and yet their importance is not one of prominence. It is either God or Nature, with the limited entities being influenced.

Becoming atomic, becoming cosmic, pertains to a form of the yogi, as well as being weightless, acquiring or experiencing through the sense organs of others, enjoying what was heard of and what was seen normally, manipulating mundane potency, ruling over others, (Uddhava Gītā 10.4)

...non-attachment to mundane influences, which results in the technique of controlling one's nature, and obtaining what is desired; these my dear friend, are considered to be the eight natural skills. (Uddhava Gītā 10.5)

- becoming atomic
- becoming cosmic
- being weightless
- acquiring or experiencing through the sense organs of others
- enjoying what was heard of and what was seen normally
- manipulating mundane potency
- ruling over others
- non-attachment to mundane influences, which results in the technique of controlling one's nature, and obtaining what is desired

The split of influences is between God and Nature, with the limited entities being in a class by themselves which is influenced by person as God or by environment as Restrictor.

The above eight mystic powers are distributed from the spread of God's influences. A limited entity shares in these powers in a proportion which is determined by his/her relationship with the Supreme Lord.

God does not draft a sketch like an architect. The powers are distributed according to the natural relationship between the Supreme Person and the others. This includes the limited entities' resistance or susceptibility to God's suggestions. In the calculation, the will of God and the desire of the limited selves, must be taken into account. It is rendered finally in the physical world with the influence of Nature being applied before there is a manifestation.

The **atomic forms** are natural for the limited entities, who are instances of spiritual radiance. However, for anyone to experience himself/herself as an atomic something, there needs to be either natural or imposed detachment.

Because of extended radiance, a limited self does not realize itself as being atomic. Rather it identifies with the spread of its radiance. According to the edge of its feeling range, it believes itself as such.

The **cosmic format** is the exclusive domain of the Supreme Person. God is such that his cosmic range is beyond the assessment of any limited entity. His radiance is so vast, that even the greatest mystics are baffled at his extent. They cannot estimate it. Still on occasion a yogi finds himself/herself to be extended to a cosmic range which renders some understanding about the Supreme Lord and about the spread of Nature.

By becoming free from its limited extent, a limited self may feel the spread of God's radiance but only to a limited degree which may feel unlimited to that limited person. This becomes possible by the action of God in linking his radiance to that of a limited self.

To **become weightless**, a limited self must disconnect or be disconnected from its adjuncts. By itself the coreSelf is weightless. However, that condition is not allowed except by special influence from the Supreme Lord.

Weightlessness is based on detachment, either self-imposed or enforced by other agency. Since the limited self is a sponge for influence, it rarely experiences weightless. There may be fear involved in being weightless because the limited self feels secure when it is attached to whatever may give it a sense of security.

Sensual wiring is such that one limited entity may **acquire or experience through the sense organs of another person**. A common example is a pregnant woman and her fetus. There is some feedback between the two. However, by psychic transfer a yogi could experience through the senses of another person.

This writer however, had many experiences of advanced yogis who were deceased, who entered his psyche, and used it to acquire sensual experience, or to acquire even physical things. It is possible. Krishna informed that this happens under his supervision. The spread of God's influence is the format through which this occurs.

To **enjoy what was heard of and what was seen normally** is the privilege of every human being. Naturally, as soon as one is born, there is the need for enjoyment. There is hesitation when contacting whatever causes suffering.

Though natural, this tendency has its original expression in the Supreme Person. It is shared to all other personSelves proportionately. God is the aggregate of it.

To **manipulate mundane potency** is another feature of person which is sourced in the Supreme Being, and which is distributed proportionately to other persons. God has the total control, the over-riding grasp of the colossal mundane potency, which influences the limited selves as it is influenced by the unlimited person, by Krishna.

To **rule over others** is another person feature which is a mystic power in its original format. This power is local to the Supreme Being. Minute portions of it are felt by other selves.

The **non-attachment to mundane influences, which results in the technique of controlling one's nature, and obtaining what is desired**, is expressed in full by the Supreme Person. The limited selves feel and express this as they are empowered by God.

Being unaffected by the sense of self identification with the body, hearing from a distance, seeing from a distance, moving at the speed of the mind, assuming any desired form, entering anyone's body, (Uddhava Gītā 10.6)

...dying as desired, participating in the sports of the supernatural rulers, perfect fulfillment of one's motive, and to command circumstances from an unopposed course anywhere, (Uddhava Gītā 10.7)

The ten mystic powers which are granted from Nature.

- being unaffected by the sense of self identification with the body

- hearing from a distance

- seeing from a distance

- moving at the speed of the mind

- assuming any desired form

- entering anyone's body

- dying as desired

- participating in the sports of the supernatural rulers

- perfect fulfillment of one's motive

- to command circumstances from an unopposed course anywhere

The ten mystic abilities, which are granted by Nature, occur in the psyche of anyone whose subtle body is synchronized into the level of existence in which those powers are shared. When any of these are manifested in the physical world, they may be regarded as miracles. It means however that the person's psychic energy shifted to a level where the subtle body automatically exhibits those abilities. Just as the infant of a monkey has limbs which allow it to swing through a forest, so if someone's subtle body shifts to a dimension in which one is **unaffected by the sense of self identification with the body**, that person will feel detached from his/her physical form.

Hearing from a distance occurs when the ears of the subtle body become detached from physical hearing and engages into subtle sound. The person hears speech which was said thousands of miles away. This is subtle speech which may or may not be emitted physically.

A yogi may **see from a distance**. This is subtle perception which is visual and clear. Rarely is this physical vision. Whatever happens physically also registers as psychic circumstance. Thus, the subtle body sees just as well as the physical eyes perceives.

A yogi may **move at the speed of the mind**. Even though a yogi may move his physical body with rapidity, the application of this is related to the subtle body. It can travel as fast as light energy can. Such experiences may occur during astral projections. They may happen involuntarily with the yogi having no control over the speed of the subtle body, except to be an observer of the movement.

On a certain psychic plane, one may **assume any desired form**. If someone desires to change his/her complexion, it happens instantaneously. Sometimes a yogi may be on an astral level, where others do not have the power to assume any form desired, but the yogi may have this ability, because his subtle body has exceptional powers, which are not assumed on that plane by anyone else.

A yogi may **enter anyone's body**. This power should be rarely used. If used, it should be with caution. Some yogis enter the body of this author. This happens infrequently. A yogi may go into my psyche to view physical objects. Sometimes, a yogi looks through the author's eye. The mystic yogi may be in the eyeball. He may peer through a corner of my eye, while I look through it head-on.

A yogi may for one reason or the other, desire to **die as desired**. In the *Mahabharata*, we read of *Bhishma* who delayed the death of his mortally-wounded body for fifty plus days. He wanted to use sun energy to usher his psyche to a supernatural world.

Someone may **desire to participate in the sports of the supernatural rulers**. To attain one of their domains, a relationship is required. The deity must specifically desire the devotee to be present in that place. Mere wishful thinking or even strong desire alone, will not cause the transfer of the psyche of someone to a deity's place hereafter.

In the physical world, nearly everyone wants **perfect fulfillment of a motive**. Nature however, usually thwarts the idea, either to alter or to demolish it. This gives one the *experience of frustration*, which is a basic energy in this creation.

Unless all factors are present and are functional, it is not possible to have perfect fulfillment of a motive. When it happens that someone gets complete satisfaction, a memory of the event is stored in the psyche. This acts to re-initiate the desire but if any factor is absent or if it is present but is disabled, the person will experience frustration.

A yogi soon realizes how the roll of time is activated. He/She no longer projects the need for completion of any stored desire. He trains the self to enjoy inactivated or partially completed urges.

The tapestry of history concerns the efforts of trillions of unit selves to **command circumstances from an unopposed**

course anywhere. Everything everywhere is a manifestation of desire which also includes the frustration of what is wanted. The success of a unit self, indicates the failure of some other.

There are five special mystic powers which are reliant on God, Nature, and limited entities to be interactive. These are listed now.

...knowing the three phases of the time factor, not being affected by heat and cold, happiness and distress, knowing the mental and emotional energy and other related privacies of others, counteracting the influence of fire, sun, water, poison and other dangers, not being conquered by others: (Uddhava Gītā 10.8)

- knowing the three phases of the time factor
- not being affected by heat and cold, happiness and distress
- knowing the mental and emotional energy and other related privacies of others
- counteracting the influence of fire, sun, water, poison, and other dangers
- not be conquered by others

To **know the three phases of the time factor,** a limited entity must be positioned in a special phase of time, where he/she derives natural objectivity, and is graced to interact, and turn to grasp what was, what is, and what will be. The Supreme Person is all pervasive. His radiance penetrates everything everywhere. He has the unlimited reach into the time spread. Others may experience the diversification of time, now and again, but not for eternity.

The Supreme Person is **not being affected by heat and cold, happiness and distress.** This is because he is outside and inside of everything. Other entities, limited beings, may have a glimpse of this now and again.

The God knows the mental and emotional energy and other related privacies of everyone else. This sensitivity does not affect him. Even though he is aware, he is detached as well. A limited entity may also know the mental and emotional energy and other related privacies of someone else. Some deities are aware of everyone who is in their domain or who relies on their energy for objectivity.

A limited being may exhibit special powers to **counteract the influence of fire, sun, water, poison, and other dangers**. This attracts persons who were threatened by a hazard of Nature or by the action of hostile people. That attraction causes the miracle worker to be appraised as a great personality.

To **not be conquered by others,** is a special power. For a limited entity it is a relative feature. Nature changes at every moment. Whatever it exhibits as being superior, it will in time demolish.

When Nature positions someone so that he/she seems invincible, it will in time withdraw its boost. No one should assume that an empowerment will last forever. One should be adaptable, taking ques from Nature, so that one can step down when it acts to degrade an empowerment which it installed previously.

These are a brief description of the mystic skills which manifest from the linking of the attention with the concentration force in yoga practice. Learn from Me, by which concentration linkage, particular skills are developed and how they will manifest. (Uddhava Gītā 10.9)

It must be understood that the mystic skills may occur spontaneously, where someone experiences a skill, but did not desire to have it, nor made an effort to derive it. Someone may have no interest in a mystic skill, or may have no information that such an ability is possible, and yet, that person may experience the extraordinary ability.

As Lord Krishna explained to Uddhava, the mystic skills may manifest from linking the attention with a concentration force. Invariably that is the situation, but there are exceptions, in the sense that there may be involuntary linking of the attention with a concentration force, in an involuntary yoga practice, where the person did not practice but suddenly finds himself/herself assuming a posture and state, which is advanced yoga. The result of which is a mystic experience.

One does not have to be a yogi to experience mystic powers or insight. It can happen to anyone anywhere with or without the effort in yoga.

This is because there may be psychic movements of Nature or God, whereby someone's psyche could shift and cause mystic experience, and even surprising mystic control. One does not have to be worthy to experience mystic power. It can happen to anyone at any time. It may last for a time or for a moment. It may be understood by the person, or he/she may have no coherence about it.

By linking his attention with the concentration force of subtle matter, which is in his psyche, and in My subtle body, the worshipper of subtle matter, acquires the ability to assume an atomic form. (Uddhava Gītā 10.10)

During the life of the physical body, a yogi should practice to link his attention to various causal realities. There will be curiosity about existence. Since it is complicated, and has numerous complex phases, a yogi cannot expect that he/she will figure it in one mystic action. One must be prepared to spend years researching this existence, to figure how it operates, and how one can negotiate in it.

The deliberate linking of the attention to any phase of reality is termed as *dharanā*. This is in contrast to when there is spontaneous linking, which occurs by natural switching, where one finds oneself to be linked either after making the effort to do so, or after doing something else, which was not related to the achievement. When there is spontaneous effortless linking, that is termed as *dhyāna*.

To link one's attention to any phase of psychic reality, the yogi must first locate the psychic object. This object may be atomic, of normal proportions, or it may be cosmic.

The yogi must collect his attentive powers, then focus them on the phase of reality which he identified with. The focus must be for a time, sufficient for the contact to be reciprocal, with the yogi gaining insight into the nature, and relationship aspects, of the reality which he contacted.

This practice should be well developed before the yogi is deprived of the use of the physical body. If somehow a yogi could not do this, his chances of achieving this after being deprived of the body, are nil.

In the astral world hereafter, the focusing power may be shiftier, where there is no stability in the focusing ability, because the sense of identity energy cannot stop the instability of the intellect, which means that focus on higher levels is not likely.

During the life of the physical body, there is the likelihood that the physical system may assist in anchoring the adjuncts in the subtle body, which may result in stability of focus, and the ability to be directional within the mind. If the yogi gained focusing stability while the physical body was alive, he can continue that skill hereafter, with the possibility of being transferred to higher dimensions.

The subtle body has this aspect, where it naturally imitates the behavior and format of the physical system. Hence if the yogi diverted the physical body to yoga practice, his subtle body will be reinforced for higher pursuits, rather than for normal materialistic achievements.

By linking the attention with the concentration force of subtle matter, which is in his psyche, and in Krishna's subtle body, the worshipper of subtle matter, acquires the ability to assume an atomic form. At first, this may happen only by linking in the yogi's subtle body. The Supreme Being's subtle form is on a higher plane and is accessed with more proficiency.

Some yogis have no idea of the Supreme Person. Their experience will be limited to their subtle form only. The yogi addressed here is one who worships subtle matter. This also means someone who by mystic penetration discovered the subtle matter in the subtle body and realized that this energy was the basis for other energies in the subtle body. This yogi will experience himself as an atomic entity in a micro-world.

Linking the attention with the concentration force in the super-subtle total material energy, which is in his psyche and in Mine, the yogi becomes situated in that super-subtle condition and achieves the ability to experience a cosmic form of either of the super-subtle elements. (Uddhava Gītā 10.11)

When the yogi practiced for many years to keep the mind in a silence mode, where no thoughts occurred in it, and its curiosity tendency was curbed, he discovers himself in a spatial consciousness, in which energy is widely dispersed. This energy shows no format of itself. It is detected by feelings in his psyche, and by the sense of touch on the edges of subtle self.

Attaching the energy which is used for ideation, to Me, as I am related to the material elements, in the composition of atomic energy, the yogi assumes a weightless form, which is based on the subtle existence of time. (Uddhava Gītā 10.12)

This does not mean that the physical body becomes weightless. This happens on the level of ideation when the yogi is connected to the Supreme Lord.

As ideation energy is insubstantial, the subtle feelings of self on the level of opinion-energy, are weightless. When a yogi becomes habituated to existence on the ideation plane, and when the need for physical surroundings is absent, the yogi experiences weightlessness of self. He does not experience a limit to his movement, but all the same there is no geography, hence no urge to be somewhere.

If the yogi fails to detect how the ideation energy is attached to Krishna, to the Supreme Being, his assessment of location and time will be that there is no other higher level. He will resume physical and subtle formats, as soon as he shifts from being afloat in the ideation plane.

Linking the attention to the concentration force which is focused on Me, on My energy of assertion and on the motivational powers of material nature, one feels self identification with sensual energies. By focusing the mind on Me in that way, one acquires the power of appropriation. (Uddhava Gītā 10.13)

It is not easy to link the attention to the concentration force which is focused on Krishna, nor on his energy of assertion. A yogi may link to the motivation powers of Nature, and to the self-identification with the sensual energies in the yogi's psyche. Doing that is an achievement but it is not the full practice.

Nevertheless, one should not think that it is easy to link into Krishna. First of all, the Supreme Being is on a higher plane of existence which is transcendental to the level the limited persons exist in. It is more than a matter of being Krishna's devotee. One may be a devotee and still not reach Krishna on a transcendental plane. Then one's meditation would be limited to reaching the motivational powers of Nature and the self-identification one feels with the sensual energies, which one can perceive and control.

One who applies his mind to Me by linking the attention with the concentration force, consisting of the sexually-charged conscious cosmic power and the primal conscious cosmic force which originated from the abstract existence, obtains the greatest mystic skill of being able to fulfill any desire. (Uddhava Gītā 10.14)

To make use of the physical body in real terms, the focus within it has to be turned, so its interests are for the most part invested in the coreSelf. Along with this, the adjuncts of the core, which are necessary perception utilities, must be discovered, analyzed, and efficiently utilized.

First the attention must be lifted from its habitual and compulsory focus on physical reality. Then the attention protrusion which normally goes outside the psyche, must be arrested. Then the attention spout must be retracted into the psyche. Then this retracted organ must remain still for a time, until it no longer lunges at every opportunity.

The interest must be directed back to the coreSelf. At first this may be done by a loop action. Then it is done by a retraction pulling force, where from the coreSelf, the movement of interest outwards, is reversed so that it aggressively goes inwards into the core.

The linking with God is the highest practice, but one must first master inner focus of the core into the core. When the coreSelf masters self focus, it is likely that the Supreme Being will grace him, causing that self to commune with the Supreme Personality.

Some authorities interpret that the linking with Krishna is done through linking with Krishna's duly installed deity form which is painted, sculptured, or even imagined. That is not the case. This process of *dharanā* is the application of the sixth stage of yoga, which is a deliberate focus into the supernatural plane of existence.

There is value in the deity worship of Krishna but that is a different practice. This process is specifically for yogi-devotees who are skilled in mystic practice, which is related to discovering Krishna on higher planes.

One who applies his mind to Krishna by linking the attention with the sexually-charged conscious cosmic power, and the primal conscious cosmic force, obtains the greatest mystic skill of being able to fulfill any desire.

One who links his attention to his ideation energy which is focused on Vishnu, the Supreme Lord of the three influences of material nature, and the One who assumes the form of Time, obtains the skill of controlling, having dominion over spirits and their psyches. (Uddhava Gītā 10.15)

To achieve this one must have a serviceable relationship with Vishnu, Krishna, the Supreme Lord. This must be a direct relationship with this deity. It should not be a promised relationship, nor one which is based on an assurance by someone, who is famous as a devotee of Krishna.

It is easy to link one's attention to the ideation energy in the psyche, but it is difficult to keep the attention there, with the mind being cleared of mundane ideas, which relate to one's physical history.

Such linking to the clear ideation energy can be done consistently, only if the yogi practiced many hours of meditation, to curb the intellect from haphazard thinking, and to cause it to remain in a stable condition, where it is not resistant to instructions of the coreSelf.

As soon as one connects with the Supreme Lord, there will more than likely be felt, some dominium over other selves and their psyches. The Supreme Being delegates authority to limited entities.

By attentively linking the mental force to Me, as Lord Nārāyaṇa, as the person who is in the fourth dimension, as the one with the most skills, Bhagavan, the yogi gets near-absolute self control and exhibits My sense of values. (Uddhava Gītā 10.16)

There are many features of God, so many that they are innumerable. To which one, should a yogi link? One needs a relationship with the Supreme Being or with someone who is aligned with and is continuously connected with him. The linkage with the deity does not occur on a whim. One may access the Lord through a spiritual master who already is connected to him, or one may do so by the sheer mercy of the Lord, where he upgrades one's nature and contacts one.

God's four dimensional, out-of-this-realm, forms, are addressed as the *Nārāyaṇa* forms. These have four arms with specific symbols held by each limb. These are addressed collectively and individually as *Bhagavan*, the person with the most skills. Each of these is a Personality of Godhead. They are plural God Persons with no conflict of interest, with no jurisdictional clashing.

When a yogi positively links with a *Nārāyaṇa*, he gets near-absolute self-control and exhibits Krishna's sense of values. The yogi's conflicting possibilities disappear. He becomes compatible with divine will.

By linking the attention, with the concentration force of the cleansed mind, which is focused on Me, Who is the spiritual existence beyond the mundane influence, one obtains the supreme happiness, wherefrom the need for pleasure is completely fulfilled. (Uddhava Gītā 10.17)

These achievements must occur either during the life of the physical body, or hereafter using only the subtle form. It is best if these are experienced while the physical system still functions. Otherwise, one must depend on going to a psychic location where there will be no distraction, such that one can complete the practice.

Desire for pleasure is ever-present in the psyche of a limited entity. This cannot be removed. It may become dormant for some time, but it will reassert itself. Hence, if possible, a yogi should deal with it by finding a place where there is a continuous stream of pleasure in the self for its fulfillment.

To achieve the connection, changes need be made in the psyche, where the mind becomes cleansed of urges from the passionate and retardative energies of Nature. A yogi when he can maintain a clarifying energy of Nature in his mind, continuously shifts to a mental condition, where he becomes content with the energy from the highest level of Nature. This rids the self of needing to feed on the passionate and dulling energies. This addiction to the highest level, will eventually cause the yogin to shift, where a level of transcendence will be experienced, now and again, during meditation, and even during normal mental operations of the mind.

When this happens, the yogi will be inspired to focus on Krishna, on the Supreme Being. He will shift from focusing on divine energy, to viewing and contacting the Personality of Godhead. This will result in bliss feeding and saturation of the connection with the God.

A person obtains purity and gains exemption from the six agonies by linking the attention with the concentration force which is focused on Me, the Person of full existential purity, The Lord of the White Island Paradise, the One Whose nature is composed of the righteous way of life. (Uddhava Gītā 10.18)

No matter what, the recommendation of the Supreme Being, if one could get it from him or from his agent, is the schematic for the righteous lifestyle. People like to acquire a rule or law, a statement which defines morality. Then they fit that into their way of dealing. They brand their actions as approved morality.

However, one must come to terms with the fact, that even though it is best to streamline one's conduct by stated morality, in the end, it is the opinion, and the live view of the Supreme Being which is the righteous lifestyle, which will not bring rejection from the God.

There are four features. One may conflict with the other, but one is the standard to follow, the absolute reference. That is the opinion of the Supreme Lord. The ultimate responsibility rests with God. His view, even if it conflicts with every other opinion and pressure, is the overriding force.

There is the opinion of the person involved, the self. There are the views of other people and the collective idea of morality. There is the pressure for fulfilment from Nature. At last, there is the will of God. If any of these conflicts with the other, or if these are in harmony with each other, still, it is the view of the Supreme Being which has the power.

Gaining purity of intent means that one is freed from everything except the view of the central person of Universal Form, who is Krishna.

By continuous linking of his attention with the concentration force which is focused on subtle sound within the mind, and on Me in the spiritual atmosphere and in the energizing energy, the advanced yogin directly hears the sounds of distant living beings. (Uddhava Gītā 10.19)

Linking the visual power with subtle light and subtle light with the visual energy, while effortlessly meditating on the linkage and on Me, the yogin can, from within his mind, see whatever is far away. (Uddhava Gītā 10.20)

This is divine eye development. A few entities experience this perception from their embryo stage, but most humans do not. They can, however, do meditation practices which makes it likely to have supernatural perception. Some yogis who experience this visual perception, did so after getting assistance from advanced gurus or from deities. This is a vision perception which many people wish for.

Since the visual sense is prominent in the human species, one is conditioned to regarding it as the final verification in any sensual conclusion. Hence psychic blindness is unacceptable. As such anyone who makes the effort to develop psychic perception, is challenged to find a method of having clear subtle vision.

One is gifted with a pair of eyes when one is developed as a new born child, but with that no psychic vision is awarded. One must endeavor in meditation to develop that. A hint is taken from some species of life, like the cats for instance. They have partially developed eyes at birth. Within a short time, the development is completed. In the humans also there are physical eyes at birth but these develop within days after parturition.

One can be confident that if one does meditation, it will result in the use of supernatural perception through supernatural sight.

The visual power is available. It must be curtailed from the tendency to hunt for color and form outside the physical body. This involves its retraction. When the yogi practiced sufficiently to curtail this power, he will experience that its ray is shortened so that it does not protrude beyond the edge of the subtle body. It stays within the confines of the subtle form and is relieved of the tendency to pursue objects.

The subtle light is inside and it is outside the subtle body. The concern here initially is to see objects within the subtle body. For this, the focus is to recognize lights in the subtle form. There are dark regions where no light is manifested in the subtle body. The yogi will discover these. He has to meditate to create a situation where the inner subtle lights become manifested inside the subtle body.

There is visual energy in the subtle body. This energy is in every part of the subtle form but its perception is not always evident. In meditation, a yogi must discover it. When the visual power is linked with subtle light and with subtle energy, the yogin sees objects inside the subtle body. After this perception becomes stable, the yogi can focus outside the subtle body into astral dimensions which are here and there.

Some yogis who are Krishna devotees, execute focus to link with Krishna and with the visual power. They see the supernatural body of the Lord. They also perceive his territories and their inhabitants.

Easily and continually connecting to Me, the mind, the body and the life air that trails the mind, and by linking the attention with the concentration energy, which is operative in the inner nature, and which is focused on Me, the spirit surely goes wherever the mind travels. (Uddhava Gītā 10.21)

Being existentially connected with the Supreme Lord, Krishna, someone becomes free to go here or there in the subtle existence. He/She may also have physical transportation whereby fate facilitates his desires for a time.

In this situation, the coreSelf does not move about on its own. It moves according to the condition of its adjuncts. Hence the purification of the adjuncts is a vital effort for increasing mystic skills.

By bringing the mind's sensitive energies to order, to quiescence, by keeping the body in a purified state where it is not exhausted by sickness and disease, by using the highest quality of life air for energizing the subtle body, and by linking the attention with the concentration energy, which is operative in the inner nature, and which is focused on Krishna, the spirit surely goes wherever the mind travels.

At first however, one must be proficient in rectifying and upgrading the condition of the coreSelf. Then the accomplished focus is applied to Krishna, the Supreme Being.

When applying the mind, whatever form one wishes to assume, that specific form he becomes, by resorting to yoga power as concentrated on Me. (Uddhava Gītā 10.22)

According to how the yogi can change the inner energy of his psyche, the dimensional switching is possible with limitations. If it is upgraded, he rises and translates to a sublime environment. If it is downgraded, he finds his consciousness to be on a lower level.

From anywhere and everywhere, directly, or indirectly, one may concentrate on the Supreme Being, but only if one has the capacity to leave the dimension one finds the self to be in.

Desiring to enter another's body, a skilled yogi, should existentially relocate himself there. Leaving the gross body, his life force which is like the wind, should enter just like a bee. (Uddhava Gītā 10.23)

The ability to enter the psyche of some other person occurs frequently in the minds of persons who recently lost a physical body. By the power of Nature and through a long log of physical history, any limited self may enter the form of a would-be parent. Therefore, the invader may emerge as the child of that victim who is regarded as the parent.

Nature operates possession of lifeforms. By that method it causes formation of species through reproduction. However, if a yogi develops a detached feeling towards his existence and towards others as well, he becomes relatively free from attachment. This gives him a penetration ability. He finds that he can enter or depart from the psyche of some other person, except for those who are on a higher level. Since the yogi's attachment energy is retracted, the possessed person may be unaware of the yogi's entry.

Blocking the anus with the heel, and lifting the vital energy to the heart chakra, then through the chest, throat and head, and by taking it through the hole at the top of the head of the subtle body, one should transfer to the spiritual existence, while giving up the gross form. (Uddhava Gītā 10.24)

Those who mastered the kundalini lifeForce generator, can train the subtle energy to be retracted from its lowest reaches into the central spine, from which it would be pulled up through the spine into the head of the subtle body. From there it would be pulled to the crown chakra at the top of the head.

When the kundalini is retracted to the crown, that infusion of energy causes shifts in awareness, such that the coreSelf resumes its spiritual energy radiance, and enters a plane of existence, which is the base spiritual energy. At that place, there is full spiritual effulgence, sheer golden lights of bliss energy in all directions.

A limited self is a speck of that effulgence. Here it realizes itself as such. It knows itself. It is shorn of adjuncts, and is not restricted by the condition of a lower environment.

Wishing to enjoy life in the parks of the supernatural rulers, one should contemplate the clarifying energy as it is based on Me, then by aerial conveyances, the celestial women whose bodies are productions of the clarifying power, will appear in aerial conveyances. (Uddhava Gītā 10.25)

Different people have different desires, based on the needs within the psyche of the individual. There is no one location or destination which each person wishes to attain.

Most human beings are obsessed with enjoyment but with variation in each case. Even persons who have similar taste, have slight or major departures in some aspect of the pleasure.

People who indulge in the same act, either jointly or singly, seek different pleasures from the same source. The afflictions of a material body are such, that it inspires most selves to desire freedom from afflictions, to want only pleasurable expressions and responses.

Thus, after hearing of a heaven in the psychic existence, or after experiencing that in astral projection journeys, someone may wish to enjoy life in the parks of the supernatural rulers. One can comply with rules for righteous lifestyle, and hope that will qualify one to be transferred to a paradise hereafter.

Otherwise, for certainty of reaching heaven later, one should contemplate the clarifying energy as it is based on Krishna as he described in *Bhagavad Gītā,* and as one experienced it because of saintly behavior, then during the life of the physical body in dreams and visions, or at the time of death, one may ride in aerial conveyances, which are psychic space travel vehicles. Males will discover themselves in the company of celestial women whose bodies are productions of the clarifying power with no lower aspects, no offensive odors in their privacies, none in their mouths or nostrils, none in their vulvas or at their anuses, no clammy smelly perspiration, no malformed parts in any part of their bodies.

Accordingly, whenever a person who is devoted to Me, has an intention within the intellect and links his attention with the force which is focused on Me and on Reality, he gets that objective as desired. (Uddhava Gītā 10.26)

A person who assimilated My nature, Me, who am the perfect ruler and controller, finds that his wish is not frustrated in any way, just as it is with My desire. (Uddhava Gītā 10.27)

To be like God is a desire of some human beings. Many have no such desire but prefer to be continuously blessed by God. The main aspect of desire is enjoyment, but that is a compounded formulation of many aspects of various energies.

It is through introspection that a yogi sorts the factors. The assimilation into God's nature is a difficult feat. If that is attained partially or near-fully, that person gets his wishes fulfilled. This is not due to his command over everything else, but rather due to the practicality of his needs, where he does not desire that which is impossible for him to attain.

The intellect of the yogi, who is reliant on the pure clarifying influence by devotion to Me, and who knows how to link his attention to the concentration force in the clarifying energy, has an increased capacity to discern the three phases of time, as well as his births and deaths. (Uddhava Gītā 10.28)

Clarity in perception and conclusion is an important achievement for a yogi. If not, he will dissipate much energy seeking the impossible. He will wish for things which a limited being cannot attain.

The yogi must shift himself from the enthusiastic and dulling phases of the natural energies. He should self-restrict to the clarifying powers, so that these saturate his psyche. From that purity, he will have the proper idea about the Supreme Lord, Krishna, whose association will further enhance the yogi's existence.

The yogi will have an increased capacity to discern the three phases of time, as well as the births and deaths in the past, present, and future.

Provided that the yogi philosopher's ideation energy is tempered by yoga austerity and made quiescent by yogic discipline to Me, his body is not destroyed by fire or other dangerous factors, just as in the case of the aquatics and water. (Uddhava Gītā 10.29)

One who effortlessly remains in the linkage of his attention and the special concentration force which is focused on My supernatural form, which is adorned with the Śrīvatsa curl of hair, with a weapon, a banner, an umbrella and a chowry fan, becomes unconquerable. (Uddhava Gītā 10.30)

Abhidhyāyan is the effortless and quite spontaneous contact with the supernatural or spiritual reality. It could be the linking with a person or environment. This is in contrast to *dharanā*, which is contact after making efforts and which ceases as soon as the focus is relaxed.

Krishna has many forms and multi-forms with each being rated as physical, subtle, super-subtle, supernatural, and spiritual. These forms may or may not be divine. Contact with Krishna on any level is extraordinary. Wherever Krishna is manifest, he is directly the Supreme Personality, and should be related to, as such. One should not feel that the physical presence of Krishna, as he was before Arjuna in the *Bhagavad Gītā*, is of little consequence.

The effortless linkage with God happens when God descends *(avatar)*, when he makes himself available to the devotee. That is a more reliable contact than the effortful contact which is only sustained by the reach focus of the devotee, which is a limited throw from a lower plane of existence.

When the Lord penetrates a lower realm and touches the devotee, that ascetic is rated as unconquerable. He is reminded of his spiritual status in relationship with the God.

Thus, to the yogi philosopher who worships Me by yogic linkage of the attention with the concentration force, the mystic skills mentioned before, are manifested in their full measure. (Uddhava Gītā 10.31)

If a devotee persists in the effort to contact the Supreme Being, Krishna, that person will in time be elevated by the Lord. Sooner or later, the mystic skills will be manifested in their full measure for that ascetic. His effort will come to fruition.

One should not think that it is reasonable to became disgusted or disappointed, if one commits austerities for a time, and do not get the result intended. It is difficult to properly estimate how much effort is required for success. One should become occupied, curtailing interest in the physical world, and applying oneself to the supernatural side of life.

What mystic skill is very difficult to achieve for the yogi philosopher whose sensual energies are subdued, who is disciplined, who controlled his breath and psyche, who linked his attention to the concentration force which is connected to Me, and who effortlessly links his attention to a higher concentration force. (Uddhava Gītā 10.32)

In the quest for discovery of the divine person and the spiritual environment, a yogi should not sit and wait. One should aggressively endeavor to be translated to the divine world. If, by the pull of God, one is drawn into that situation, that is preferred.

However, one should exert the self to reach divinity as soon as one can. One must

- subdue the sensual energies
- have self-discipline
- control the breath and psyche
- linked one's attention to the concentration force which is connected to Krishna
- effortlessly link the attention to a higher concentration force.

While waiting for the grace of God to manifest, in the form of having direct access to the spiritual environment, the *chit akash*, a yogi-devotee should subdue the sensual energies, by attenuating their reach into the physical existence and its psychic copy. The sensual energies must be trained to remain contained in the psyche. When they are quelled, that is the beginning of their reversion to the self, and the end of their resistance to being indifferent to physical nature.

There should be self-discipline which is spontaneous, where much effort is not required, to cause the sensual energies to abandon their interest in physical pleasure.

It is necessary to control the breath and the psyche, because otherwise these will motivate the self to pursue physical interest, which shroud the spiritual core, and block existential vision.

Initially there must be an effort to inFocus, to sort the adjuncts from the core. When these practices become proficient, the yogi-devotee becomes qualified to make contact with the transcendental Lord.

The authoritative yogis say that these mystic perfections are obstacles. For one who habitually practices the linking of the attention with higher concentration forces, which are connected to Me, and who seeks the higher achievement, and whose mind is focused on spiritual well-being, they are a waste of time. (Uddhava Gītā 10.33)

This means that as a focus, as an objective, the mystic skills may serve as a distraction from the issue, which is that the person should sort the coreSelf and its adjuncts. He should bring these to order. Then he should discover the Supreme Being and know his relationship with God.

However, this does not mean that every yogi-devotee can avoid having and using mystic skills. Sometimes, accidentally, a mystic skill is evident and is used by the yogi. This may be spontaneous even with no desire for it by the yogi. Hence one must be prepared for using and not abusing that skill.

An important hint however is that a yogi should use any mystic skill which is manifest to him, for advancing further on the path of liberation. Mystic skills should not be the focus of any serious practice, and yet, one should be prepared to use a skill which develops. As the subtle body is upgraded, it will display mystic abilities, which are advanced ways of interacting with environment and people.

Each body type, and each unique body of one body type, has abilities which are native to that form. One should take note of this, and use a body constructively for the achievement of accessing divine persons and environments.

By yoga practice, one achieves all those mystic skills, which may otherwise be gained by birth, herbs or drugs, austerities, and special chants, but one cannot achieve the actual objective of yoga by those other means. (Uddhava Gītā 10.34)

Mystic power, or extraordinary actions and influence, may be caused by taking a certain type of body, or by taking herbs or drugs, reactive chemical substances, or by disciplines besides yoga, or by making sounds or vibrations. But Krishna stated that the actual objective of yoga cannot be attained by those other methods. Yoga is unique in this regard. It is the only method which allows deep penetration into the coreSelf, and reach into divine world.

I am the cause, the master and Lord of all mystic skills. I am the Lord of Yoga and of the Sāṅkhya philosophical analysis, of righteous duty and of the teachers of spirituality. (Uddhava Gītā 10.35)

I am the interiorized self of all embodied beings. Being unconfined, I am outside of the bodies as well. As the elements are inside and outside the living beings, so am I. (Uddhava Gītā 10.36)

The residents of heaven and those of hell hereafter, desire this world which yields the achievement of thinking and emotional experiences. Both heaven and hell are locations which are incapable of yielding an achievement. (Uddhava Gītā 15.12)

This physical world has value because efforts made here may result in the achievement of self-realization. The tension here could result in the perception of the coreSelf in contrast to its adjuncts.

In the heavenly world, which one may attain by righteous conduct, there is no idea of making an effort to change anything. In the hell one may be consigned to after physical mistakes here, one will not think about striving for a divine environment. One only thinks of escaping from the unpleasant condition. Thus, one should use this earthly location for self-realization, and for discovery of the whereabouts of the Supreme Lord.

A wise human being should pursue neither the course of heaven nor that of hell. And he should not desire this world either, for here he is bewitched from the habit of dwelling in a body. (Uddhava Gītā 15.13)

One should desire neither the earthly location, nor a heaven one where one may be transported to if one behaves in a saintly manner, nor a hell where one may be compelled to reside, due to criminal activities. And yet, one should use the physical body and the circumstantial opportunity to become self-realized and to know the Supreme Being.

Knowing this, and being without bewilderment, he should before death, strive to be free of mundane existence; knowing that even though the body will die, it is capable of assisting in the goal of perfection. (Uddhava Gītā 15.14)

Observing that the tree, on which its nest was built, was being cut down by cruel persons, a bird, being without attachment abandons its home and achieves well-being. (Uddhava Gītā 15.15)

There are sufficient alarms about the death of one's body. There is no excuse for not preparing for the event of losing access to physical history. One's parent, grandparent, or great grandparent is dead. One's child, or grandchild, endures the features of infancy and youth. That is the evidence that one cannot remain here as a contributor of physical history.

Seeing that time is vicious, and that it has no leniency or favorites, that it spares no one not even the saints, one should develop detachment from the essential factor which is the physical body and the opportunities which it enjoys.

Figuring that his life span is being reduced by the passing days and nights, someone trembles in fear and freeing himself from attachment, he realizes the Supreme. Without endeavor for anything, he becomes peaceful. (Uddhava Gītā 15.16)

Seeing the foremost form, the human body which was easy to obtain, but which may be difficult to secure again, which is very useful like a boat, which has a teacher for the steersman, and which is pushed by Me, as by favorable wind, he who does not cross over the ocean of material existence, is a killer of his own soul. (Uddhava Gītā 15.17)

One should act in self-interest and not be conned by anyone or any force which encourages one to ignore impending death.

When he is disgusted with cultural activities and attained detachment, having controlled his senses, the yogi should, by practice, hold the mind steady on the spirit. (Uddhava Gītā 15.18)

The first stage in self-realization, the initial accomplishment is to become thoroughly disgusted with the ever-new presentation of opportunities for participation in physical history. There is this promise which is presented by Nature, but it is a route to disappointment.

One is born with little control of the bodily senses. That is given freely by Nature. Somehow one should gain control of the sensual energies. One should reduce the quest for physical participation.

One was born from a woman's vulva. One is encouraged to return to that place for the next body. One should reconsider the opportunity. It is enticing. It seems to be a free adventure. Still, at some point one should become disgusted with the cultural activities.

Mental steadiness, inFocus, should be achieved. It is a difficult accomplishment however. Each person must strive for it, individually. It is not a collective effort.

When the mind is being linked to the higher concentration force, and it quickly wanders off, not being steadied on the desired place, then being alert, he would bring it under the control of the soul, by a process that takes into account its own waywardness. (Uddhava Gītā 15.19)

The process of mind control happens after many attempts at meditation. Each yogi must struggle within his mind for gaining rulership over the adjuncts.

He should not lose the focus on the objective set for the mind. Having mastered the life energy and conquered the senses, he should bring the mind under control by using the intellect, which is surcharged with the clarifying energy of material nature. (Uddhava Gītā 15.20)

Some devotees, some advanced ones who have many followers, disavow these instructions of Krishna. The idea is that currently, this process of mind control is too difficult to achieve.

However, one would be a fool to ignore what Krishna says here to Uddhava. To say that this practice is irrelevant currently, is a silly notion. If, however one can ignore this and use a simpler method, then that is good for oneself.

Please, however, consider what was said above about mantras (*mantrair*) and their usage in contrast to yoga. Here is that statement.

- *By yoga practice, one achieves all those mystic skills, which may otherwise be gained by birth, herbs or drugs, austerities, and special chants, but one cannot achieve the actual objective of yoga by those other means.* (Uddhava Gītā 10.34)

This tight control of the mind is said to be the highest yoga discipline like the curbing of an unruly horse, by one who knows the creature intimately and who tries to make it confirm always. (Uddhava Gītā 15.21)

For success in the spiritual mission of life, one must attain tight mind control. This means direct control by command of the mind, and not indirect control, by using props, because one finds that one just cannot control it.

The mind must be confronted. If one is to be successful in having the coreSelf command its psychological adjuncts, there should be no roundabout method for mind control.

By the Sāṅkhya information on the origination and dissolution of all existential factors in their retrogression and progression, one should remain in the stage where the attention is effortlessly linked to the relevant concentration force, until the mind becomes stilled. (Uddhava Gītā 15.22)

Some people are of the opinion that, without having to achieve these particulars, which are listed by Krishna, one can become liberated. The idea is that liberation should come with less effort and naturally. However, that idea does not serve the purpose. Our indulgence with Nature is complicated.

A complex problem requires a matching complex solution. If one is reluctant to apply a difficult process, that indicates that one is under the influence of the dulling retardative energy of Nature. This power supports a sluggish easy course which will not result in the objective.

Regarding a person who is disgusted with material existence, who assumed a detached mood, and who understood the teachings of an educated brahmin, his mind gives up its bad inclinations by his repeatedly being absorbed into the concentration force. (Uddhava Gītā 15.23)

By moral restraints and other preliminary stages, by the path of yoga, by logical analysis, as well as by effective techniques or attentive service to My worship ceremony and by no other means, the mind should be absorbed in the objective of yoga. (Uddhava Gītā 15.24)

Whatever tight rein the mind should be harnessed in, that should be applied. But if one cannot successfully control the mind, by directly confronting it within the psyche, one should realize that one must practice repeatedly, until the mind yields to the self.

If through carelessness, the yogi does a disapproved act, he should completely remove the offence by yogic discipline alone. There is no other effective method for this. (Uddhava Gītā 15.25)

Morality has its value in keeping human society from becoming an animal kingdom. Still, morality is not the issue. Social prestige is not the achievement. The conflict is within the psyche. It is a struggle between the coreSelf and its adjuncts. The kingdom which is to be ruled is the one in the psyche.

Firm attachment to one's duty is definitely declared as merit. By this declaration of merits and demerits, a restriction is made pertaining to cultural activities, which are by nature impure. This is done by a desire for the removal of social attachment. (Uddhava Gītā 15.26)

Even though righteous conduct is appraised, and is necessary, still it contains a flaw which is that it constructs more and more attachment to physical existence.

Hence one should observe moral constrains with the understanding that it is flawed. It will not in the long-term cause detachment from history. The mix of the actions which comprise history causes avoidance of focus on the psychic aspect of the self. That is the fallacy.

One who has faith in true stories about Me, and who is disgusted in being involved in cultural activities, who knows that the nature of cravings is misery, but who also is unable to give up those cravings, (Uddhava Gītā 15.27)

...that faithful devotee, having firm conviction, should at that stage, lovingly worship Me, and should continue to satisfy those cravings, while condemning all that ends in misery. (Uddhava Gītā 15.28)

A devotee should acknowledge his short comings and work with himself to upgrade the psyche, so that eventually he can directly confront the mind, and bring it to order under the control of the coreSelf, as stipulated by Krishna.

Regarding the yogi philosopher who constantly worships Me as instructed for the application of yoga to the emotional experiences, all cravings in the core of his being, are destroyed by me, who is positioned in his core self. (Uddhava Gītā 15.29)

This statement directly addressed the devotees of Krishna (*bhakti-yogena*). God from within the psyche of the devotee will destroy the cravings. Krishna says that he will do so from within the coreSelf. How can it be that with Krishna's grace, the devotee cannot directly command the mind, and must use a proxy for mind control?

The blockage to his causal body is penetrated. All uncertainties are sorted out. His cultural obligations are dispelled, having put his vision on Me, the Self Who is the basis of all. (Uddhava Gītā 15.30)

Therefore for the yogis who are habitually practiced in devotion to Me, whose self is focused on Me; knowledge and dispassion may not be of a benefit in this world. (Uddhava Gītā 15.31)

Whatever is to be gained by cultural activities, by penance, by dispassion and by theoretical understanding, by yoga disciplines, charity, righteous duty and even by other methods designed for one's well-being; (Uddhava Gītā 15.32)

...My devotees gets all of it by applying yoga techniques to devotion to Me, even if perchance he desires heaven and liberation to My Abode. (Uddhava Gītā 15.33)

Saintly persons who have accurately-perceiving intellects, who are devoted and who are singularly dedicated to Me, do not desire the complete isolation of their spirits from its psychological equipments, such that they are never to be existent in the material world again, even if such privileges were offered to them by Me. (Uddhava Gītā 15.34)

The statement here is that the confidential devotees of Krishna are focused on their relationship *(bhava)* with Krishna and not with achievements, unless those attainments will service the Lord. Whatever should be done to bring the self to terms with what Krishna requests, will be practiced by such a devotee.

Not caring for anything is called the highest and fullest well-being. Therefore the devotion of one who has no desires, of one who does not care for anything, is developed in relationship to Me. (Uddhava Gītā 15.35)

Mundane influences which produce virtues and flaws, do not affect those devotees, who are singularly dedicated to Me. They are saintly. Their mental and emotional energy are similar in purity to their spirits, and they achieved what is beyond the intellect. (Uddhava Gītā 15.36)

Thus, those who practice these methods of achieving Me, which was taught by Me, attain My abode, which is full well-being. They realize the Supreme spirit. (Uddhava Gītā 15.37)

The culmination is relationship to the divine Lord. Whatever one must do to achieve and sustain that, should be committed immediately and with fervor.

It is not born, nor does it die. It is not by the instrumentality of its cultural activities, that this human being is born or dies, for it is deathless. It is perceived so, by misconception, just as the fire is regarded when burning wood. (Uddhava Gītā 17.45)

Krishna's information begins with the declaration of a perpetual self, a person unlimited. If one cannot realize this by direct perception, then to follow Krishna's presentation, one should accept this as a premise. The support for this idea is that one should make efforts to realize this, as one practices self-realization and Krishna Consciousness.

Impregnation, embryonic stage, birth, infancy, childhood, youth, middle age, old age, and death are listed as the nine stages of the body. (Uddhava Gītā 17.46)

This happened before. It will spontaneously occur again, unless one takes steps to interrupt the natural process.

The superior or inferior bodily status is created by the imaginary power of the mind, and is of something pertaining to something else. Due to attachment to the influence of material nature, the spirit assumes these. Sometimes however, someone does cast that aside. (Uddhava Gītā 17.47)

There is a natural attraction between the person and the Nature force, which conducts the appearance, and disappearance of physical life forms. Somehow one must study that natural attraction, and find a means of disrupting it.

One's own birth and death can be figured from those of one's son and father. The observer of things affected by birth and death is not characterized by those two features. (Uddhava Gītā 17.48)

Nature will continue its routine. No limited being will stop it. Even the Supreme Being allows it. However, one should make the effort for exemption from it.

A person in knowledge who sees the birth and death of a plant, from seed to final stage, is distinct from the plant. Similarly the witness of the body is separate from it. (Uddhava Gītā 17.49)

The evidence is the witness to the variations of Nature. That observer can step aside. It happens by inner detachment with intellectual support to analyze the strikes of history.

The ignorant person, failing to correctly ascertain his spirit from material nature, is deluded by sensual contact and by the substances. He is drawn into the process of birth and death. (Uddhava Gītā 17.50)

It is important to sort the self, so that one locates the core of it, and the adjuncts which provide assistance to it. One must do meditation, to figure how to reduce the dominance of the adjuncts over the core.

The sensual energies are the electric currents which convey ideas across the psyche. When the coreSelf becomes objective to these emotions, it begins to understand how the psyche was configured by Nature. Then it sees how it can seize control to reduce its slavery to Nature.

Being made to transmigrate, by the force of cultural action, a person by affiliation with the perceptive energy in material nature, goes to the yogi sages or to the supernatural rulers; or by affiliation with the impulsive motivations he goes to the wicked personalities or the human beings; or by absorbing the depressive energies, he goes to the ghosts and animal species. (Uddhava Gītā 17.51)

Just as when seeing a troupe of dancers or a choir of singers, one imitates them, just so upon observing the operations of the organ of the intellect, that factor, which is indifferent and essentially neutral, patterns itself after them. (Uddhava Gītā 17.52)

As trees reflected in moving water, seem to be moving, so that landscape is seen moving about by whirling eyes. (Uddhava Gītā 17.53)

As imagination, the intellectual conception and sense experience are also false, so also, O son of the Dāśārha, is the transmigrating existence of the soul. (Uddhava Gītā 17.54)

The factor which transmigrates is the subtle body. The coreSelf does not move from one physical life form to another. However, it appears that it is, just as a man on a dock whose eyes use the boat as a reference, feels that the dock moves away from the boat.

For thousands of years, many human beings were of the view that the sun orbits the earth. Now with superior instruments which are more accurate than our eyes, scientists know that the earth orbits the sun.

Even though it is in fact, unreal, the material existence of changing bodies in ignorance of previous ones, does not cease for one whose attention is linked to the attractive mundane objects, just as the undesirable circumstances continue in a dream. (Uddhava Gītā 17.55)

Therefore, O Uddhava stop experiencing the attractive mundane objects with the temporary senses. See the perception of the delusive varied world as being the cause of the lack of clarity and the non-perception of the spiritual self. (Uddhava Gītā 17.56)

Those dedicated to the Vedic principles, become elevated higher and higher through the clarifying energy. But through the retardative mode one moves head first, lower and lower. Through the impulsive force, one transmigrates in-between the two. (Uddhava Gītā 20.21)

Those whose bodies are destroyed while they are in the clarifying influence, go to the angelic world. Those whose forms pass on while in the impulsive mode, go to the human world. Those who pass on from the depressive retardative influence, go to hellish places. But those who transcend the subtle influences of material nature go to Me. (Uddhava Gītā 20.22)

All this which concerns a person's transmigration through various bodies, is formed through cultural activity which is sponsored by material nature. O good man, a person who is not subdued by these mundane influences which occur in the mental and emotional energy, is by virtue of application of yoga expertise to devotion, qualified for being dedicated to Me and for the intimate existential linkage with Me. (Uddhava Gītā 20.32)

Therefore, having acquired the body, which is productive of information and actual experience, having thoroughly discarded the association with material nature, persons with spiritual insight should worship Me. (Uddhava Gītā 20.33)

Being devoid of attachment, the wise person should worship Me, without bewilderment. Having mastered the senses, the yogi philosopher should effectively suppress the impulsive energy and retardative force by cultivation of the clarifying influence. (Uddhava Gītā 20.34)

Index

About the Author

Michael Beloved (Yogi *Madhvāchārya)* took his current body in 1951 in Guyana. In 1965, while living in Trinidad, he instinctively began doing yoga postures and tried to make sense of the supernatural side of life.

Later in 1970, in the Philippines, he approached a Martial Arts Master named Arthur Beverford. Michael explained to the teacher that he was seeking a yoga instructor. Mr. Beverford identified himself as an advanced disciple of Rishi Singh Gherwal, an Ashtanga Yoga master.

Beverford taught the traditional Ashtanga Yoga with stress on postures, attentive breathing, and brow chakra centering meditation. In 1972, Michael entered the Denver Colorado Ashram of *kundalini* yoga Master Harbhajan Singh. There he took instruction in *bhastrika pranayama* and its application to yoga postures.

In 1979 Michael formally entered the disciplic succession of the Brahmā-Madhava-Gaudiya Sampradaya through *Swāmī* Kirtanananda, who was a prominent sannyasi disciple of the great Vaishnava authority *Swāmī* Bhaktivedanta Prabhupada, the exponent of devotion to Krishna.

However, yoga has a mystic side to it, thus Michael took training and teaching empowerment from several spiritual masters of different aspects of spiritual development. This is consistent with Krishna's advice to Arjuna in the *Bhagavad Gītā*:

Most of the instructions Michael received were given in the astral world. On that side of existence, his most prominent teachers were *Swāmī* Shivananda of Rishikesh, Yogiraj *Swāmī* Vishnudevananda, *Bābāji Mahasaya* - the master of the masters of *Kriyā* Yoga, Yogeshwarananda of Gangotri - the master of the masters of *Raja* Yoga (spiritual clarity), and Siddha *Swāmī* Nityananda, the Brahmā Yoga authority.

The course for kundalini yoga using *pranayama* breath infusion was detailed by Michael in the book *Kundalini Hatha Yoga Pradipika*.

Michael's preliminary books relating to meditation are *Meditation Pictorial*, *Meditation Expertise*, and *Meditation ~ Sense Faculty* (co-author). Every technique (*kriya*) mentioned was tested by him during *pranayama* breath infusion and *samyama* deep meditation practice.

This is a result of over fifty years of meditation practice with astute subtle observations intending to share the methods and experiences. The information is published freely with no intention of forming an institution nor hogtying anyone as a disciple.

A reviewer suggested that this book be titled, *Michael Beloved's Book of the Dead*. That would be appropriate because it is based on the psychic experiences of the author in a lifetime of mystic research for chanting the passage from the world of the dead to that of the living.

Publications

English Series

Bhagavad Gītā English

Anu Gītā English

Markandeya Samasya English

Yoga Sutras English

Hatha Yoga Pradipika English

Uddhava Gītā English

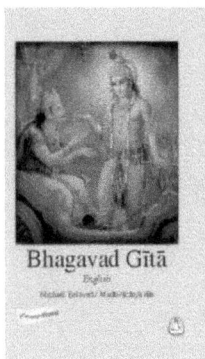

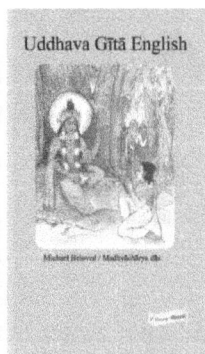

These are in precise and exacting English. Many Sanskrit words which were considered untranslatable into a Western language are rendered in precise, expressive, and modern English.

Three of these books are instructions from Krishna. **In Bhagavad Gītā English** and **Anu Gītā English**, the instructions were for Arjuna. In the **Uddhava Gītā English,** it was for Uddhava. *Bhagavad Gītā* and Anu Gītā are extracted from the *Mahabharata*. Uddhava Gītā was extracted from the 11th Canto of the Srimad Bhagavatam (Uddhava Gītā Bhagavata Purana). One of these books, the **Markandeya Samasya English** is about Krishna, as described by Yogi Markandeya, who survived the cosmic collapse and reached a divine child in whose transcendental body, the collapsed world existed.

Two of this series are the syllabus about yoga practice. The *Yoga Sutras* of Patañjali is elaboration about ashtanga yoga. Hatha Yoga Pradipika English, is the detailed information about *asana* postures, *pranayama* breath- infusion, energy compression, naad sound resonance and advanced meditation. The Sanskrit author is Swatmarama Mahayogin.

My suggestion is that you read **Bhagavad Gītā English**, the **Anu Gītā English, the Markandeya Samasya English,** the *Yoga Sutras* English, the Hatha Yoga Pradipika and lastly the **Uddhava Gītā English**, which is complicated and detailed.

For each of these books we have at least one commentary, which is published separately. Thus, one's particular interest can be researched further in the commentaries.

The smallest of these commentaries and perhaps the simplest is the one for the Anu *Gītā*. We published its commentary as the Anu Gītā Explained. The *Bhagavad Gītā* explanations were published in three distinct targeted commentaries. The first is *Bhagavad Gītā Explained*, which sheds lights on how people in the time of Krishna and Arjuna regarded the information and applied it. *Bhagavad Gītā* is an exposition of the application of yoga practice to cultural activities, which is known in the Sanskrit language as karma yoga.

Interestingly, *Bhagavad Gītā* was spoken on a battlefield just before one of the greatest battles in the ancient world. A warrior, Arjuna, lost his wits and had no idea that he could apply his training in yoga to political dealings. Krishna, his charioteer, lectured on the spur of the moment to give Arjuna the skill of using yoga proficiency in cultural dealings including how to deal with corrupt officials on a battlefield.

The second Gītā commentary is the Kriya Yoga *Bhagavad Gītā*. This clears the air about Krishna's information on the science of kriya yoga, showing that its techniques are clearly described for anyone who takes the time to read *Bhagavad Gītā*. Kriya yoga concerns the battlefield which is the psyche of the living being. The internal war and the mental and emotional forces which are hostile to self-realization are dealt with in the kriya yoga practice.

The third commentary is the Brahma Yoga *Bhagavad Gītā*. This shows what Krishna had to say outright and what he hinted about which concerns the brahma yoga practice, a mystic process for those who mastered kriya yoga.

There is one commentary for the **Markandeya Samasya English**. The title of that publication is Krishna Cosmic Body.

There are two commentaries to the *Yoga Sutras*. One is the *Yoga Sutras* of Patañjali and the other is the Meditation Expertise. These give detailed explanations of ashtanga Yoga.

The commentary of Hatha Yoga Pradipika is titled Kundalini Hatha Yoga Pradipika.

For the Uddhava *Gītā*, we published the Uddhava Gītā Explained. This is a large book and requires concentration and study for integration of the information. Of the books which deal with transcendental topics, my opinion is that the discourse between Krishna and Uddhava has the complete information about the realities in existence. This book is the one which removes massive existential ignorance.

Meditation Series

Meditation Pictorial

Meditation Expertise

CoreSelf Discovery

Meditation Sense Faculty

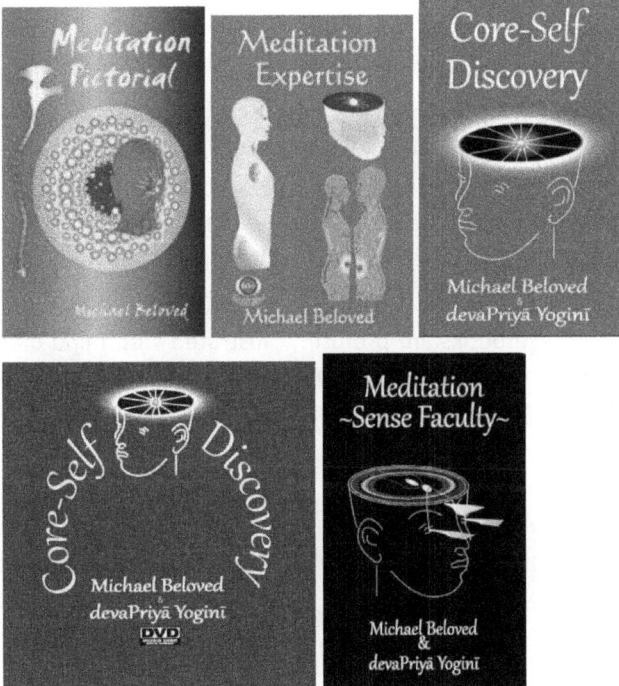

The specialty of these books is the mind diagrams which profusely illustrate what is written. This shows exactly what one has to do mentally to develop and then sustain a meditation practice.

In the **Meditation Pictorial**, one is shown how to develop psychic insight, a feature without which meditation is imagination and visualization, with no mystic experience.

In the **Meditation Expertise**, one is shown how to corral one's practice to bring it in line with the classic syllabus of yoga which Patañjali lays out as the ashtanga yoga eight-staged practice.

In **CoreSelf Discovery**, (co-authored with *devaPriya Yogini*) one is taken though the course of *pratyahar* sensual energy withdrawal which is the 5th stage of yoga in the Patañjali ashtanga eight-process complete system of yoga practice. These events lead to the discovery of a coreSelf which is surrounded by psychic organs in the head of the subtle body. This product has a DVD component.

Meditation ~ Sense Faculty (co-authored with *devaPriya Yogini*) is a detailed tutorial with profuse diagrams showing what actions to take in the subtle body to investigate the senses faculties. The meditator must first establish the location and function of the observing self. That self must be screened from the thoughts and ideas which usually hypnotize it.

These books are profusely illustrated with mind diagrams showing the components of psychic consciousness and the inner design of the subtle body.

Explained Series

Bhagavad Gītā Explained

Uddhava Gītā Explained

Anu Gītā Explained

The specialty of these books is that they are free of missionary intentions, cult tactics and philosophical distortion. Instead of using these books to add credence to a philosophy, meditation process, belief, or plea for followers, I spread the information out so that a reader can look through this literature and freely take or leave anything as desired.

When Krishna stressed himself as God, I stated that. When Krishna laid no claims for supremacy, I showed that. The reader is left to form an independent opinion about the validity of the information and the credibility of Krishna.

There is a difference in the discourse with Arjuna in the *Bhagavad Gītā,* and the one with Uddhava in the Uddhava *Gītā*. In fact, these two books may appear to contradict each other. In the *Bhagavad Gītā*, Krishna pressured Arjuna to complete social duties. In the Uddhava *Gītā*, Krishna insisted that Uddhava should abandon the same.

The Anu Gītā is not as popular as the *Bhagavad Gītā* but it is the conclusion of that text. Anu means what is to follow. In this discourse, an anxious Arjuna request that Krishna should repeat the *Bhagavad Gītā* and again show His supernatural and divine forms.

However, Krishna refuses to do so and chastises Arjuna for being a disappointment in forgetting what was revealed. Krishna then cited a celestial yogi, a near-perfected being, who explained the process of transmigration in vivid detail.

Commentaries

Yoga Sutras of Patañjali

Meditation Expertise

Krishna Cosmic Body

Anu Gītā Explained

Bhagavad Gītā Explained

Kriya Yoga Bhagavad Gītā

Brahma Yoga Bhagavad Gītā

Uddhava Gītā Explained

Kundalini Hatha Yoga Pradipika

corePerson ~ Krishna Sāmkhya

Yoga Sūtras of Patañjali — Yaṣ Madhvācārya / Michael Beloved

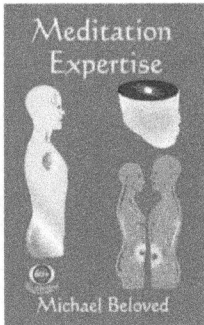

Meditation Expertise — Michael Beloved

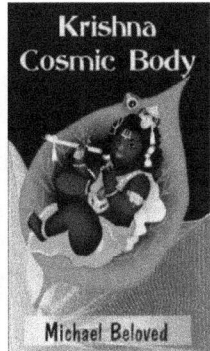

Krishna Cosmic Body — Michael Beloved

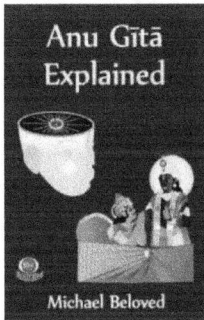

Anu Gītā Explained — Michael Beloved

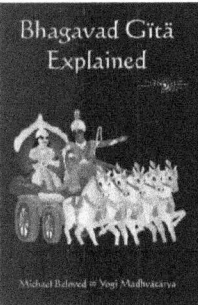

Bhagavad Gītā Explained — Michael Beloved & Yogi Madhvācārya

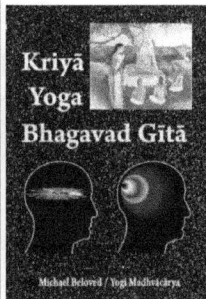

Kriyā Yoga Bhagavad Gītā — Michael Beloved / Yogi Madhvācārya

Brahma Yoga Bhagavad Gītā — Michael Beloved & Yogi Madhvācārya

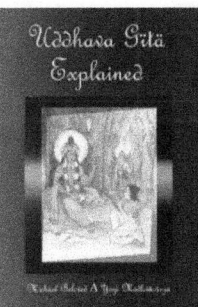

Uddhava Gītā Explained — Michael Beloved & Yogi Madhvācārya

Kuṇḍalinī Haṭha Yoga Pradīpikā — Michael Beloved

Yoga Sutras of Patañjali is the globally acclaimed textbook of yoga. This has detailed expositions of yoga techniques. Many kriya techniques are vividly described in the commentary.

Meditation Expertise is an analysis and application of the *Yoga Sutras*. This book is loaded with illustrations and has detailed explanations of secretive advanced meditation techniques which are called kriyas in the Sanskrit language.

Krishna Cosmic Body is a narrative commentary on the *Markandeya Samasya* portion of the Aranyaka Parva of the *Mahabharata*. This is the detailed description of the dissolution of the world, as experienced by the great yogin Markandeya who transcended the cosmic deity, Brahma, and reached Brahma's source who is the divine infant, Krishna.

Anu Gītā Explained is a detailed explanation of how we endure many material bodies in the course of transmigrating through various life-forms. This is a discourse between Krishna and Arjuna. Arjuna requested of Krishna a display of the Universal Form and a repeat narration of the *Bhagavad Gītā* but Krishna declined and explained what a siddha perfected being told the Yadu family about the sequence of existences one endures and the systematic flow of those lives at the convenience of material nature.

Bhagavad Gītā Explained shows what was said in the Gītā, without religious overtones and sectarian biases.

Kriya Yoga *Bhagavad Gītā* shows the instructions for those who are doing kriya yoga.

Brahma Yoga *Bhagavad Gītā* shows the instructions for those who are doing brahma yoga.

Uddhava Gītā Explained shows the instructions to Uddhava which are more advanced than the ones given to Arjuna.

Bhagavad Gītā is an instruction for applying the expertise of yoga in the cultural field. This is why the process taught to Arjuna is called karma yoga which means karma + yoga or cultural activities done with yogic insight.

Uddhava Gītā is an instruction for applying the expertise of yoga to attaining spiritual status. This is why it explains jnana yoga and *bhakti* yoga in detail. Jnana yoga is using mystic skill for knowing the spiritual part of existence. *Bhakti* yoga is for developing affectionate relationships with divine beings.

Karma yoga is for negotiating the social concerns in the material world. It is inferior to *bhakti* yoga which concerns negotiating the social concerns in the spiritual world.

This world has a social environment. The spiritual world has one too.

Currently, Uddhava Gītā is the most advanced and informative spiritual book on the planet. There is nothing anywhere which is superior to it or which goes into so much detail as it. It verified that historically Krishna is the most advanced human being to ever have left literary instructions on this planet. Even Patañjali *Yoga Sutras* which I translated and gave an application for in my book, **Meditation Expertise**, does not go as far as the Uddhava *Gītā*.

Some of the information of these two books is identical but while the *Yoga Sutras* are concerned with the personal spiritual emancipation (*kaivalyam*) of the individual spirits, the Uddhava Gītā explains that and also explains the situations in the spiritual universes.

Bhagavad Gītā is from the *Mahabharata* which is the history of the Pandavas. Arjuna, the student of the *Gītā*, is one of the Pandavas brothers. He was in a social hassle, and did not know how to apply yoga expertise to solve it. On the battlefield, Krishna gave a crash-course on yogic social interactions.

Uddhava Gītā is from the *Srimad Bhagavatam (Bhagavata Purana),* which is a history of the incarnations of Krishna. Uddhava was a relative of Krishna. He was concerned about the situation of the deaths of many relatives, but Krishna diverted Uddhava to the practice of yoga for the purpose of successfully migrating to the spiritual environment.

Kundalini Hatha Yoga Pradipika is the commentary for the Hatha Yoga Pradipika of Swatmarama Mahayogin. This is the detailed process about *asana* posture, *pranayama* breath-infusion, complex compressions of energy, naad sound resonance intonement and advanced meditation practice.

This is the singular book with all the techniques of how to reform and redesign the subtle body so that it does not have the tendency for physical life forms, and for it to attain the status of a siddha.

corePerson ~ Krishna Sāmkhya is from the Uddhava Gita. It renders the Sāmkhya teaching of Krishna, which was given to Uddhava. It is distinct from other Sāmkhya itemization teachings which abound in India. To understand the Bhagavad Gita, one should study this.

It departs from the Upanishads in that it renders value to the person factor, the purusha, Unlike Advaita Vedanta and even Buddhism, it does not erase or undermine the person. And yet it does not over-value the coreSelf.

These books are based on the author's experiences in meditation, yoga practice and participation in spiritual groups:

Specialty

In **Spiritual Master**, Michael draws from experience with gurus or with their senior students. His contact with astral gurus is rated. He walks you through the avenue of gurus showing what you should do and what you should not do, so as to gain proficiency in whatever area of spirituality the guru mastered.

sex you! is a masterpiece about the adventures of an individual spirit's passage through the parents' psyches. The conversion of a departed soul into a sexual urge is described. The transit from the afterlife to residency in the emotions of the parents, is detailed. This is about sex and you. Learn about how much of you comprises the romantic energy of one's would-be parents!

Sleep Paralysis clears misconceptions so that one can see what sleep paralysis is, and what frightening astral experience occurs, while the paralysis is being experienced. This disempowerment has great value in giving you confidence that you can, and do exist, even if one is unable to operate the physical body. The implication is that one can exist apart from, and will survive, the loss of the material form.

Astral Projection details experiences Michael had even in childhood, where he assumed incorrectly that everyone was astrally conversant. He discusses the lifeForce psychic mechanism which operates the sleep-wake cycle of the physical form, and which budgets energy into the separated astral form which determines if the individual will have dream recall or no objective awareness during the projections. Astral travel happens on every occasion when the physical body sleeps. What is missing in awareness is the observer status while the astral body is separated.

Masturbation Psychic Details is a surprise presentation which relates what happens on the psychic plane during a masturbation event. This does not tackle moral issues or even addictions but shows the involvement of memory and the sure but hidden subconscious mind which operates many features of the psyche irrespective of the desire or approval of the self-conscious personality.

death You! is derived from the author's current experience in the psychic existence. It is not a text for supporting religion or for making indoctrination. It presents your likelihood when you are eventually deprived of using the physical body which you now identify as.

inVision Series

Yoga inVision 1

Yoga inVision 2

Yoga inVision 3

Yoga inVision 4

Yoga inVision 5

Yoga inVision 6

Yoga inVision 7

Yoga inVision 8

Yoga inVision 9

Yoga inVision 10

Yoga inVision 11

Yoga inVision 12

Yoga inVision 13

Yoga inVision 14

Yoga inVision 15

Yoga inVision 16

Yoga inVision 17

Yoga inVision 18

Yoga inVision 19

Yoga inVision 20

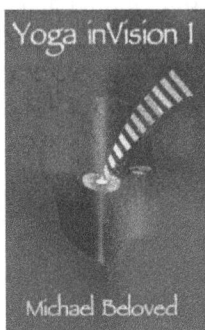

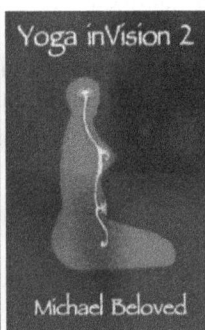

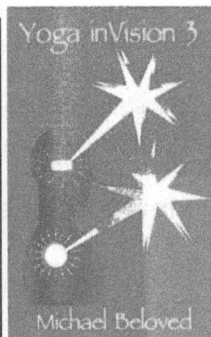

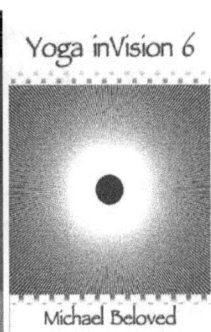

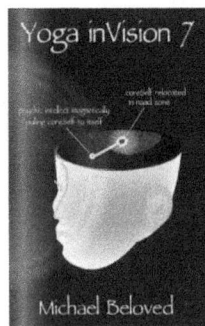

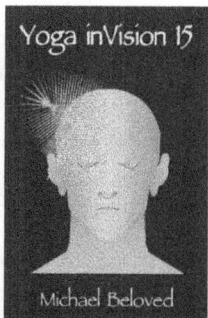

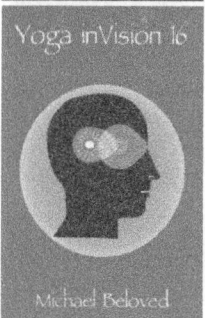

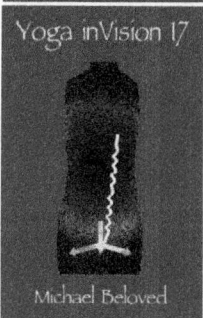

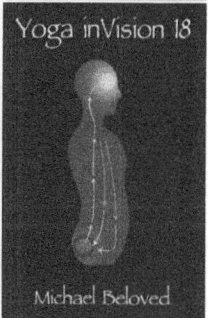

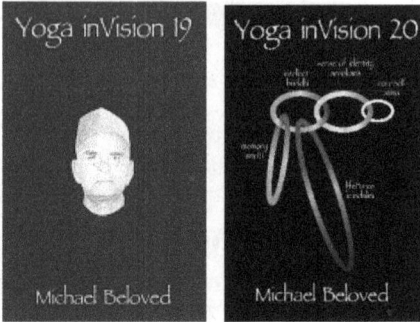

Yoga inVision 1, the first in this series, describes the breath infusion and meditation practices during the years of 1998 and 1999. There are unique, once in a lifetime, as well as recurring insights which are elaborated. inFocus during breath infusion, and the meditation which follows, is an adventure for any yogi. This gives what happened to this particular ascetic.

Yoga inVision 2 reports on the author's experiences from 1999 to 2001. Each day the experience is unique, illustrating the vibrancy of practice. Many rare once-in-a-lifetime perceptions are described.

Yoga inVision 3 reports on the author's experiences from 2001 to 2003.

Yoga inVision 4 reports on the author's experiences from 2006 to 2009.

Yoga inVision 5 reports on the author's experiences from 2006 to 2008.

Yoga inVision 6 reports on the author's experiences in 2010.

Yoga inVision 7 reports on the author's experiences in 2011.

Yoga inVision 8 reports on the author's experiences in 2011.

Yoga inVision 9 reports on the author's experiences in 2012.

Yoga inVision 10 reports on the author's experiences in 2012.

Yoga inVision 11 reports on the author's experiences in 2012.

Yoga inVision 12 reports on the author's experiences in 2012-2013.

Yoga inVision 13 reports on the author's experiences in 2013-2014.

Yoga inVision 14 reports on the author's experiences in 2013-2014.

Yoga inVision 15 reports on the author's experiences in 2014.

Yoga inVision 16 reports on the author's experiences in 2014-2015.

Yoga inVision 17 reports on the author's experiences in 2016-2017.

Yoga inVision 18 reports on the author's experiences in 2017-2019.

Yoga inVision 19 reports on the author's experiences in 2019-2021.

Yoga inVision 20 reports on the author's experiences in 2021-2022.

Online Resources

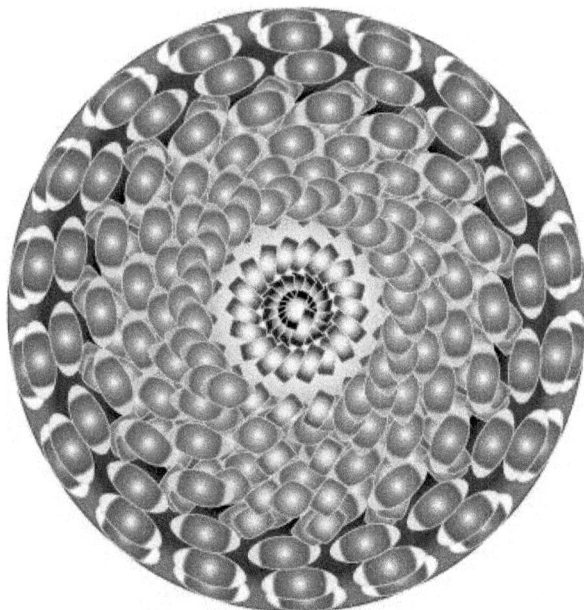

Email:	michaelbelovedbooks@gmail.com
	axisnexus@gmail.com
Website:	michaelbeloved.com
Forum:	inselfyoga.com
Posters:	zazzle.com/inself

www.ingramcontent.com/pod-product-compliance
Lightning Source LLC
Chambersburg PA
CBHW072337090426
42741CB00012B/2816